Single Women, Alone and Together

Single Women

alone & together

LUCIA H. BEQUAERT

Beacon Press   Boston

Copyright © 1976 by Lucia H. Bequaert

Beacon Press books are published under the auspices
of the Unitarian Universalist Association

Published simultaneously in Canada by
Fitzhenry & Whiteside Limited, Toronto

Printed in the United States of America

(hardcover) 9 8 7 6 5 4 3 2 1

Library of Congress Cataloging in Publication Data

Bequaert, Lucia H
    Single women, alone & together
    Bibliography: p.
    Includes index
    1. Single women—United States. 2. Single
women—United States—Case studies. 3. Divorcees—
Case studies. 4. Widows—United States—Case studies.
I. Title.
HQ800.B46   301.41'2   75-36038
ISBN 0-8070-2756-1

CONTENTS

ACKNOWLEDGMENTS

$\mathcal{S}$INCE THIS is a book about women, and in particular about women helping women, it is gratifying to record my indebtedness to so many competent women. I am grateful not only to colleagues and close friends, but to the many scholars, activists, and feminists whose efforts on behalf of women are recorded in these pages. Some of these contributors are not known to me personally, except through their work. Others are friends of long standing—clients, fellow counselors, teachers, administrators, housewives, students. It is not possible to mention all those whose ideas are incorporated into this work. Some have insisted on remaining anonymous, in any case, and others may be inadvertently omitted.

Much of the original research took place in libraries, and I have been fortunate to have access to some good ones: the Boston Public Library, Guttmann Library at Harvard, the Schlesinger Library at Radcliffe, and the Cary Memorial Library in Lexington, Massachusetts, which ordered countless books for me. The Women's Bureau at the Region I Federal Offices was especially helpful in supplying me with reliable statistics on the status of women. Books-on-the-Green, an all-women enterprise, gave me much bibliographic help, at no cost.

The interviews with Margaret Adams, Dorothy Burlage, Vivian Buckles, Helena Lopata, Miriam Krieg, Phyllis Silverman, the Rev. Polly Laughland, Roberta Kevelson, Mary Rowe, Betsy Zitrin, and many others have given me invaluable support and a real depth of reference. Many women's centers and associations contributed their time, their writings, their own experiences with single women's lives. Among these, I wish to thank the Child Care Resource Center, the Massachusetts Feminist Credit Union, the Women's Cooperative of Newton, the Somerville Women's Health Center, the Women's Inner-City Educational Resource Service (WINNERS), the Paulist Center for Divorced Catholics, New Environments for Women Associates, the Women's Center at Bristol, the Women's Opportunity Research Center (WORC), the Women in Transition Project, MOMMA, the Widow-to-Widow Project, and many others.

The interviews with single women form the essential core of this book. Without Deahdra, Leslie, Wilma, Liz, Peg, Helen, and all the others who wished to go unnamed, but who gave so generously of their time and lives, there would be little real substance to this study. It is their words, rather than mine, that are important here. My research associate, Ma'Carry Hull, was responsible for many of these interviews. She also had the somewhat novel research task of attending innumerable "singles" groups and meetings, for which I am most grateful.

My colleague and close friend, Laurie Saunders, reviewed some of the work in progress and offered many helpful insights. My husband, Frank Bequaert, a competent writer (and far better typist than I), helped out with much of the final-draft editing process. My editors at Beacon Press, MaryAnn Lash and Joyce Tovell, have been consistently helpful and sensitive to the particular demands of advocacy research—and have taught me how to write my next book!

It is customary to mention here the person who prepared the final manuscript, in a brief tribute to her patience and manual dexterity. I would like to say that my assistant, Joan Sturgis, exemplifies all those hard-working, under-paid, seldom-thanked women (and invariably they are women) who bring their own intelligence and sensitivity to such exacting work. I am especially indebted to her for the transcription of some fifty hours of tape recordings, which called for both technical competence and objectivity.

Finally, I would like to dedicate this study of single women to the young woman I know best, my daughter, Rebekah Kingery, and to all the young women of her generation who are fashioning hopeful new lives from the crucible of the women's movement.

INTRODUCTION

"As soon as the inhabitants of the United States have taken up an opinion or a feeling which they wish to promote in the world, they look out for mutual assistance; and as soon as they find each other out, they combine."—De Tocqueville

*T*HIS BOOK is not a tract against men and marriage nor is it primarily about the women's movement, although the movement is permeating the lives of most women today. It is a book about women, single women, and it is a book about change—about the ways the women in our society who are not married survive, about the ways they are creatively responding to the circumstances of their lives, about the ways they are pushing toward a public policy that takes account of the profound changes taking place in the status of women in family life. It is a book which looks at the interaction of two very powerful social trends—the growing numbers of single women, and the rising tide of the new feminism.

It is not easy to write a book about a rapidly changing society that is in transition. It is difficult to make predictions about the future, to discern signs that can suggest where the transition will lead. But it is vitally important to understand the present, to look at the most striking evidence of the transition, for there is no other way to begin to know what that unknown future might possibly hold. And the most striking signs of the profound changes that are taking place in this period of transition are found in the lives of single women, women who are widowed, separated, divorced, or have never married, who live in a society that is yet largely a married society. This book examines the lives of these single women: who they are, how they live, and what they need.

It also analyzes some of the strategies and resources they are devising and using to survive in a society that offers few guidelines for their behavior and minimal support for their concerns.

In the course of the book we will periodically focus on the lives of a number of single women who have shared with us some of their thoughts about their perceptions of the values, feelings, and beliefs which are forming and transforming their own roles and the communities in which they live. Each speaks individually, but they also address the common concerns that bind all single women together just as they point to the realities that divide them. We will also look at the traditional networks of support for women—the church, the law, the community, the workplace—to see how they are adapting to changing social attitudes about women and the family. We will look too at life planning that recognizes that a growing number of women will be single for substantial periods in their adult lives, at life plans no longer made "just in case something happens," at plans made instead as commitments to training, work, and new lifestyles, commitments being made by social planners and by women themselves. Even more importantly, we will look at the new approaches that women have developed to make the realities of singleness manageable, at the new voluntary associations, the grassroots, self-help, community-based organizations addressing the issues and concerns of single women in an indifferent, if not hostile, society.

The topic of single women is complicated by a loose terminology. Most social scientists feel that the critical definition of a woman lies in her marital status, so that single women, women living without husbands, are often referred to as women alone. But obviously single women are not *ipso facto* women without men; there can be and often are fathers, brothers, sons, and lovers in their lives. And it is even less likely that they are alone; there are mothers, daughters, sisters, and friends. (And were we to reverse the emphasis, it's equally obvious that some married women are women alone, functioning as the head of their households because of the disability or default of husbands who nevertheless live with them.)[1]

For the purposes of this book when we speak of single women, we will be talking about all those women who are not married—whether widowed, separated, divorced, or never married—who are alone in charge of their households. Some of these women live alone, some live with other adults, and some with their dependent children or aging parents.

These women and their families represent a sizeable percentage of the population, and that percentage is increasing. A Russell Sage Foundation study that is probably the most comprehensive analysis of the statistics on women notes there has been considerable difficulty in reaching exact figures on single women from the available data. There are errors of primary census collection, particularly from nonwhite households; there is confusion over the term "separation," and a separation without a legal agreement is often unreported; husbands may be absent for extended periods because of military service, imprisonment, or institutionalization; and desertion, particularly after a second marriage, frequently goes undocumented. Divorce statistics too are probably incomplete; certainly the figures are conservative. The Bureau of Vital Statistics established Divorce Registration Areas in 1958, following the 1957 Marriage Registration Areas, but while the marriage data-collection facility now covers some forty-two states, the divorce data-collection covers only about twenty-six states. All these statistical difficulties are matters of great concern, particularly because accurate statistical information is an important tool in attracting the interest and advocacy of public policymakers and the support of government funding. [2]

The source of the figures we use to describe any population or subgroup in this book will, of course, be identified, but rather than belabor statistical problems it is important simply to note that it is apparent that single women are increasing in both absolute numbers and in their ratio to the general population. Female-headed families have increased some 33 percent over the past decade. The number of children living with a single parent (usually the mother) is estimated at anywhere from 10 to 14 million, or one out of six. The median income of these families was $5,114 in 1970, as compared to $10,930 for male-headed families; one-third had incomes below $3,000. And though there are twice as many white female-headed families as black, the black families are poorer and female-headed families of all races are poorer than two-parent black or white families. Divorce rates are accelerating at the rate of 10 percent in each of the past five years. The number of widows has increased with each decade, and the poverty of elderly widows has become a growing issue of national debate. And the young women between the ages of eighteen and thirty are simply not marrying—some 48 percent by some estimates. One last vital statistic pointedly documents the sweeping changes in family composition; in 1975 the census Bureau announced that for the first time in our history American households now contain, on the average, fewer than three persons. Thus it is clear that single women and their families represent a sizeable percentage of the society, a percentage that is increasing. A good working figure would be the estimate that at any one point in time around *one-third* of the adult women in the population are not married.[3]

Journalists and social scientists tend to focus on one or another subgroup of single women, writing books about divorced women, studies of widowhood, and innumerable analyses of the female-headed welfare family; and single women themselves often identify with these subgroups, minimizing the common concerns that could bond them together. A book about "single women" as they are defined here might be criticized for casting too wide a net. Perhaps this book has, but the very nature of the broad definition reinforces the point we wish to make—that many different women, in varying situations, will be single at some time in their lives, and that they must begin to plan for that singleness through systematic and proactive approaches. There are basic common concerns, basic bonding agents, in the social situations of all single women that transcend the issues which divide them. As one writer put it, single women share their womanhood, their singleness, and, in many cases, their poverty.[4]

The rising feminism in the sixties has coincided with the dramatic increase in the numbers of single women, and some observers see a causal relationship between the two phenomena. Few of the early feminists in the nineteenth century dared to attack marriage and the family, few dared even to perceive alternatives for women outside of marriage. But the single women of today, whether forced into new roles or liberated by them, are challenging these values, making a public debate out of private issues.

Nowhere is this debate more visible than in the new voluntary associations which women themselves are building. Each chapter includes some discussion of some representative programs and organizations that illustrate a variety of approaches to the concerns of single women. These new social inventions which give us a chance to analyze both the strengths and weaknesses of the new collective experience of feminism take many forms; there are women's centers and women's studies, small support groups and national networks, employment agencies and legal advocacy organizations. Together, they translate the rhetoric of the women's movement into activism and planned action. They are the means by which women's new roles, needs, and lifestyles are defined and made visible to the larger society. They are helping to connect the individual to the complex resources of our pluralistic nation. And finally, they provide women with the skills they need to meet obstacles, overcome barriers, and reach new objectives of independence and community acceptance.

The literature in the general subject area of single women is large but uneven. There are many studies of divorce, relatively few about widowhood, and almost nothing about women who have never married. The poorest women—elderly widows and welfare mothers—have been studied more than the working poor; yet the majority of single women fall into the latter category. The pathology of some female-headed families has been emphasized, while the viability of many more has remained largely invisible. And textbook definitions from the literature of marriage and the family lag behind the social realities. Traditionally, "family" and "marriage" have been linked to mean the two-parent nuclear family with one or more children while other forms of families are described as "broken homes" or "deviant families," labels that ignore the increasing numbers of voluntarily childless marriages and parents who choose not to marry or not to continue a marriage.[5] Whether those choices are decisions to divorce, to adopt, or to remain single, there is no longer reason to label the numerous families so ordered as pathological or deviant.

Because much of the literature is problem-centered it tends to stress the negative factors of single life for women. The "father absent" family is analyzed but not in its positive aspect, "mother present," and popular writers expound at length about the dissolution of marriage but write little about the task of reorganizing one's life.

Thus while we gathered background data from this literature and the available demographic statistics, it seemed important also to find new sources of information from the raw material of the new feminism. So we observed and participated in a number of conferences, workshops, group sessions, and social gatherings concerned with widows, divorcees, and never-married women. We visited offices and had interviews with women developing services and programs for single women. And finally, we interviewed thirty women who fell into some one of the categories of single women.

These interviews are the real core of the book. In each chapter, we refer frequently to the words of single women themselves, to clarify, to explain, to bear witness to the social situation of single women's lives. And throughout the book are some longer stories from the lives of single women, stories we call "Voices," that come solely from transcriptions of the interviews in which each woman told about her life.

Twenty-seven of the interviews are used; there are five widows, including one who had remarried and divorced; seven never-married women; two women who were separated; and thirteen divorcees. One woman had lived in a common-law relationship before marrying the man from whom she was presently divorced. Many had children living with them; there were around fifty altogether. Although no attempt was made to draw a scientific sample, we did make real efforts to find women who were from a variety of backgrounds in a large urban/suburban region. They came forward willingly, having heard about the project through women's centers and from professional colleagues. They were not formally screened, but, to be frank, we were looking for "copers," women building innovative and working lives for themselves out of the pressures and constraints of their own situations. One important study of educated women has four main descriptive categories: planners, recasters, adapters, and unsettled.[6] We found these divisions useful, too, but the "unsettled" woman was underrepresented in our group.

We felt a mandate to have the women speak for themselves. Most of the experiential literature we had surveyed was written for and by upper-middle-class, well-educated, and highly articulate persons; many messages have gone unheard, many other women are invisible, and, as we have noted, many subgroups have had a particularly "bad press" (especially low-income and minority populations studied by middle-class male sociologists). We therefore conducted interviews and site visits in a blue-collar and working-class community, the inner-city, and exurbia. We talked to some elderly women in a public housing unit and toured their apartments, and interviewed young "movement women" involved in women's activities on the campuses in the region. We talked to many suburban women and found not all were affluent and well-educated; single women and their families frequently form small pockets of poverty in communities where everyone is assumed to be solvent.

The interviews lasted two to three hours each. No fee was paid, but the respondents were offered a free vocational counseling session at a time of their choice; in a few cases, we paid child care expenses. Most interviews were taped, except in a few cases when for reasons of preference or technical problems they were recorded by hand.

The interviews were largely unstructured. In almost every case, the woman to be interviewed had read our prospectus prior to the meeting and we made a point of sharing our own experience with single life—

that we had raised children, had jobs, were underpaid, took courses, and sometimes felt lonely. After writing down essential background information on age, marital status, income and income source, number of dependents, and household data, we asked a few questions about education and work histories. Then we would turn on the tape recorder and ask several open-ended questions: "How does it feel to be a single woman in your community?" or "What kinds of community supports have been helpful to you?" We also asked, "How's your social life?" and received much more information than we had expected. We asked about family, friends, and neighbors, about feelings, hopes, and expectations for the future, including one familiar question of children (and adults who admit to fantasies): "If you were granted three wishes, what would they be?"

These questions were not intended to lead to conclusions, but rather to help us begin to understand changing lives, to tap fantasies, to hear firsthand the voices of women surviving, even enduring. The answers we heard seemed to cut across categories of singleness in spite of many individual differences, and began to group into some common areas of concern—singleness in a married society; economic and social barriers which must be overcome; legal and governmental policies which demand advocacy, change, and group action. Visibility and an awareness of each other and the common bond of womanhood seemed essential to these concerns.

These women are not narrow, male-baiting partisans; some do not even consider themselves feminists, nor activists. Many have not chosen consciously to be single. They are all, however, in one way or another, questioning the values and functions of prevailing lifestyles. They have become more demanding about the quality of the lives they feel they are entitled to; they are more apt to be active in helping themselves, more knowledgeable about ways to achieve their objectives.

Our report of these women and their organizations is neither completely consistent nor comprehensive; it is rather an attempt to understand one group of women in a time of transition. We have no ideal solutions to complex issues of marriage and family styles, nor have we even tried to deal with the changing roles of men. For this book is not always objective, nor does it always strive to be so. There is a real need for advocacy here—and research itself can be an advocate when it focuses on a specific group and then translates that experience to a wider audience through the sharing of lives. Finally, the most important lesson to be learned from the lives of single women is that singleness is an experience that is by no means unique, or deviant, or accidental; that it can be planned, chosen, survived, endured, and enriched through personal self-directed change and collective action.

part One

In the simplest terms they are that large group of women who are living without husbands. Yet like any group defined by only one common feature they are ultimately diverse individuals. Some are pleased with their lives, others are discouraged, some are old, others are young, and some cannot be placed in any of those categories. But there are certain obvious groups—some have never married, others are separated or divorced, and others are single because their husbands died. We shall look at them in those three groups first, and then we shall turn to other features that define their lives as they define the lives of all people in our time; but the problems that accompany old age, being in a racial minority, and homosexuality have a special impact on the lives of single women. Finally, however, the best descriptions of the lives of single women come from the women themselves, and so this section begins and ends with the "Voices" of two single women telling us about their very individual lives.

V O I C E S

"I love it. . . . I have enough time for myself, enough time for friends, enough time to take care of my work, enough time to be with my children."

The speaker is a young mother of two children, divorced three years ago, who lives in a middle-class suburb, where both children attend the public schools. A college graduate, she works full time at a professional level job, earning the major portion of the family income which is supplemented by regular child support payments. She lives in a single-family dwelling, owned jointly with her former husband.

I love it. I'm very busy but I've always enjoyed being busy and I feel that I can extend myself in each area adequately. Sometimes I feel that I don't have enough time for one thing or another, but in general I feel that I have enough time for myself, enough time for friends, enough time to take care of my work, enough time to be with my children. It works. I think the hardest part was during the time I was making the decision that I needed a change, that I was dissatisfied with my marital situation on many levels. Until it became clear to me that I had to do something about that, there was a lot of upheaval—constant arguments and fights which were physical and verbal and involved tremendous tensions in the house. There were a lot of upsets with my running out of the house with a suitcase, that sort of thing.

The children at that time had a lot of difficulty. Both of them had difficulties in school. My son started wetting his pants and my daughter spent most of her time in her room with the door closed writing in her diary. Now she tells me she's glad she has it all written down. She realizes how unhappy I must have been and she's looked back on it herself in an effort to realize what she's gone through too. We've talked about whether she's feeling her pain or my pain or whose pain she's feeling that makes her upset about it still.

By the time my husband and I separated, he had already been moved out of my room for six months or so. He went on a trip. When he came back, we made a tentative separation agreement because during the time he was gone I was able to really think clearly about the fact that not only did I not miss him, but that I was much healthier and happier when he was away. He was only gone for about three weeks, but it was wonderful, just a joy not to have to think about another adult who was, at that time, taking a tremendous drain on my energies without returning very much. Seems like all our energies became freed up in a physical sense as well as emotional. I did speak to the children at that time about it briefly, and they did know we were unhappy at that point.

We made an agreement that we would lead our separate lives and that we would not encumber the other person by attempting to socialize together as a couple. And that we would live in separate rooms until he felt comfortable about moving out. And that we would not be negative about each other's lifestyles with the children. And that we would try to show respect for each other.

It was hard for him to accept this, but he knew by that point that I really meant it. He finally took me seriously and moved out of the room. For the next six months, he went through changes in his own mind of accepting it and looking for an apartment and trying not to feel sorry for himself, and he came to some good decisions. One was that he wanted to live close by so that the kids could see him when they wanted. The children could go there after school, and when they stayed there during the week, they could go to school from his apartment; it made sense. At the time I was incensed that it took him so long to move out and I thought it was terribly immature, but in the long run I think it was okay. It gave the kids a real chance to realize that this was going to happen and they could anticipate it. And the fact that he was able to spend that time profitably and find a place nearby made it good too.

Now my son is apt to go there frequently on his own after school. On Wednesday nights he goes there and he often just goes after school. He's allowed to have a key and he just goes in and makes himself comfortable until his father comes home from work and they have dinner together. It's like having a grandparent or an uncle that's close by, especially for my son, because there are three women in this house and there's a fair amount of feminist talk going on. And when he feels the need to get out, I don't blame him.

He calls first if there's any question. His father has a woman that's been living with him for the last year or so and there's no problem there. She's been friendly enough with the children so that they have their own relationship with her although my daughter has been very quick to come back and tell me that she doesn't feel it's a real relationship. But she's critical of relationships *I* have with people as well and she's very quick to tell people when they're not being themselves in a situation.

There's another woman here who lives on the third floor who is a friend of mine. She insists she's part of the household and in some ways even part of the family and she spends time with the children and has her own relationships with them as individuals. I needed the rent for some extra income. We share our meals and we share the kitchen. We share everything. She pays one third of the utilities but I pay for major repairs to the house. It works pretty well. We started out on a trial basis, and she's been here almost three years.

Money's no big problem. It never has been and I feel very fortunate because of that. When we were separated originally, I was able to say, "I have this much that I make, I need this additional to make it work." He paid me voluntarily the exact amount on the first of the month ever since he moved out. I wouldn't mind having a cost of living increase at some point in there, because my raises haven't been all that adequate. But I have full medical coverage and I also have a pension plan, if I live that long! That's one of the good things about belonging to a professional association. And I have disability insurance too.

My work is very satisfying to me. The only time when it isn't is when I start to think, "Am I really going to keep doing this, having done it now for thirteen years?" I feel if I want a second career, I'd better start thinking about it now. There's nothing specific yet—I just may at some point prefer to work with adults in some other setting. It may not be feasible if I can't afford to go back to school, or if the job market remains tight, or if I don't have the imagination to conceive of the type of job that I would prefer.

I think I started off being separated and divorced with having what I consider a healthy balance of male and female friends. And I was dating enough. I had women friends that I spent a fair amount of time with, whom I felt close to, who were supportive of me, and I was supportive of them. One of the men I was dating at that time, I started to see more frequently. I'd been seeing him once a week and I decided to make it twice a week. And another person, who had been out of town, came back and I was no longer interested in him. I was still enjoying this other man and we still have a relationship.

But I've changed a lot since then. I'm a different person than I was. He's also changed, but less drastically. I think he's uptight about the possibility of my counting on him in some way to be a substitute father. He likes the kids a lot, but he's not a very verbal person. And I'm going through a process now of deciding whether this is still giving me as much opportunity for continued growth and support as it was in the beginning. Maybe I'm just questioning it more. I think that's true of any long-range relationship—there are ups and downs, good and bad times and there may be moments when you want to reevaluate it. I haven't decided to make a change.

At this point I feel as though I enjoy the company of women a whole lot more than men except for this one man, and for my son.

And so I'm realizing that if that's true, then if I end this relationship with this person, there'll be quite a gap between this and the time I get involved with anybody else. Maybe it'll be a woman next time, not a man, just because I think I'm spending more time in those circles right now. Socializing in a group is probably what I'd be doing, going to the movies with people, which is something I do with women, but not with an eye out to really being involved with any one person intensively.

My activities, outside of my work and my children and my social life, are the Women's Group, and the Feminist Credit Union. I'm a participating member of that, and I haven't decided if I enjoy it because it's a credit union or because it's a feminist organization, or because it's just the people I like. And I'm also active in my professional association. There are not many women who are involved and I'm on the Negotiation Committee, working on a new contract. Until I came on the committee, there was only one other woman. I had said to her, "Isn't it upsetting for you to be the only woman on this committee?"

She said, "Oh, it's devastating. Those men don't listen to me. They don't pay any attention. They just pretend they haven't even heard me." And she's the president! So I got on that committee, and that's been very time consuming. But, it's worth it.

I don't know my neighbors very well. I feel the way I lead my life is different from most of the people here. I feel I could count on them in an emergency. I think people in general are not too pleased about divorced women. And divorced women who seem happy and healthy and who have friends coming and going—well—they raise their eyebrows even more, particularly as quite a few of them are elderly—they just unfortunately spend a lot of time at home looking out the window.

I do have some family nearby. I see both my parents from time to time. They're both quite old, but they're in good health and they both still work. Their support has been very good on some levels. They've always been very open about sexual issues, which is, I think, because they had a healthy sex life, and they wouldn't want to deprive anybody —they're open about that. But other things—they want me to try hard to conform and I don't fit that mold. They often view me as an extremist. They were not happy about the divorce. I feel they were not happy because *they* were upset. *They* did not want to tell *their* friends that their daughter's marriage wasn't lasting. They're not against divorce, but they're against it for people they know well or are close to them because it bothers them, makes it harder for them. They spent a lot of time talking to my ex-husband and telling him maybe he should have given me flowers and that maybe I would still love him if he did—this kind of thing. It was hardly that simple.

I feel that really the most support that I received has been from my women friends and from my children. That means that my children understand me as a person and view me as a person. I'm still their mother, they have that in their heads, but they call me by my first name. They're understanding of me in terms of my needs. I think that's healthy. In terms of my support from other women, it's meant that I could escape to their homes when I needed to before he moved out and we could spend some time together, making meals or something.

Our pediatrician has been helpful. He's a psychologically oriented physician anyway. He's very much aware that the parents' mental health has an awful lot to do with the children's physical and mental health. And he talks extensively with the parents to get their feelings, attitudes, how their lives have been going, even before he looks at the children. So when I went to him and said we were getting a divorce, we talked about it. He asked me how I felt and I said that I was pleased, that it was going to be a good thing in my life. And he asked me how my husband felt. I told him, "He thinks I need a psychiatrist, because if I'm not happy with him, I must be nuts."

He said, "It sounds to me like you need a lawyer." I found that supportive—that he realized I was being honest and direct, that I wasn't falling apart, and that I really did need legal advice.

And the legal advice was helpful, but not as much as it might have been. I'm sorry that I'll have to pay off half the investment on this house if I remarry. I'm punished. The lawyer explained that this was an emotional issue, a way of paying off the person so that they don't make trouble.

I think my own interests have supported me a lot. One of the first things I became involved in was my health because I realized that I couldn't afford to be sick, I couldn't afford not to have the energy to do all the things that I needed to do. So I started to read about nutrition and vitamins and health and diet and I started to take vitamins, watching what I ate. I stopped eating meat gradually, and stopped eating sugar, stopped eating so much white-flour products, and I feel more energetic than I did ten years ago. My doctor and dentist keep saying, "You're getting healthier every year." They can't believe it. I went off the pill about a year ago, and I think my health has improved a lot because even the vitamins weren't enough to take care of the side effects of the pill. After ten years I was starting to get worried. I was approaching my thirty-fifth birthday, and I thought, "Wow! This is too big a chance to take."

The future could go various ways. I could change my job and conceivably find something that would financially suit my needs and still be able to stay here, maybe fill up the children's rooms with people. Or, I could envision having a child with the person that I'm still close to. He has no children and is getting older and is interested. It would be a drastic change in my life because I would have to get married. I would not want to. I would prefer not being married, but here we go again. I couldn't hold the job I do and not be married if I had a child.

So, it's even more probable that I will get some retraining in some area or go back to school if I can find a way to finance it, and change my job. It's just a matter of getting my priorities straightened, deciding what I want to do most. I've considered doing something in the law. I'm not sure I could afford it, but I could go in the summers and at night; people do. But then it would mean taking myself away from the things I'm now interested in. I really wish that women could have the opportunity—and men too—to grow up to be who they really want to be without society being so intent on forcing conformity. I want most of all to be independent.

Chapter 1

SINGLE LIFE: A CHOICE

"There is something I want to add for the sake of . . . those
who are not married: it is a good thing for them to stay as they
are. . . ."—Saint Paul to the Corinthians (from *The Jerusalem
Bible* translation)

*U*NTIL VERY recent times, "single" was syn-
onymous with "never married" in our society. Widows were widows,
divorced women were "grass widows," married women were matrons,
and single women were spinsters—barren, lonely, and sexually chaste.
Women who never married were seldom assumed to have consciously
made that choice. A common assumption persisted that they were
physically unattractive or psychologically incapable of marriage. Ridiculed as "old maids" and relegated to the margins of society, where
they lived out narrowly defined lives as schoolteachers, menial workers,
or members of religious orders. Deviations from these few options were
penalized by the married majority, particularly by other women; the
unmarried woman had to watch her behavior within the community
lest she be judged a lesbian or a loose woman.

But singleness is now being redefined as women's roles are changing.
The growing fragility of marriage ties, the emphasis on new social and
work roles for women, and the access to safe methods of birth control
have drastically increased the options of women; they may be single or
become single at all ages. "Single" has, in fact, in common usage come
to mean those who are "in the ardent and anxious state of trying not to
be alone. It implies a very gay and hip advocacy of free-wheeling unattached contact."[1] And this kind of worldly unsavoriness clearly relates more to popular ideas about the *formerly* married than to *never*
married persons.

In this chapter we will be examining the lives of women who have never married, who are living alone and on their own, and are single through their own decision rather than by default. We talked at length with seven women who had never married. They range in age from twenty-four to fifty-six; all but two are white; two are also parents, each of a little girl; and all work full time at white-collar jobs that have some relation to human services. Three can be called professional women and have graduate degrees; one has a B.A. degree; one is a graduate student; and two are still studying at the undergraduate level. All the women are totally self-supporting, and have been for their entire adult lives.

These women are not easily put into categories. Unlike the elderly widows or the young divorced mothers we talked with, their paths have been diverse and individual. They come from sharply different backgrounds—a small New England milltown, the urban ghetto, and from Europe; from semirural communities and middle-class suburbs. It can be argued that the single women presented here are exceptional—strong, articulate spokespersons, speaking from a firm base of good educations and jobs. Certainly these qualities are remarkable and do present a positive picture of never-married women—which is one of our goals—but one can also argue that their decision to remain single was in itself a source of their strength. For example, all these single women financed their own educations, some over a considerable period of time, and the two students are still working and studying concurrently.

What they share in common beyond their obvious strength is that they chose not to marry and were comfortable with that choice. Indeed, this seemed to be the most striking theme running through all the interviews, that of freely elected choice, of patterns of planning in which marriage is seen rationally as only one of several important life options. This sense of decision was critical to the outcome of their lives. The fifty-six-year-old woman talked about making decisions:

I have made tremendous changes in my life, but I have always had the control. I never had anyone say to me, "we don't want you anymore." I don't want to sound conceited, but I've kept the reins on my own life, obviously sometimes at a relatively high cost. I don't think I can analyze the ingredients. I was sometimes seen as a loner, which wasn't true. I like to do things on my own, which *was* true. There's a certain sense of doing things my way, finding out for myself what it's all about. I think that I've known what I wanted to do all along.

And another woman, ten years younger, said:

I don't just define myself as never married. I define myself in terms of problems I'm coping with, goals I have, my relationships with other people. When I was young, I decided I did not want to get married. I made a conscious decision, which, I guess, is one of the big things that is different from a lot of other women my age who are not married.

Young women now have total choice about babies, which we really didn't have. We had—what?—a 90 percent choice and that 10 percent was a very big determinant of behavior. So they have now a 100 percent choice, and it's a hard decision to make.

In those days the way to have a good marriage was for the woman to be able to just give, give, give, and I knew I couldn't do that. I was too crotchety, too demanding, too self-centered, and as I looked around at marriages everywhere—the people who were in trouble, and many marriages seemed to be—this was what the hassle, who was going to give to whom. And I didn't want that kind of hassle. So one of the things I had to do, having made that decision, was to get out of the small town where I grew up because the pressures there to get married were unpleasant. I can see in retrospect that I really worked at a lifestyle where being married was not an issue.

These women, so unlike one another in age, lifestyle, and family background, were also alike in one other very crucial way. They were all planners, and plan they did, every aspect of their lives, and we shall see later how carefully they approached such concerns as work and social life.

But first, how many never-married women are there in this Noah's Ark society? The question can't be answered easily for the reporting of marital status is notoriously inaccurate. It is safe to assume some women conceal their never-married status if it is a barrier to social acceptance as it often is, for example, though decreasingly so, for an unwed mother raising a child biologically hers. Thus the 1972 figures of the Women's Bureau that indicate there were nearly three million women in the country who had never married probably are conservative. And one other factor may be enlarging the ranks of the never-married: there has been in recent years an extraordinary decrease in marital decision among young women ages twenty to twenty-four. Some estimate that almost half of these women in the most marriageable years are not yet married (obviously in many cases representing deferred decisions rather than life plans).[2]

The implications of these numbers for predicting the size and the composition of both families and the work force are staggering. It means, to take the second instance first, that many more women are staying seven to ten years in the work force *before* marriage and child-rearing. One can project, therefore, longer, more stable work histories for women, more career identifications that will persist throughout the lifespan and that as slots in the traditional careers in teaching and human services become filled, more women will opt for nontraditional jobs. One can even argue that work will acquire the same importance to women as marital status does now, determining a host of other decisions in their lives, such as family size, level of postsecondary training, and indeed, whether or not to marry.

Never-married women have characteristics other than marital status which distinguish them from married women. Several substantial research studies comparing the happiness or unhappiness of married women with single women have found that married women reported themselves happy more often than single women, though the separation of the percentages is never as great as one would suspect, and in at least one study, the same percentage of both groups reported themselves very happy. But, how happy is happy? More married than never-married women were bothered by feelings of depression and anxiety, were plagued with imaginary ailments and feelings of impending death. More married women were reported to be passive, phobic, and depressed, and almost three times as many married women exhibited severe neurotic symptoms. (Incidentally, husbands also demonstrated better mental health than wives in most of the studies.)[3]

In one of the few studies that included a large sample of never-married women in religious life, Yale professor Douglas Hall found the way these educated women coped with role conflicts was quite unlike that of married women.[4] Most working married women had developed strategies to reduce conflicts between work roles and the demands of home and family, the most common being an attempt to change or reduce the expectations of other persons in their lives, such as husbands, children, and coworkers. To the never-married church women in the study, however (largely Catholic women in religious life), work and career were central to their lives, and they experienced relatively little role conflict with individuals, because they were not members of nuclear families. Consequently they did not need to devise coping strategies in the same frame as did the married women who worked.

"The religious life has a lot of support for you as a single person," the former nun whom we interviewed told us. Although she would not return to it, she thought it was

very helpful to have a community or family of people who go through every day's rhythm with you, who are intelligent people and creative, and not so intelligent and not so creative, all sorts of people who can live with you and, at the same time, you can be very free. You owe them a lot but you don't owe them your whole life. You're not responsible for them in the same sense that you would be if you were married or had to be responsible for children. You can function freely. You don't have to bother about a lot of things that I now have to bother about, like supporting myself, cooking for myself. You know, they're little things but they're things I didn't have to deal with. I miss the community support sometimes.

At a recent conference on elderly women, attended by many women in religious life, professionals for the most part, working in both government and private projects for the aging, the women exchanged notes on lifestyles. One nun who was approaching retirement commented on another sister's decision to live in a communal apartment. Personally, she said, she found the convent life very convenient; if she had to do all that housework, she'd never get her own work done!

The women's movement has come as a welcome change to most never-married women, for it has confirmed their own early decision for autonomy. While some of the older women did not consider themselves militant feminists, they felt that the renewed emphasis on female independence, at the least, lent a new dignity to their status, and gave a badly needed boost to their self-esteem. One woman told us she "had paid no attention to the women's movement until recently. But then I got very interested in it. My saying I was not involved or didn't need the women's movement was like house slaves before the Civil War who said they didn't need freedom because they had freedom. Somehow I made that connection and could look at myself in the women's movement." At the beginning, she said, she had been

turned off by all the militancy, and also by the fact that an awful lot of liberated women seem to be anti-men. There's only now just beginning to be a lot of talk of "women's liberation is also men's liberation." Having worked all my life, and having worked mostly with men, I don't see that men have all that much freedom of choice either. My women friends who are stuck in the suburbs with kids were saying, "But he goes out to his interesting job all day." But you know, work can be a hassle. Many wives won't tolerate mid-career ambivalence in their husbands.

When a friend asked her if she was interested in a network of women's support groups, she discovered

just what I was looking for. As a matter of fact, my life is much more filled with women lately than it ever was before in my whole life. But

I also see that there are a lot of very nice men around whose inclination to be egalitarian and considerate is being freed up by what's going on. Also, I think men now feel free to talk about their needs, whereas in the old days they were supposed to have no needs, but you were supposed to be meeting their unspoken needs. Now, they can ask and you can ask and it's a whole other thing. So, that's where I'm at now. I'm uncomfortable, but I'm really very interested in it.

So far, we have tried to stress the assets of singleness, the autonomy in making life plans, the relative freedom from conflicting demands of work and home life, better mental health—assets somehow ignored by those who would penalize women for the choice to remain single. The force of the myths surrounding marriage and the nuclear family has in fact created enormous problems for women who dare deviate from the majority. Their public image has been almost wholly negative. We have been socialized to regard never-married women as failures or eccentrics. The autonomy of a few women who never marry can be tolerated, but the emergence of singleness as a workable and attractive lifestyle is very threatening to traditional values of family life. In addition, since few people have had positive role models of never-married women in their lives, there is little sense of how such lives are led, and this ignorance, as much as any other single factor, nurtures the myths of deviancy.

The self-sufficiency of single women has presented a further dilemma to a society that fosters widespread female dependency. It is one thing to be a victim of death or an errant husband. Society must pick up the mandate of support, however grudgingly, and become if not the husband at least the provider of last resort. But never-married women, once seen as a financial drain, have been expected in this century to provide for themselves, and frequently they fulfill this expectation very well, in spite of the barriers of wage and job discrimination that all women face. All the never-married women we spoke to were very invested in their work life. Financial independence was essential to them, but it was equally important that the job be a satisfying one in itself, given its central role in their scheme of things. One woman effectively spoke for all the others when she said:

I don't feel I should even tolerate a job that is not interesting to me, and I know that very few people can say that. But I feel that I can and must say that because I'm educated. I have capacities. I've met wonderful people and I have advantages. I think it pays to demand a lot. For me it pays to try to create a job that I'm interested in rather than just going through the ritual of pulling in my daily bread. That's meaningless to me. What I'm really saying is I think I owe it to myself to find a good job, an interesting job, and also to ask for the money I feel I deserve.

Loneliness has long been the focus of much discussion about the lives of single women. We asked all our respondents whether they ever felt lonely. No one, it seems, ever really wants to admit to the state or condition of loneliness, since such an admission carries its own stigma. Americans abhor loneliness. It is a confession of some kind of personal failure; it is our own *fault* if we are lonely. And in fact none of the never-married women found herself immune to the human experience of loneliness; yet far from being a negative or destructive force, they found loneliness to be a universal teacher, a great clarifier of values and goals. Out of their loneliness, they have forged their lifestyles and philosophies. The former nun, living alone after some years in a convent, had this to say:

What bothers me about loneliness is that in a sense you're wasting time. That's the one sin, I think, wasting time. I don't mind loneliness if it's creative or if it generates an action even out of something negative—even if I'm so lonely I do something just because I don't want to be lonely. It's generative, you know. I have deliberately lived a life without a roommate, without being married, because there's something I want to do with myself that requires that I be alone. It's been hard but it's the only way that I can work things out.

A black woman, living by herself in the crowded inner city, made a distinction between loneliness and solitude. She liked being alone, she told us. "I like privacy. I like solitude because it gives me time to think and to write my poetry. I'm not afraid to be by myself. It's not that I don't like people—I just like to have a place to go where I can close the door."

So many women are never alone during their youth and young adulthood. They go directly from their original homes into marriage and the rearing of children. An experience of aloneness—private, generative, creative—such as these two young women are describing, is relatively rare in women's lives. Women still tend to shun solitude, and the risks they assume are implicit in that state. Energies which could be released lie dormant, for until recently most women have had little opportunity to hear about such private concerns of single women.

Loneliness, of course, used to carry the added implication of sexual abstinence for women who lived alone. It is apparent that this, too, is moving from the area of moral dictum to that of personal choice, as contraceptives have become both safe and accessible, population pressures dictate smaller family size, and new moral values are explored by large numbers of the society. Too many choices can be bewildering to many women, especially when the only controls are from within, but the never-married women seem, once again, to be taking a planned and structured approach. One of the women, who is also a single parent, said:

Being without a man—that worries a lot of women. They say, "Oh wow, I've got to have somebody. I'm incomplete unless I have somebody." And it's not true. A lot of women deal with it on the basis of sexual needs and that's fine. But when you look at the overall picture of how your child is going to benefit, I personally don't find it that difficult to sacrifice that particular part of my life. I can deal with that. And I think that a whole lot of women are going to just have to deal with it too. The whole physical thing is nice, it's beautiful, and I'll be glad when it comes in the person of somebody I can respect and love. Until then, I'm patiently waiting.

This woman is twenty-four, the youngest of the never-married women we interviewed. There is some indication that the enormous increase in women who choose to remain unmarried during the age period of twenty to twenty-four may be due to a new awareness of sexual needs that acknowledges their role in the whole lifespan of women. Even more important is the increasing dialogue among women of all ages and marital statuses. The women's movement has forced us all to a consciousness of our own sexuality, and to the realization that our anatomy is not our sole destiny. In the early years when movement women were largely young and unattached, their discussions were held apart from their more traditional married sisters. But in an age of instant mass media and a growing feminist press, women of all ages are learning about sexual alternatives and choices, including that of abstinence.

The new morality is also beginning to remove the stigma from even the most outcast of women, unwed mothers. Public attitudes are slowly changing, especially toward those women who do not become public charges in their communities, but give up their children for adoption or somehow support themselves independently of public agencies. The majority of all unwed mothers now are not the highly publicized teenagers, but women in their mid- to late twenties, most of whom support themselves with their own earnings. In a study of the Greater New York City area, in the period just prior to legalized abortion, it was found that two out of three unmarried women decided to keep their babies, and raise them alone.[5]

Many young unmarried mothers, however, need social services for such real needs as housing, education, job training, and maternal and infant care. While there has been some progress toward support, particularly in the public sector, true advocacy for these single women has been virtually nonexistent, because of profound social aversion to their plight. [6]

In this attitude, we are considerably behind other western societies. In Sweden, for example, the word "illegitimate" has not been used in public support programs or in the law since 1920. "One-parent" families are entitled to state support, and the child in such a family may be assigned to a child care supervisor, if this is desired by the mother. In England, bed-sitting room apartments in cooperative housing are available for an unmarried mother and child to provide a supportive environment while the woman adapts to her new life. [7]

This country, with the exception of the federal Maternal and Infant Care program offering services regardless of marital status, has provided few societal supports for these women. There are a few outstanding projects aimed at "rehabilitating" high school girls, notably in Iowa and Massachusetts. And in Philadelphia, the Berean Parental Vocational-Educational Program has developed a model training program for unmarried mothers already out of school, providing high school equivalency diplomas and business training in conjunction with group day care for the babies, so that the separation between mother and child is minimal, at least during the training period. [8]

But, in spite of the official sanction of such programs, there is a striking lack of mutual self-help voluntary associations founded by unmarried mothers themselves. The necessity of maintaining a low visibility in the community has until very recently prohibited any such bonding among women for mutual support. For the most part, these women have gone it alone. One of the women spoke out courageously on this point. She had made it the basis for her lifestyle:

I'd like to explain how it feels to be single and have a child; the reason being, personally I think there's a uniqueness with that in the fact that I have my freedom. I'm very used to making decisions for myself, for a long time. I like that, especially being a black woman, I guess. We're constantly looking for a man who's stronger than we are, who can be stronger than we can, and that's very seldom and very rare. We'll wait until that comes or we'll just go through relationships that don't mean anything, or we'll marry somebody and get separated from that person, or we'll be living with somebody and really not making things work. And rather than go through that, I have my daughter. I found out that

I was pregnant, and I realized that I did not love the baby's father. I could not see myself sharing a life with him, not even for the sake of giving the baby a name. What's a name, when there are so many other things I have to think about for her? Although my first thoughts were— she's never going to see him, she's never going to know about him. I don't even want anyone to know he even existed. I'll get married and someone else will adopt her. She'll have another name and for all she knows, that'll be her father. But, I've seen what that does, and I don't want to screw her up any more than she's going to be. My family never talks about it because they know it's a strong decision that I made, and that's all it is. If they have any opinions, they've kept them to themselves, and that's the way I'd rather have it, and they know that about me. I could ask their opinions, but so far, I haven't.

Recently, there has been an upsurge in advocacy groups and self-help programs for single mothers. The Consortium on Early Childbearing and Child Rearing publishes a newsletter on teenage mothers called *Sharing*. In addition, they are strong advocates for educational programs for young mothers still in school. They act as a clearinghouse for information on adoption, and on the options unwed mothers have for keeping their babies.

The Sisterhood of Black Single Mothers was originally organized as a support group for black unwed mothers in the New York area. They have expanded their clientele to include single mothers who are separated or divorced, some men, and other sympathetic supporters. They distribute a montly newsletter and operate a Big Sister program to assist pregnant single women who may need extra support before and after delivery. They are trying to establish a home day care program for their members. And the Big Sister League has recently begun encounter groups for unwed mothers who are keeping their children.[9]

The largest organization for single mothers is a California-based group calling itself MOMMA, with chapters in nearly twenty states and Canada. For three years they have published a newsletter for single mothers, with a national circulation. MOMMA also sponsors a resources handbook, special classes, and support groups for mothers. While MOMMA serves more women who are separated and divorced, it is one feminist group which extends services and real advocacy to single mothers of all marital statuses, including unwed mothers.

In contrast to the stigma attached to the unwed biological mother, there is a kind of community generosity and goodwill toward the single adoptive mother, indeed, toward all adoptive parents. The media have been especially willing to take up the cause, under such sympathetic headlines as "Unwed Parents—and Proud of It!" or "Single Fathers

Grateful on Father's Day." Single adoptive parents, although they are few (estimated at fewer than a thousand in all the country), have formed a network of local self-help organizations to support each other, and to promote the adoptive-single-parent way of life.[10]

Since these parents have usually gone through the scrutiny of adoption agency workers, they are, by most definitions, middle-class, stable, self-supporting persons; and frequently are human service workers. They are thus articulate spokespersons in the debate of singleness as a life choice. As advocates speaking from a position of strength and respectability within their communities, they represent a new transitional family model, an alternative to some of the penalties of singleness. And there is no question that such new single-parenting styles, adoptive or biological, present an alternative to present definitions of singleness.

Several of the respondents said that they would not rule out marriage sometime in their lives, as part of a new life plan. In fact, one woman in her mid-thirties was startled by our use of the term "never-married." It had, as she heard it, "something terminal about it, and I hope someday to be married; so I would like to be classified as 'not yet married.' I'd like a partner with whom I could work out a life's project. That would be preferable to what I'm doing now. But I choose to be unmarried now."

And another woman said, "The thing I'm really thinking about now, for the first time, is getting married or the equivalent. I still can't see *marriage*, but getting into somekind of a long-term involvement is, for the first time, something I really want to do. But it means that all those things I thought of when I was young and had rejected then, I'm now really thinking about trying."

Thus today's never-married woman is radically changing the definition of singleness. Some are more committed to remaining unmarried than others, yet for all unmarried women the options are broadening. Women's lifestyles are no longer dictated so stringently by marital status. Even women in religious life, traditionally the most committed to their lives, are choosing new domiciles, new career patterns, even new clothing that no longer sets them apart from other women. Women who decide to forgo marriage entirely nonetheless now feel that they have a right to parenthood. Young and not-so-young single women are now regulating the role of sexuality in their lives on the basis of personal preference, secure from the fears and stigma of an unwanted pregnancy.

Even more important, the new wave of feminism has made it legitimate to remain unmarried, a process which has been reinforced by the inexorable pressures of rising world populations. Or, one can marry considerably later than tradition and community have decreed, and for reasons unrelated to issues of support and protection. And freedom from the *mandate* to marry will release many more strong and competent women into a world where achievement and personal commitment have at least the same priority once given only to homemaking.

In spite of the general support of the feminists, however, there has been virtually no public identification of the needs of never-married women, as a special group. Our government has not pressed for social planning which would make it convenient or even desirable to remain in that status. The assumption seems to be that one will either put up with singleness, or one will marry, and solve the problem that way. No special advocacy groups seem to coalesce around the concerns of never-married women. In England, however, just such an organization was formed in 1965. The National Council for the Single Woman and her Dependents provides services and information for never-married women, particularly those who have or have had the care of elderly or infirm dependents. As the council's brochure says:

Many single women shoulder the three-fold burden of running a home, caring for an elderly dependent, and going out to work. Many have given up prospects of promotion, financial security, an independent life of their own—even the chance of an occasional night out and an annual holiday—so that their dependents can live their old age in their home surroundings. Many women face severe problems after the death of their dependents.[11]

The council operates as a voluntary, nonprofit, charitable organization, serving as a national clearinghouse and maintaining local branches in many major cities throughout the British Isles. It provides direct services to single women and their dependents, studies legislation affecting their interests, campaigns for increased home care and suitable housing, publishes both research studies and a bimonthly newsletter. The council has also established legislation to insure property rights, interest-free loans, tax allowances, compassionate grants, and nursing-home services for single women with elderly dependents. Local branches identify single women and their families in the area, encourage social gatherings and educational programs, and help to further government support for domestic care.

The council's particular value has been to bring to public attention the existence of single women, as well as generating concern for their needs. It functions as an informational resource for single women in a way which is unique on both sides of the Atlantic. While the family and economic structures of the two countries are by no means similar, this model of a voluntary association which works for the interests of single women is one that can well be copied here in the United States.

All of these remarks must be considered highly tentative and speculative. There are many gaps in our knowledge of women who never marry, or remain single long past the "marrying years." With the exception of some biographies of a few outstanding women writers and artists, academicians, and professional women, we know almost nothing about lifestyles and personal values of single women. The women interviewed for this chapter were not all middle-class or white, but they all are working toward professional careers. One new study on single women should add many insights to this discussion, but the author, Margaret Adams, talked mainly to and about never-married, articulate middle-class women. Obviously we still have little knowledge of the lives of single working-class women, or those who are black or Hispanic. And in Mirra Komarovsky's definitive study *Blue Collar Marriage*, an otherwise exhaustive survey of working-class attitudes toward marriage, no one asked the respondents, "Would you have preferred to have remained unmarried?" Apparently it was simply not thought of as an option, either by the respondents or the research team.[12]

Women who do not marry and are attached to extended families, once a common lifestyle, have almost disappeared from the small nuclear-family home. If the renewed interest and experimentation in communal, collective, and group-family styles continues, such single persons may again find suitable shelter and supports within family systems, yet remain relatively independent of the pressures of traditional domestic roles. Communities and housing developments deliberately constructed to contain three generations could also offer feasible alternatives for single women. All these areas need much more study and innovative social planning before singleness can at least achieve a legitimate status.

Chapter 2

DIVORCE REVISITED

"Divorce is a chapter in the history of the American Family."
—William O'Neill

*I*F DIVORCE is only a chapter, then it surely is the longest single section of the book. No aspect of marriage and family life has invited so much scrutiny or provoked so much controversy as has divorce. Divorce is considered by some a *cause* of moral looseness, and *effect* of family breakdown, while others hold the reverse to be true. For the individuals involved, divorce has been likened to a *death* and to a *rebirth*. Divorce rates receive scare headlines as they "spiral" and "accelerate," yet at the same time one authority on family life no longer considers divorce "newsworthy." We know more about the problems of divorce than we do about its benefits; more about the process of separation than about building new postdivorce lives; and we know little about the women who head more than 85 percent of all postdivorce families except that almost half of them are poor and most of them remarry.

We do, however, have some solid statistical data on the numbers of divorced persons, which help anchor the headlines in fact. But once again, the data are subject to many interpretations. For example, if 75 percent of the divorced eventually remarry, as one writer estimates, the number of persons actually living as divorced persons in any one census tabulation is far from an accurate guide to the number of people who have been divorced. On the other hand, some divorced persons never remarry, particularly women over thirty with children. And not only do

37 percent of all first marriages end in divorce, but 59 percent of all second marriages fail also.[1]

A more useful figure in a study of divorce is the rate of divorce per one thousand population. That thousand, however, refers to total population (men, women, and children), but the change of rate over time is useful as an indicator of recent social trends. Its use in predictions for the future is more doubtful, yet such predictions will be made and will play an important role, not only in determining public policy, but in shaping the views women have of divorce as an alternative and a solution. If the rate continues to rise, as it seems will be the case in the seventies, then divorce may reach a tipping point in terms of community acceptance; if a sufficient number of persons have been divorced at some time in their lives, the experience of divorce will become assimilated into the society, as Jessie Bernard, the authority who finds it no longer "newsworthy," thinks it already shows signs of doing.[2] At present, our society permits, but does not sanction, divorce; it is a legal solution to marital conflict, but not an *approved* one. In a nation so heavily invested in marriage and the nuclear family, and the pursuit of happiness through those institutions, divorce is commonly viewed as a disaster, a deviant choice, a last resort to insoluble personal problems, and much that is written about divorce derives from these essentially negative definitions. The literature is problem-centered and prescriptive rather than neutral and analytical.

Our present view of divorce is undergoing considerable change, due to the influence of several strong forces working in the society. The striking rise in the divorce rate immediately after World War II (the 1946 rate per thousand is nearly double the 1962 rate) spurred many

Year	Divorce Rate Per Thousand Population
1860	1.2
1900	4.0
1926	7.4
1935	6.8
1946	18.2
1956	9.8
1962	9.4

*Adapted from divorce data cited in *The Courage to Divorce*, by Susan Gettleman and Janet Markowitz (New York: Simon and Schuster, 1974).

social scientists to revise the traditional view of divorce and to take a more rational look at the institution of marriage and its alternatives. A philosophy of divorce began to be articulated by many writers and spokesmen in the fifties and sixties. These writers came to represent a new orthodoxy, what Bernard calls "the ideology of the avant garde," [3] that aimed to eliminate the bias in scholarly writings about divorce.

A historical view was expressed by William O'Neill in his study of divorce during the period 1880-1920, which reviewed the changes in family expectations in a period when most paid work moved out of the home into factories and offices. Divorce, in his opinion, did not represent a moral revolution but "the first in a series of adjustments by which the patriarchal family and the Protestant ethic have accommodated themselves to the demands of an urban, industrial society." [4] Divorce was a safety valve in an essentially married society where the old taboos still existed in subtler form. Since the family was still the principal unit of consumption, the nation had a vested economic interest in preserving marriage.

As time wore on, anthropologists, too, began to examine divorce in this and other cultures, to search for clues to new models and workable solutions to the problems of marital instability. When the pill made family planning a realistic goal, Margaret Mead suggested a two-stage design for marriage which would directly counter the pernicious effects of early marriage, unwanted pregnancies, and rising divorce rates. The first stage would be

a marriage between childless partners with no commitment to continuity. Such marriages should be easy to contract, should involve no automatic economic relationships and should be capable of dissolution by mutual consent, without undue delay, cost or supervision from the constituted organs of society. On the other hand, marriages which are parental should be placed in a different category, and have built into them once more the conception of what a marriage with children is— a lifelong relationship which will only end with death. [5]

Mead's view that parents must commit to marriage for life aims at encouraging men and women to think through their expectations of marriage and at controlling unwanted pregnancies. Yet, as another author suggests, her plan is "probably unworkable. Many marriages are the result of pregnancy, and this is particularly the case with younger couples. . . . To lock women in such circumstances into a lifelong commitment at such an early age would seem to defeat Ms. Mead's purpose." [6]

William Goode, one of the foremost writers on family sociology, wrote the first major field study on women in divorce.[7] Based on samples of over four hundred divorced urban mothers, aged twenty to thirty-eight, his aim was to document how women "adjusted" to the catastrophe of divorce in the absence of any institutionalized supports for divorced persons. Women stepped into a social limbo when they divorced, he felt, and had no social guidelines for their conduct. But his warning that women were penalized both emotionally and economically far more than men has had the effect of a self-fulfilling prophecy, for his research had a profound effect on other social science writers. His findings have frequently been used to justify the traditional bias of professionals for marriage and two-parent families.

While scholarly literature carries great weight with professionals involved in social policy, the values of average Americans are most clearly articulated in the popular press. The position of the media is well known. The idealized nuclear family has been so glorified in soap opera and serious drama, in situation comedies and the discussion panels, that the arrival of the two new television programs with single female heroines, "One Day at a Time" featuring a divorcee and "Phyllis," a widow, was headline news in most television reviews. And women's magazines have over the years carried even more weight. The well-known feature, "Can This Marriage Be Saved?" which appears regularly in the *Ladies Home Journal*, capitalizes on the drama of separation and has had a major though incalculable effect on women readers. One must note that the title doesn't reflect the question, "*Should* the marriage be saved?," nor in fact do many of the real-life cases end in divorce. The format varies even less than the outcome; each spouse tells his or her story, the counselor suggests some strategies (frequently another baby), and the marriage is saved, obviously the only goal worth consideration. One is struck by how little the woman's own goals are fully aired or met in the counseling process. Personal adjustments are stressed at the expense of some basic structural planning. No attempt is made to rebuild the family along more egalitarian lines although the wife is sometimes encouraged to get an outside interest which does not, of course, impinge on family needs, and husbands are never counseled to work part-time in order to share homemaking and parenting equally with wives. Yet this is a magazine for women and a powerful molder of women's personal values and images.

It has fallen to the women writers and social scientists to try to clarify the issues and role of divorce. Anne C. Schwartz, a social caseworker writing in a professional journal, has raised the basic question:

Is divorce a social reality that is here to stay and therefore requires our efforts to be directed towards altering the present-day conception of it? Can divorce be seen not solely as a consequence of a person's rigidities and inability to adjust, but as a legitimate, valid, moral, sanctioned social invention; a creative, rather than destructive act; and orderly instrument of change?[3]

An increasing number of women writers have responded to this and other questions which challenge the limitations of marriage and the traditional assumptions about divorce. Before we look at these radical new responses, however, some attention must be paid to a new literary phenomenon in the popular press recently, where there has been a spate of books, mostly by women, describing the experience of divorce, often in dramatic, highly emotional accounts. The titles carry the theme, *Women Alone, The Woman Alone, Facing Life Alone.* Many of these books move on from individual histories to offering practical guides to postdivorce behavior and situations, a worthwhile attempt to help women through the social limbo of a married society. Most try to emphasize some positive approach to the divorce experience, but in tone and mood they unfortunately convey the same well-worn myths: divorce is the ultimate experience of failure, carrying with it severe penalties of suffering and loneliness; women *can* rebuild these shattered lives, however, by admitting failure to themselves and their children and returning to an active social life as soon as possible. And that new social life resembles as closely as possible the former lifestyle of middle-class married mores; dinner parties, cruises, dances, and clubs forward the objective of securing another partner. These writers show little sense that women can do very much for each other or for themselves, alone, or that a new lifestyle might be created out of the single experience, while many otherwise reputable books contain specific references to the threat of lesbians who prey on single women and their daughters. And virtually none of the writers addresses the realities of poverty and aging which characterize the social situation of so many single women.

The how-to books, another category popular now, have an inherent paradox as guidebooks for single life directed at changing that singleness as soon as possible. While such titles as *Creative Divorce* and *Life After Marriage: Divorce as a New Beginning* stress an affirmative view of divorce, finding and keeping new partners still figures much more importantly than all the helpful hints on financial and legal management, or what to tell the children.

The new kind of study, however, now appearing in social-service literature attempts a more radical definition of divorce. One example, a series of studies made by the Women's Research Center, a group of women clinical workers and sociologists, focuses on case histories of twenty-two divorced families headed by women, analyzing the social situation and coping strategies of divorced mothers, with the assumption that the one-parent family can be a healthy alternative rather than a deviant or trouble-ridden "broken home."[9] These cases are an important contribution to the study of women in postdivorce lives.

A second work that has even more potential as an agent of change among professionals is *The Courage to Divorce*, written by two family therapists, Susan Gettleman and Janet Markowitz.[10] They document both the forces that have opposed divorce as a reasonable alternative to bad marriages and, using both their own clinical experience and the available literature, argue that it is valid to describe divorce as a time of life-transition and family reorganization rather than of family breakdown. They make a convincing case for the positive role divorce can play, offering a second chance for a happy, useful life. Those who take the steps to dissolve a bad marriage are, in this view, at least as mentally healthy as those who remain in miserable family situations, often reinforcing the neurotic needs of one or both partners.

Other writers have looked at the increasing incidence of dissolution of seemingly happy marriages where, for example, no third person was involved. One writer, Sonya Rudikoff, feels that it is women, who stand to lose the most in present-day marital models, who are seriously questioning both the permanence and the exclusivity of marriage. She sees few options other than divorce to resolve those questions of equality and justice raised by feminists, for only the upper-middle class, with its ample resources of time, money, and privacy, can even consider the more radical alternatives such as group marriages and the so-called "open marriages" popularized by the Bells and the O'Neills.[11]

How many people will choose divorce as a reasonable solution to a bad marriage will depend on a number of both public issues and private attitudes. We need to look closely at how women live as divorced persons; what they see as the benefits of divorce as well as the liabilities; and how they manage the daily problems of parenting, social life, and earning a living. What has helped them in their postdivorce life? What makes remarriage attractive to so many divorced women? And how do divorced women differ from widows and those who have never married?

Some answers to some of these questions were provided by sixteen women with whom we talked; there were thirteen divorced women, two who were separated, and one woman, widowed earlier, who had divorced after a second marriage. All these women had received some training after high school, but not all were college graduates nor did all have specific career skills. Two were students, one full-time, and many had taken some courses since they were divorced. Several had been on welfare at some point; one was still receiving benefits and was able to work only sporadically. The occupations these women held included secretary, schoolteacher, nurse—the classic trio—but one was a community volunteer and another a Unitarian minister. All were mothers; among them they had more than thirty children, from preschoolers to grown men and women, and all had been or were now the custodial parent, with the major responsibility for providing a home.

Their average income was less than $15,000 a year from all sources—alimony, child support, state aid, and their own earnings; and three women received $6,000 or less per year and received such aid as food stamps, subsidized housing, and Medicaid. Their housing ranged even more widely, the more affluent women typically living in single houses, often from the former marriage, while others had moved to apartments or other multiple dwellings, usually for financial reasons but often for the sake of convenience, or for anonymity, or with some notion of starting a new life. (Difficulty of home maintenance and repairs was a common thread with all the women, although at least one former husband came periodically to clean up the yard—and others were learning new skills for themselves.)

None of them divorced for frivolous reasons. While many of these women would agree with the affirmative view of divorce expressed in the new literature, there are some very real, nonneurotic problems women have that keep them in bad marriages—barriers to equal opportunity, heavy burdens of home management, deeply held religious convictions, and the sense of "coupleness," the image two people present to the world at large—all can and do keep many more women than men in unhappy households. Some of these needs were evident when the women spoke about their decisions to divorce.

"One of the things at issue in my marriage was that I set up a private savings account for myself which infuriated my husband," one woman told us. "Just something to do what I wanted to with . . . a little puddle of money." After the divorce she found, "Money is close, yes—it *isn't* agonizing. One of the reasons I wasn't going to step out of my marriage—I figured it *would* be agonizing. I had very little money of my own."

Often the decision is a slow, drawn-out process. One separated woman found she was essentially still "living the same kind of life I was living before we separated. It really isn't that different except that I don't have the marriage status—it's just like when he used to come back from a trip and he'd fall asleep on the sofa." She told us she'd been "head of the house in many ways for a long time because my husband traveled in his job so that I had many of the responsibilities a lot of the time since we moved here." Having him out of the house wasn't that much different, except for the repairs in the house and financial things she had to learn about. "Things are evolving," she added. At first her husband had slept overnight in a basement room when he visited, but she

found it too upsetting emotionally. I'm not emotionally divorced yet. Until I find someone else, or something that is really truly satisfying or engrossing, I guess I won't be.

But it doesn't seem as though we're divorced until he leaves and then I know we're divorced and I go through that whole dying process all over again. So, I've just issued an ultimatum: no more will he stay in this house, which he can't understand at all. But we'll see what happens.

For many of the women the "courage to divorce" was hard won. One who told us, "I'm still not through this whole process," frankly admitted her fears. "Every single time I have to make a major decision like go down and sign papers for the car or go and sign for a loan on the car or give someone the first and last month's rent and sign a two-year lease it scares me a little. I think if it didn't scare me, I really ought to worry—but, it's the idea of *knowing* you're alone."

The separation period is a most painful and chaotic time, and many of our divorced and separated women, like the separated woman whose life seemed to have changed little, felt that the end of their marriages was like a death from which they would gradually recover, after a period of mourning. The phraseology of death and dying appears regularly, but the usefulness of this "fashionable psychological analogy" as a tool for understanding divorce is being questioned. No matter how sympathetic the analogy is intended to be, the authors of *The Courage to Divorce* feel that the mourning rituals of death thus prescribed are just not appropriate.[12] Postdivorce life must build on the reality that the ex-spouse is alive and well, especially if he is also the children's father. Grief and mourning for a "dead" marriage can mask the rational relief many women justifiably feel at terminating a bad situation, and the allied belief that "grief work" will be completed only when one finds a new partner may be even more destructive. And, as we shall see in the next chapter, most widows strongly object to the death analogy applied to divorcees, for the presence of the ex-spouse is a reality which even remarriage cannot erase, nor is it beneficial to pretend that it will.

All the women, as we noted, had raised or were raising the children. Many of them considered the fathers to be inadequate or downright unfit, and none of them would have had things arranged any other way, but at least one mother suspected that she felt the way she did because of the way sex roles had been parceled out in early childhood:

I think our society prepares women for being parents, because from a very early age, little girls want to grow up and be mommies and carry dolls around, but boys want to be firemen or policemen. No little boy says, I want to be a Daddy. I don't think it equips women to be parents, but I especially feel that this society certainly does not bring up boys to be good husbands or good fathers. They just don't give them that kind of responsibility in the home. They don't teach them that this is a very valuable thing, to be a good father or a good husband.

She found many of her friends told her their husbands were unwilling to do household chores—"just day-in-day-out things that need to be done in order to live, things like food shopping, emptying the garbage, giving a child a bath." She thinks this is changing, but "I just sort of wonder about how we bring up boys in this society—that it's the woman who's expected to do all these things, plus hold down a job if she has one. That's what's bothering me."

One of the most persistent myths has been that divorce is bad for the children involved. Many couples stay together for the "sake of the children," but recent research has confirmed the commonsense conclusion that bad and chaotic marriages are far more damaging to children than divorce itself.[13] The majority of the divorced women who talked with us felt that while the period just prior to the separation had been very hard on the children, their children were nonetheless adjusting extremely well to postdivorce life. Since some of the women had only recently separated and others had led stable single lives for several years following their divorce, the difference in family tone and mood that time seemed to make was reinforced. One young mother, recently divorced and struggling to come to terms with the past, manage three small children, and live on welfare checks and food stamps, told us her children were very upset. One problem had been their father's visits, so "I finally told my husband that he had either to see them on a regular basis or not see them, because I couldn't stand the way he was doing it. He'd come by the house, stop by and come in and talk to them for two minutes and get up and leave. I couldn't stand it—they were just completely confused, they couldn't understand it at all."

Matters were improving, however. She found that a parents' support group at her children's nursery school was very helpful; she had "a lot more understanding of children—seeing where they're at instead of just stopping the behavior I don't like." And while her plans for the future were vague except for a firm intention to work, her present concern was clear—"the overriding thing in my head has been to get myself together so that I'm comfortable with myself and my children."

Her worries about her children, however, don't support the myth that divorce hurts the children so much as they confirm another commonsense conclusion—that all major changes require a period of adjustment. The difference that time can make is clearly shown in the conversation we had with another mother, who was self-confident but realistic—and divorced for nine years:

The children are doing extremely well. I'm very comfortable with them. I think this whole idea of "deprived child in the single parent family" is a thing of the past. Yes, it sometimes happens, but then it happens in a two-parent family, too—I don't think there is that much of a problem. My kids are very good students. One of them is more introverted than the other and I imagine he is still supersensitive about the divorce. In the school he used to be in, about fifty percent of the children came from divorced families. Now, in this new school, only a smattering are, and I see him tending to associate with the few kids that come from a divorced family.

Another important factor is involved in the differing attitudes of these two women, however; the second woman's former husband pays child support regularly, she runs a small business of her own, and she and her children live in some comfort in an attractive suburban neighborhood. If the first mother were not beset with financial woes, her voice would undoubtedly sound more confident. Money is important; in fact, some kind of minimal financial security is the crucial variable in family survival in a recent study of single mothers who have managed to stay off welfare. [14]

One effect of the prevalence of the myth that divorce hurts children is a distorted focus upon children rather the parents that shows up in an almost mandatory feeling of guilt. "I had awful feelings of guilt about depriving my children of a father," one mother told us. "I took all the blame, that *I'd* done this awful thing to my kids." But the relationship between the adults is what is at stake in divorce, and another woman who acknowledged concern for the children as a complicating factor felt that "in the end when it comes time to make a decision as to whether or not you're going to stay with this man, the decision is usually based more on the relationships with the husband."

The issues in that relationship are changing. In only two cases had the presence of "the other woman" been critical; the far more frequent theme was a sense of the husband's inadequacy as a life partner, a feeling of needing relief from the demands of an unjust, unequal relationship. The women were reexamining their expectations of marriage and the process of divorce became for many women a time of learning and growing, a time to test one's sense of autonomy and self-worth.

This experience is not limited to the middle-class women we spoke with. The extent of the fanning-out of feminist rhetoric from a small group of young educated women to the general public can be measured by the size of the opposition; "Women's Lib" is no longer a joke but a threat to some and an operating reality in the consciousness of many wives. The traditional blue-collar marriage too is crumbling, largely because the women, no longer willing to accept dominant male values, place a premium on companionship, the sharing of marital tasks and burdens, and the realization of their own self-esteem.[15]

One area of postdivorce life which urgently needs redefinition is that of altered family relationships, particularly with the ex-husband and his family. This concern obviously sets the divorced single woman apart from widows and never-married women. The enmities that surround most divorces tend to disrupt these relationships, yet the resource system of the new family needs these connections that are relations of the father—the grandparents, cousins, aunts, and uncles who can be that extra support a single mother can count on. Some of our divorced mothers felt quite comfortable with these new relationships and encouraged the children to feel the same way, but others were either hostile or bewildered, unable to devise any appropriate ways to handle the situation. Often children never saw their grandparents or fraternal cousins. And we talked with several women who had moved to a new community far from the old relationships, in effect, burying their former lives, just like those parents who tell children the ex-spouse is dead that some studies find (although such a "death" may also reflect the desire to enjoy the higher status of the widow).[16]

Most divorced women must deal with the legal question of custody, an ordeal that widows are spared. Somewhere between 85 and 90 percent of all children of divorced parents live with their mothers, the result of a potent socio-legal mandate assigning the prime parenting task to women. This may be changing; of late more fathers appear to be the prime custodial parent, but it is difficult to document this change. This difficulty is compounded by the fact that most legal custodial arrangements are not totally observed by either parents or children over a long period of time. Since divorced and separated women we interviewed were the custodial parents they all spent much more time in child-rearing than did the fathers, but there was great diversity in the kinds of arrangements these parents had devised.

One mother, divorced for some ten years, whose former husband moved from the area three years ago, said her daughter told her that she starts not to care for him anymore but she still can't help missing him. Before he moved he visited regularly although he never took the children out. "That," she said, "was one of my problems when they were smaller—he just came here and sat on the couch and read magazines. *That* was visiting the children. But I thought it better than the children not seeing him at all."

Another more recently divorced mother whose children saw their father on Wednesdays and Fridays and alternate weekends said, "He's a much better father to them now. He does more things with them— he gives them more quality time when he's not living here. He's basically interested in the children."

Still another reported that although the arrangements had had changes, "Their father is definitely around. We've worked it out. It took a while. He had a hard time when my son was an infant with the two of them. Then it was good for a while. Now, it's hard again."

And at the other end of the spectrum another young mother talked of the time she "had to call up three bars before I could reach him to tell him his baby was in the hospital. And then he didn't want to come. I told him he had to, or else."

Many factors are at work here: the geographical distance of the father from the family; the degree of friendliness, frequently linked with the financial issues, between the ex-partners; the age of the children; the children's own feelings about the divorce; closeness to or distance from other relatives. All helped to determine what kind of shared parenting would develop. Another important determinant was the psychological maturity and stability of the mother, and her sense of self-worth. Class and lifestyle may also have been influential, but that is difficult to document. Finally, time proved to be a great healer, and more shared parenting seemed to occur as the families moved away from the transitional trauma of the separation and divorce, and toward new family styles.

Some blue-collar women from a single mothers' group and some divorced Catholic mothers we spoke with saw their parenting roles in a much more traditional and inflexible light than did middle-class suburban wives. The divorced Catholic women could not conceive of prolonged separation from their children so that they could spend time on their own pursuits; the best arrangement they could come up with was the Sunday visitation ritual, often grimly tolerated by all participants "for the sake of the child." These women too had not divorced lightly or amicably; their stories were long histories of bitter conflict, even physical abuse, and few of them worked at rewarding jobs. One Catholic with a large number of children had been married to an alcoholic, who recently had undergone treatment, was now sober, and was beginning to build some real relationships with the children. Her resentment was palpable; having to surrender a share of the parenting to a despised ex-partner after so many years of "going it alone" was infinitely painful.

The mothers from the single mothers' group were even more embattled. Two were presently involved in custody disputes and all indicated that at one time or another the fathers had threatened to bring custody suits. Visitations, if they did take place, were stormy occasions, and held to no regular pattern. The mothers on welfare, however, typically seldom if ever saw the fathers. And regardless of class factors, all those husbands who were in arrears in support payments were never seen.

It is important to note that many of the middle-class mothers as well had been threatened with loss of custody, particularly at the height of disputes and tensions preceding actual separation. Predivorce discussions of custody frequently were not rational discussions, and financial considerations and "fault" and "blame" were all too often mixed into custody decisions and arrangements. Confronted with tangled laws and sanctions, parents make their own arrangements in haste and bitterness, seldom with the child's best interest in mind. While the current trend in custody awards is away from tests of fitness of the parent and toward the best-interest-of-the-child approach, parents, particularly mothers, are poorly informed as to what kinds of alternatives are available. Many divorced women, locked into traditional images of themselves as mothers and primary parents, cannot accept shared parenthood outside of marriage; even less can most women decide to relinquish custody totally, despite the fact that traditional views of custody reinforce women's economic and psychological reliance on the ex-husband.

With new styles in family living, new approaches to custody are being developed. The women we interviewed are wrestling with these issues, discussing with increasing frequency their own ability to decide how their children will be raised and by whom. They are informally devising new ways to share parenting, recognizing that divorce need not deprive their children of healthy, close, and loving relationships with a father who is also an ex-husband. Single parenting is a heavy responsibility; sharing that task relieves divorced mothers of many burdens, and free and accepted movement between two homes can be a positive force in a child's life.

RESOURCES

In the past, women who were separating from their husbands sought out professional services to help them through an unknown experience with few guidelines. If they rejected the role of the "gay divorcee" of the Hollywood films, they remained invisible in a married society, although they could also become a patient or client by going to a doctor or a lawyer and often women went to both. The divorced women we talked with still sought out these two professional sources of help, with mixed feelings of helplessness and frustration that led to mixed results. One woman decided to go to her family doctor, realizing she "was a mental and physical wreck. I was down, hardly ever up—I couldn't sleep. I realized that I couldn't stay that way forever. I had to pull myself out of it. Nature finally did it. I had that awful bronchitis, and I went to see our doctor. I told him what was going on. And he said, 'Why, that son of a bitch.' It made me feel great. I'd been so angry, but just feeling it; it felt good to hear someone else say it." She added, however, that the pills he gave her didn't help her sleep.

Another woman who went to a lawyer to deal with her former husband's custody threats still felt ignorant of her legal rights.

One thing I do not think most lawyers give you because they don't have the time and you don't have the money to pay for that kind of time is to really let you know what your legal rights are. Any husband going through this—whether he wants it or you want it or you both want it—is going to try to tell you what your rights are and are not. And if you don't know what they are, you're in trouble. Every single one of us in the support group has been through the same things, our husbands trying to intimidate us, trying to tell us they don't have to give us this, they don't have to give us that, they don't have to do this, that we have to do such and such. They hit you at your weakest point. My husband knew I'd never give up my son and so he would keep telling me that he had a lawyer for him and he had a lawyer for our son, he had all this counsel and that he could in fact get custody. There's just *no way* at this age that he is going to get custody of that child, but it took me a long time to realize that.

HELPING YOURSELF

Into this partial vacuum have come some new social inventions, designed by women for the support of women. The new and expanding voluntary associations began to look specifically at the issues of divorce with which women needed the most help—emotional supports and legal resources. Later chapters will examine the responses formal institutions are making to these needs, but two women's advocacy groups designed to serve those women separating from their husbands suggest some realistic and compassionate ways to provide help. These organizations have met with mixed success in their communities. The reader is warned that one is no longer in existence, and the other is facing a fiscal crisis that jeopardizes its survival. They can best be described as grassroots responses to human needs, and buffers against bureaucratic helping institutions which are no longer helpful.

Justice for Divorced and Separated Mothers, Inc. · In 1971 in a Northeastern city, a group of young divorced mothers formed a voluntary support group to share with other divorced women, particularly those with children, the information and resources that they found helpful.[17] They began to work with other women's advocacy groups in the area, especially those with some legal expertise such as guilds of women lawyers and women law students on nearby campuses, and a task force of NOW helped them begin a needs-assessment of the region to locate the area where service was needed most. The goals of the group were threefold: to provide short-term services to meet the immediate needs for information and support; to act as liaison to the community and existing institutions involved in any way with divorce while raising public awareness of the needs of divorcing mothers; and to provide women with opportunities for personal growth, particularly in terms of home management and employment.

JDSM planned to develop a professional staff from its own clientele and to train a large pool of volunteers who would work in newly formed support groups, act as court and legislative monitors, and become community resources persons. They hoped to set up a hotline for information and referral services, staffed by trained volunteers, and proposed to collaborate with educational institutions in the design of courses on women and the law.

Their proposal was well thought out; the funding demands were modest and spread over several sources for a defined period of time; and an evaluation design was built into the proposal—an element frequently overlooked in new service designs, but critical to objective views of results. A service membership had already been identified and was paying token dues to the organization, and, even more important, JDSM had the support of many women lawyers and other prominent local leaders who were included in an advisory board to the agency. But foundations and other funding sources were unresponsive to requests for either seed money or the more elaborate pilot program, which probably says as much about conservative community attitudes toward divorce as it does about struggling new women's groups.

JDSM struggled along for a short time after it failed to find funding, but the need to earn a living wage became crucial for these young mothers and the group has disbanded. Ironically, the very needs these women had come together to address were the stumbling blocks to reform—working mothers with inadequate child support and low salaries have little time or energy to engage in activism. The wonder is that so many women have accomplished so much, since time is such a valuable commodity. As one of the women we interviewed told us, "There's never enough time for the children. The job comes home with me. I try to bring as much work home with me as I can so that I can see more of my children, which means that I'm doing a great deal once they've gone to bed, and by that time, of course, I'm very tired—the same syndrome that any working mother left alone has—doing the laundry at one o'clock in the morning or any of the other household chores in addition to holding down a job and supporting a family."

JDSM was an innovative approach to a specific social ill, tied to goals of community self-interest. Yet two factors worked against its success—there was no widespread community acceptance of the support needs of women in divorce and those who sought reform were prevented by those same needs from implementing the project.

Women in Transition, Inc. · This program, started as a resource project for women experiencing separation, divorce, and single-parenting, was originally staffed largely by women from the Philadelphia Women's Center, which had been receiving many requests from women requiring a new kind of informed response.[18] A task force was formed to seek funding for a separate office and gained the support of local churches and church councils, some family trusts, and a substantial grant from the Sachem Fund. The original staff, two paid workers plus some volunteers, expanded to seven full-time workers, four doing legal work and three working in the emotional supports component of the program; and was supported in major policy decisions by a planning group made up of lawyers, mental health professionals, and other interested citizens. The WIT project saw itself as an alternative to formal institutions that provided emotional, social, legal, and financial supports to women in separation and divorce. To expand their services beyond the Philadelphia area, they first published a handbook, the *Women's Survival Manual: A Feminist Handbook on Separation and Divorce*, which incorporated the project's experience and research.

Their clients have been women from all backgrounds, from ages seventeen to sixty, married two months or twenty years; the majority are from the thirty-to-forty decade and few are widows. Two special groups served have been women relinquishing children to the custody of fathers and gay women divorcing their husbands. Not surprisingly, the needs of these two groups of women rated low in the community priorities of most funding sources, nor have these foundations appreciated WIT's no-fees-for-service policy (although it charges a modest sum for the manual and accepts consultation fees from other professional agencies).

Much of the outreach work has been devoted to building close ties with other community agencies. Joining with other "movement" groups to attract United Fund support, WIT received some seed money from that source. They have earned new respect from many professional social service workers—and much hostility from the local bar association—for their self-help legal training program for women. The response of the clergy has been mixed; some priests and ministers have been trained by WIT in their group methods while other churches have opposed any support to divorce or divorcing women.

Last June, their major funding was not renewed. The staff is continuing with curtailed services as of this writing, partially supported by unemployment compensation and by an emergency grant from the City of Philadelphia. They still resist the idea of charging direct fees for service, and the one promising new source of funds is income from their updated, nationally oriented version of the manual.

What can be drawn from the experience of a project like WIT? First, the teaching and learning experience that these women have shared has given them a new sense of competence and clearly demonstrates women's collective ability to address some of their own problems. Equally important is the record WIT offers to other service programs—a strong grassroots model of an alternative agency. Third, projects like WIT are useful testing grounds for community values, attitudes, and biases, especially in an area where there is little consensus. Separation, divorce, and what may be termed the future of marriage and family styles are sensitive, controversial issues. The outcome of the public debate may depend on the participation of women in small, change-oriented advocacy groups.

Chapter 3

SURVIVING WIDOWHOOD

"The life styles of American widows vary so greatly that it is impossible to define 'the American widow' beyond the simple statement that she is a woman whose husband has died."
—Helena Lopata

"It's as necessary to learn to be a widow as it is to learn to be a wife or mother."—Phyllis Silverman

*E*VERYONE KNOWS what a widow is, but almost no one knows much about the social situation of widows. Widowhood is a topic no one wants to discuss and few professional researchers of human behavior want to investigate. The very word "widow" has a melancholy sound. Hearing it, we respond as if we intuitively know what Lynn Caine pointed out, that it comes from a Sanskrit word meaning "empty." We live in a society that would like to deny death; since that's impossible, we instead avoid thinking about it. There are few traditions and guidelines for women that tell us how to behave when we lose a husband, nor are we told what kind of life we should plan for the years afterward. We frown upon overt expressions of grief, encouraged in other cultures, and for years the nation's most compelling image of a widow has been a vision of Jacqueline Kennedy, the magnificent and stoic queen-widow. But even this sort of self-contained mourning we admire is limited to an incredibly short time; afterward the widow is assumed to feel as she did before and expected to act as she did before—although the slightest hint of frivolity "too soon" evokes public disapproval.

Unlike other cultures, where widows assume traditionally prescribed clothing, behaviors, status, even housing, we in this nation refuse to anticipate widowhood as a normal transition in the life history of the family. Nor do we treat bereavement as part of our human lot. We isolate the dying in hospitals and nursing homes and keep family members away from the event of death. Yet since most women tend to marry men older than themselves and women in general have a longer life expectancy, there is every likelihood that most husbands will die before their wives and therefore that the experience of being a widow is one a very large group of women will have.

There are twice as many widows as there are women who are divorced or separated, but widows too have few role models from which to create new definitions of themselves. The popular stereotype is either the "merry widow," young and carefree, or the elderly, resigned grandmother whose life is over anyway. Neither reflects reality. Obviously there are many elderly widows, but the *average* age of widows at the time of their husbands' deaths is fifty-six. Though that age is hardly young, it reminds us there are significantly more younger widows than our usual association of death with advanced age leads us to expect. This is made even clearer by a recent estimate that one out of every five children in the United States will lose one parent to death before the child reaches the age of sixteen. And it is even more significant that three-fourths of the women who become widows at age forty-five can expect to live at least twenty-five more years.[1]

What do widows themselves say about their life situation? We talked at length with five widows; three were in their early forties, one was almost fifty, and one was in her late seventies, and one had also been divorced from a subsequent marriage. Three had adequate, even comfortable, incomes from their husbands' insurance and investments, another was barely solvent, living on insurance money and a small salary, and the elderly widow and her friends in the housing project where she lived, also widows, were all low-income persons (although she told us some of the residents had hidden assets which, if known, would disqualify them for the subsidized housing). All the women had children, but only the three younger had children at home, most of them teenagers.

The information these women exchanged with us was supplemented by the experiences of forty-five widows who shared some of their thoughts with us during a five-week "Widows' Conference" that was designed to offer practical resources for widows on financial and legal concerns, parenting, and the possibility of training and future employment, and included sessions of small groups in which the widows shared the more personal concerns of bereavement.[2] The participants were overwhelmingly white middle-class—women who probably could easily afford the $15 fee—but the first session was attended by one recent widower who did not return and one black woman, widowed for nine years, who attended regularly.

The principal needs and concerns these fifty widows voiced can be sorted into those that are acute and may be short-term and those that are chronic and long-term. At first they are acute. In the period of bereavement the woman whose husband has died must change roles from wife to widow, a painful process that Lynn Caine has movingly described from a very personal, experiential viewpoint.[3] Both she and her dying husband, responding to the cues of people around them, had played out a drama of incredible stoicism, self-defeating in the end because it never addressed the realities of loss and widowhood which she alone finally faced—the sense of matelessness, a loss of self, and the need for structure in a new role.

This period of mourning has been described by many writers as a three-stage process, and the new widow first experiences the time of impact, feeling numb and unable to conceive of herself as a woman no longer a wife. When the terrible realization of loss can no longer be avoided, when the real grieving begins to be experienced as such, she has moved in effect into the second stage, of recoil, able to *feel* the incredible intensity of her pain. Yet precisely at this time when she feels her hurt so acutely, she and the caregivers she encounters are trapped by logical consequences of the three-stage description. The next stage is recovery and both the widow and those who would help her are anxious to see the pain end. They are in effect apt to nudge the person into "recovery" while her real feelings lag behind. But as Phyllis Silverman, who has studied the experience of grief in hundreds of widows, points out, one should not expect to "recover" from grief as if it were a disease; the self changes during loss and gradually accommodates or adjusts to the past event, as a preparation for the future and a new way of life.[4]

Many widows we talked to said that the caregivers they had encountered—clergymen, family, friends, and doctors—depended too heavily on this "timetable of grief." Told that they must show signs of recovery by a certain time, that they would be "as good as new" a year later, that they were "in trouble" if they grieved too long, they were doubly troubled by the recurring episodes of grief that mark certain times, the family milestones when the departed husband is keenly missed. One widow, for example, whose husband died on her son's birthday told us the remaining family has had difficulty with that anniversary ever since.

Helena Lopata, author of the seminal research on widowhood, has also criticized the helping professions for insisting on a "timetable of recovery."[5] She feels it does not recognize individual differences, nor can it provide a substitute for the natural, supportive networks which the widow needs and seldom finds.

What makes the difference for the widow in her ability to adjust and accommodate? For her acute needs during the transitional process from wife to widow, Silverman says:

The evidence points to another widow who has coped and accommodated as the best caregiver. Very often the first question a widow helper is asked is, how am I going to manage? The second question is, how did it happen to you? The new widow seems to be seeking a role model, someone with whom to identify. This other widow can be a friend, a neighbor or a relative. . . . She can provide perspectives on feelings; she provides a role model; she can reach out as a friend and neighbor—not someone defined as concerned with abnormal or deviant behavior.[6]

Each widow needs time for the process of grief to run its course. She needs to organize her life financially and socially so that she is once more engaged with her life. She needs companionship and help with solving immediate short-term problems—money, housing, her children. She needs to be allowed to recognize her grief as a normal human condition, not an occasion for repression or guilt.

The long term and chronic needs of widows also vary with each individual and are related to a number of interlocking factors. Lopata has suggested that "the way in which different types of women re-engage in society following the death of the husband reflects their location in the modern social system."[7] It is a complicated process to fit comfortably in a new role, especially when that role is defined by society as essentially a negative one. Yet each widow must bend to considerations of age, health, level of education, ethnic and religious tenets, geographic location. And whether one is affluent or, like most older widows, poor, can mean the difference between adjustment and despair, for the lack of money exacerbates such primary problems as ill health and the need for secure, convenient housing. In addition, the style of the former role as wife is critical to the building of a new identity as a widow—younger and better-educated women were more apt to have had companionate marriages, while the older, more tradition-minded women were more likely to have lived in male-dominant, wife-submissive relationships. Some of the other differences can also be sorted out on a continuum of age, it seemed to us, from the widows whose lives we looked at. Two of them, one forty-six, the other in her late seventies, present many of these issues of widowhood in an especially striking contrast.

The younger woman, widowed for three and a half years, is the mother of two teenagers and has lived in her urban/suburban city for eight years.

How does it work out to be a mother and by myself? One's very busy, I assure you. There's not very much time left for oneself, for the essential kind of what's going on inside. Every now and again I just feel I have to split. I went to Europe for a year—I don't know how I would have survived that first year if I hadn't had that at the end of the tunnel. Also, my husband is buried over there. You see, when we came home all the preparations had been for his coming with us—dates marked on the calendar. One day he and my daughter sat in the dining room and *made* this calendar, and he wrote down the date of his death and didn't know it. This just *killed* me. I used to look at the calendar and I couldn't bear it.

I used to feel that people's faces used to change when they saw me. They didn't know how to handle me. They'd have this terribly solicitous tone. Some women even told me they went out and raised their insurance after hearing what happened to us. I got to the point where I avoided people. I felt as if every window had a face behind it, peering at me. I felt so exposed, as though there was some kind of visible stigmata.

My social life is nonexistent, really. You see, everyone assumes that of course what I'm doing is palpitating for a lover or husband or something, which is not at all the case. With as good and as happy a relationship as I had, I'm certainly not in any hurry to get into one which would be less fulfilling. I wouldn't mind some reasonable fellow squiring me around to a concert, or the movies, but I don't know—I think I know what we both had in mind for the children and I feel possessive about them. And they feel very strongly about this, too. We knew someone who was widowed and remarried—they were shocked at the shortness of time involved.

It would be nice to have a little more money. I have my little job, which I find boring as hell, if you want to know, but we really don't manage too badly, simply because I really don't spend any money at all on anything except food, gas for that damn car, living expenses like heat and taxes. I don't go to the theater, I don't go to the hairdresser, I don't smoke. I drink. By that I mean that I have sherry and wine, and stuff in the house. It's been there for weeks. I don't drink to excess, but I would hate like hell if I couldn't afford to have a bottle of wine when I have friends over for dinner.

But my main problem is money. That's where I was this morning, at the bank. You know how one hears all one's life this business of the first step down the primrose path is invading one's capital—from then on it's down all the way! So I went to the bank and said, "Look. I'm going to worry anyway. How much should I worry on a scale of one to ten? At the moment, I'm worrying on a scale of nine and a half." So he said I could worry on a scale of maybe three. He said I could get a new car if I wanted to. And here I've been driving this eleven-year-old car!

The way I see things, I have two alternative futures, or even several alternative futures. The one that really scares the hell out of me if you really want to know is the one like Mrs. Jones over there. I think to myself, "Are you going to be like Mrs. Jones? Fourteen rooms, all alone, every now and again toddling out in a pale blue Buick?" No way. This street is lousy with widows, and I don't want to do that. I don't want to be a relic, a survivor, hanging on to something that we started out to be quite different. What I never thought of was that my time with my husband would be coming to an end. It always seemed to be going on so gloriously into the future.

I could stay here, and the children will grow up and go away, and I would sit out my life. Or, I can wait until the children finish high school and then they're both in college or whatever it is they do after that, and then I can wind up the house and move, feeling by that time that I served my time, as it were. It's rather scary. I really don't see myself staying on here in this big house which is expensive to run when they're in college, because it's too difficult to live in a settled suburban community. It's not set up for people like me.

I'd like the children to be able to cope with what comes. I'd like to look forward to being contented without being static and dull—not to be always wanting something, always wanting something new. It's very unsettling.

This widow is yet looking to her future, however painful the change of her plans may be. Her thoughts are markedly different from an elderly widow's, as the following description of one woman whom we spoke with several times suggests. (Because she was not comfortable with the tape recorder and had an accent she didn't want recorded, we have not tried to phrase her story in her own words.)

This woman, in her late seventies, lives alone in a public housing unit for the elderly located in a community where her son and his family once lived. When she was first widowed, over fifteen years ago, she moved from a small rural town in the Midwest to her son's home in this suburb. She had her own room and was able to supplement her income through dressmaking and needlework. She joined a Lutheran church with many parishioners of her own ethnic background, and through it she joined a sewing group and made some friends in her own age group.

She was quite active, both through her church and her new friends and in the busy growing family in which she lived, and her daughter-in-law and grandson provided the transportation her activities required. But inflation decreased her fixed income and her son's family, growing older, needed more living space, so the attractive new low-income housing for the elderly that had been built in the community seemed an ideal solution. Though the apartments were little more than bed-sitting room suites, each had a little porch and a small garden area, and after some of her friends had moved in, she followed.

Now after seven years in the project her situation has changed considerably. Her son was transferred out of state and now she is cut off from her family and is dependent, like most of the project residents, on the project station wagon for transportation. She finds her present social situation lonely; many of her original friends have died or gone into nursing homes. But it is out of the question for her to move again; her income is barely sufficient, her son has had to borrow money to send his children to college, and her health has deteriorated so that she feels she cannot leave her doctor or pastor, while her increasing arthritis keeps her from doing the handiwork she enjoys and from joining project trips in inclement weather.

When we visited her in her tiny, spotlessly clean apartment, she gave us a tour of her neighbors' homes in the building, which houses eight residents, all single women. Each immaculate little flat was adorned with family memorabilia—photos of grandchildren, graduations, and weddings. She told us the few men in the project were very spoiled by all the ladies. One summer weekend, she said, when she had been by chance alone in the building, the only resident not away visiting or vacationing, she found herself talking to the television set—and to herself.

She told us of no plans for the future—and we didn't ask her if she had three wishes. It was a rainy day on our last interview. As we drove away, we looked back to wave and saw, one at each picture window, eight elderly ladies looking out into the rain.

Some conclusions are clear from these two contrasting histories. These two widows are at vastly different points in the life cycle. One is in the process of disengaging from active life roles, a process which is typical of many elderly women who have led traditional lives as housewives and are poor, in ill health, and alone. The younger widow, still actively grieving for a beloved companion who is missed, is yet painfully planning—sorting out her options for a new self-definition, a new direction to travel. And in many ways she is not unlike divorcees of similar age and family situation—she has to deal with the challenge of single-parenting, housing, and finances, without a partner who can help her validate her decisions and share her anxieties.

Yet, without exception, the widows we talked with did not identify with the problems of the divorcees and, in fact, in some cases were quite critical of them. "Fault" was in fact quite prominent in these discussions; like most Americans, these widows felt that the divorcees had personally failed and must work out their own problems. They, perhaps understandably, did not want to share in a status even more negative than their own, while the fact that no divorced woman we spoke with ever criticized widows may be an indication of the higher esteem widows have in the community. And the divorced women who were actively involved with women's self-help groups were regretful that the widows did not join their programs.

"Before my own experience I would have been closer to saying that there weren't that many differences," one widow who's a leader of support programs in her community told us. But she had decided

There are differences between the divorced person and the widow. The widow has not controlled the loss, has not created the situation unless she has committed murder, so the situation is beyond her. My own feeling now is that divorced women, even if their husbands aren't talking to them, still have somebody, an intermediary who could communicate with the husband. There are avenues open to them because this person is alive, avenues that are not open to the widow. Widowhood has a finality that the divorced woman is not facing as long as that person is alive. When we talk about divorce, we're talking about problems in marriage; we're not talking about survival. I'm not saying that every marriage where a spouse dies is good, but what I am saying is that at that particular point we're not talking about what led up to it but about the finality of death. There isn't the bitterness that you see in the divorce situation, because even though there's a sense of rejection and you have guilt, anxiety, and anger, they are expressed differently. We're dealing with someone who is dead, and this I see as a major difference.

And another widow, voicing the feelings of anger and despair that Lynn Caine wrote about, told us, "A divorcee has someone to fight with, or fight with through a lawyer." She has a direction for her anger, whereas "the widow is just spread all over everything—it just hits everything. A divorcee can channel her anger easier, but there is a point when a widow is very, very angry, just mad at the whole world, and asking 'Why me?'"

Another factor reinforcing this sense of apartness from the concerns of divorced women is the obligation most American widows apparently feel to sanctify the memory of their husbands. For example, the widows at the conference were adamant about continuing to use their husbands' names; nearly all intended to remain "Mrs. John Smith," though a few of the youngest planned to follow the feminist style of "Ms. Mary Smith." One woman who had thought of using her own name found her sons objected—it was unfaithful to the memory of their father. And Lopata found that the widows she studied, most of whom were working-class older women, considered their marriages "above average," impossible to duplicate, and each felt her late husband was an "unusually good man."[8] This persistent appearance of the saintly husband has its uses. It seems to palliate the crisis of grief and loss, to insulate the widow from extremes of loneliness—it is as though her husband is still with her in some way.

If it does alleviate loneliness it may not be so odd that some divorced women employed much the same device in referring to their ex-husbands, especially when speaking with the children. Women otherwise extremely realistic about their divorce experience insisted on telling their children that the ex-husband was basically a good man, one who wished them well, and whom they regretted divorcing. These dishonest platitudes were typically offered to children who also knew that the support checks were overdue and that they hadn't seen their fathers in a year. Many of the children were urged to remember Daddy in their prayers, and while praying for someone's welfare *is* different from regarding a person as saintly, the processes are similar enough that one sociologist is currently applying the "sanctification scale" Lopata used for widows to a sample of divorced women.

That there are real differences between death and divorce is clear. It would be cruel and unnatural to question genuine bereavement at the loss of a loved husband and father, but the common burdens that single women share could be viewed in a more rational, less biased light. Even though our society has encouraged judgments that married women are superior, widows pitiable, and divorcees deviant, women today need not accept these judgments at face value. They owe it to themselves to reexamine what they can do for each other.

VOLUNTARY ASSOCIATIONS FOR THE WIDOWED

Many widows and some service organizations have been increasingly involved with setting up voluntary mutual self-help groups to meet the needs and concerns of the widowed. This is a relatively new effort, for the older generation of widows still living today was socialized to be passive, nonvoluntaristic, and inflexible.[9] These oldest widows, for the most part, do not see themselves as self-sufficient women and find it hard to respond to these new styles of help, yet old support systems which formerly eased the lot of the widowed have disintegrated. For some years it has been true that no one helps the widow; there may be pity, but there is no intensive exchange of services except at times of illness, and there's little emotional support from friends. The extended family system of former years simply is not in existence, although there are indications that a new form may be emerging. Religious organizations in general are not seen as helpful, and many Jewish respondents in Lopata's study went to great lengths to mention their rabbi only to emphasize that he had *not* been helpful. And one survey of service-response in one urban area showed that widows do not typically seek out formal social-service agencies for help unless they had been involved with them prior to the event of widowhood.[10]

Yet some widows, notably in the thirty-five to fifty age group, have begun to form some kinds of groups which address the unmet needs they were experiencing in their own lives. Seeing that the elderly withdrawn widow needed outreach to maintain her contacts with the outside world, they've set up hotlines for emergencies as well as for information and referral services. Women's centers have formed support groups and social clubs, while community college systems have responded with continuing education programs especially designed for the widow. And all these new efforts are distinguished by the use of volunteers drawn from the widowed population.

The new widows' programs have had some problems, most importantly those of finding money and establishing a legitimate status in the community. In addition, because they have tended to maintain an exclusivity, they have appeared to ignore the other women who are alone in their communities, and, finally, they have had trouble in reaching some of the neediest in their own defined target population.

Finding money is always crucial to the viability of voluntary associations. Money means staff, it means service, and it means community recognition as well. This community recognition seems to be more readily accorded to widows than other single women. Churches and funeral directors, legal associations and government agencies have responded, if not generously, then at least with fewer reservations than they might demonstrate if asked to support programs which include never-married and divorced persons.

There are several reasons behind this. Certainly the number of elderly widows alone, their poverty a matter of national concern, demands a concerted response to their needs. It has also been established that the newly widowed are a "population at risk" in terms of both physical and mental well-being.[11] Finally, the huge welfare caseloads which support large numbers of separated and divorced women has produced a counterreaction in public opinion that projects the idea of "fault" and "blame" of individuals onto the group while widows continue to represent an unconfusing "deserving" population.

Many of the new groups are serving widows on the basis of a specific period of widowhood, such as the critical time of intense bereavement, which has been the focus of some innovative new programs combining service with research that gauges the effectiveness of these services.

Widow-to-Widow Project · This program, originating in the Laboratory of Community Psychiatry at the Harvard Medical School, under the direction of Phyllis Silverman, was a response to the finding that most helping professionals expected to aid the widowed were actually fearful of the newly bereaved and attempted to shut off the period of grieving prematurely and withdraw while there was still great unmet need.[12] As Silverman says, "The doctor disappears the minute the minister or rabbi appears. The clergyman himself is not trained to deal with his own fears about death. Psychiatrists are not trained to help people cope with normal life crises."

Because it is important to establish public acceptance of any mutual self-help program, particularly one combined with academic research, understandably suspect at the level of personal intervention, the first, experimental program was promoted through local churches and service agencies so that the community, not Harvard University, was perceived as the direct source of intervention. The program was designed as a public-health model of intervention; that is, its goal was to reach every newly widowed woman under the age of sixty in a lower middle-class community of 250,000. Each widow was contacted by another widow for the purpose of providing her with friendship and help during this critical period after the death of her husband. These contacts varied from a few visits to sustained friendships over a period of years. In a period of two and a half years 430 women were reached, over two-thirds of whom chose to involve themselves in the program.

Although it was directed by a professional social service worker, it was staffed by nonprofessionals, mature women who themselves had made successful adjustments to widowhood. They offered sympathy, understanding, and an exchange of common feelings. They acted as bridges back into the real world, inviting the new widows to social events and group discussions, helping them find resources to aid in specific problems, and even providing transportation to those who were shut-ins. The widow aides met in a group session once a week with the program coordinator, to report on their visits and exchange experiences.

As the research funds ran out, the original paraprofessional staff developed a "Widowed Service Line," a hotline approach designed to reach that part of the widowed population that still had chronic and residual adjustment problems. This was subsequently funded by a grant from the National Institute of Mental Health and during the nine months of funding received over 750 calls. While the line could not fully reach the needs of the newly bereaved—even seeking help is often more than a grieving person can do—the hotline service reinforced the lessons of the Widow-to-Widow design: the importance of early out-reach, of being readily available to the newly bereaved, of identifying the needs of widowed persons at different points in the process of loss.

The Widow-to-Widow project has reached national attention and has been the model for many new grassroots programs. Some have received funding and support from local government human service agencies that are, along with funeral directors and clergymen, referring their widowed clientele to these support groups. They typically serve the widowed between the ages of thirty and sixty and have a high turnover in membership as the individual finds her way back into a real life for herself and her family and comes to terms with her new role as a single person.

What is needed in metropolitan regional areas is some coordination of these scattered groups so that services complement rather than duplicate each other. To further this, the original staff persons of the Widow-to-Widow project now hope to establish an all-volunteer Widows' Resource Center which will act as a network builder and coordinator for local programming.

Church-Sponsored Organizations for the Widowed ·
Local and regional church organizations have been the official sponsors of a number of clubs, groups, and educational programs for the widowed that vary widely in the age group served, the period of widowhood they are concerned with, and organizational style. While the religious council or local clergy are the official sponsor of these groups, the real initiators of the programs have typically been parishioners,

themselves widowed, who have "felt the need, and insisted, nagged and generally pestered the organized religious body until it responded with the offer of sponsorship and assistance in forming such a group." [13]

Many of the groups have a strictly social and recreational purpose which poses problems of age-segregation and may neglect the elderly withdrawn widow. Like all social clubs for unmarried people, its members tend to marry, thereby putting their membership eligibility in question.

Some groups maintain or are developing outreach services to the isolated and housebound who are members of their church, but relatively few initiate visits after the Widow-to-Widow design, depending instead wholly on referrals. Other groups are forming regional councils and establishing coordinating networks through newsletters and public education programs. Some of the groups have officers, bylaws, advisory boards of prominent citizens, and membership dues while others are unstructured. The vast majority are totally volunteer organizations and depend for professional services on the pastor or minister who is the official sponsor.

Some church-sponsored organizations for the widowed have become nationally known and widely emulated. THEOS (They Help Each Other Spiritually) was founded in 1962 in Pittsburgh, Pennsylvania, by Ms. Bea Decker, who was then a recent widow. Primarily involved with younger widows and their families, providing both direct outreach services and educational resource programs, THEOS has through the Lutheran Service Society conducted training seminars for those who work with the widowed and ten-week group experiences for the widowed who need to work through their grief. There are ten chapters throughout the country, and the organization reaches many other interested groups through its monthly newsletter.

The Catholic Church has also been involved in service to the widowed. Post Cana, an association of widowed persons in the Washington, D.C., area, founded in 1960 as part of the Family Life Movement in the Church, offers both local service and social groups, and a central body which acts as a coordinating council. Every newly widowed person in the parishes served by Post Cana is contacted personally by the clerical moderator of the local group. The emphasis of Post Cana has been on group therapy and mutual self-help.

NAIM Conference was also founded by Catholic laypersons and clergy. Since it began in 1957 at St. Patrick's Church in the Chicago area, it has grown to twenty-seven chapters in the metropolitan region and a coordinating council which provides overview to the local groups. The newly widowed are reached through informal Sunday afternoon meetings which widowed people are urged to attend, frequently by a neighbor or relative. The Conference sponsors social and family activities for its membership, and welcomes non-Catholics as guests. Widowed persons who remarry are encouraged to maintain an advisory relationship to their original group.

One is struck by the basic conservatism of these self-help programs. The majority of these widows are not professed feminists, nor do they question the often blatant male domination of the church-oriented groups, which often have a strict orthodoxy of values imposed from above by the spiritual advisor. For the most part these widows recognize little identity of concerns with other women's problems and while it is understandable that many older widows do not empathize with such issues as day care, abortion, or welfare reform, there are many points where their needs intersect with many women. They are all alone, many are poor and badly housed, and, as women, are dependent on a system which gives them a second-class status.

Yet of equal significance has been the really remarkable effect of these spontaneous voluntaristic experiences on the women who have actively participated in them. While serving others, they have found the means of recovery and redefinition for themselves. The volunteer-widow not only works through her own personal crisis, but she also learns valuable new skills in community organization and advocacy which readily transfer to other, larger issues. There is of course always the danger that some workers will become set into the mold of what Lynn Caine calls the "professional widow," unable to move on into a new postwidow life, but this has not been the case with the majority of widow aides we talked with.

Community College Service Programs · A promising new approach to voluntary and mutual self-help for widows has been developed through community college service programs. These programs have several advantages in serving widows. First, by their institutional setting, they tend to convey positive educational values. The process of transition from wife to widow becomes in part a learning experience for the individual. Second, the community colleges serve a broad base of people in their designated regions, and thus bring the widowed into contact not only with other widows, but with women (and men) from a variety of lifestyles and experiences. In addition a community college carries a strongly legitimate status, as both a training and service institution, and as a secular institution, working pragmatically in a secular setting, it avoids the clerical supervision that otherwise potential users of the church groups reject. And, most practically, such programs have the added advantage of being able to attract public funding.

One outstanding program seems to illustrate these assets well. The Widows' Exchange Program was instituted in 1974 through the Women's Center of Bristol Community College, Fall River, Massachusetts, long a clearinghouse for women's concerns in a broad two-state area.[14] The program's central goal is to help widows return to active participation in community life. Personal counseling for the recently widowed, problem-solving workshops, social activities, and information and referral services are offered while the membership meets as a whole at monthly meetings at which guest speakers address such issues as continuing education opportunities, legal and financial resources, and training for community volunteer work. Widow aides maintain a telephone contact network and a visiting committee that goes to see withdrawn, isolated, or housebound women.

Widows in this program are engaged in a "learning by doing" process. As volunteers, they have developed a scholarship fund, a needs-assessment survey, and a leadership training program, to be funded under Title I, Project Impact, of the Higher Education Act of 1972. This program makes a point of reengaging widows into the complex resources of the urban community—never an easy task for any group of women. Lopata feels that such reengagement is critical for widows and can rightfully be assigned to existing government agencies such as the Social Security Administration.[15] Such agencies could do far more for the newly widowed than they do, since they are positioned strategically to act as resources to the newly widowed—often the visit to the Social Security office is the first social contact of the new widow. At this point, trained counselors could help them to interpret and utilize the resources for their new life alone by helping with immediate short-term problems like housing and financial management. A short-term problem-solving intervention can be enormously useful, not only in meeting crisis needs, but in building in women a sense of competence and self-confidence they badly need as single women.

Chapter 4

DIVISIONS OF THE COMMON GROUND

*T*HE GENERAL categories of marital status—widowed, separated, divorced, never-married—are useful tools for exploring the differences and common concerns of single women; and they also quickly indicate some kinds of personal relationships that most people, women included, identify women by. But clearly there are other dimensions of the lives of single women, other critical life experiences and social situations that may enrich their lives or create special problems for them as single women. The problems, by their very nature, demand unique alternatives and solutions. Sizable numbers of women alone have needs that are not even close to being met because the women have until very recently been virtually invisible. These women, when they have sought support, have tended to form separate pockets of advocacy directed toward specific goals, narrowly defined. This is now changing and one is beginning to see dramatic new approaches to mutual self-help and group action which involves large numbers of single women.

The experience of an elderly woman who has never married, for example, differs from that of the young woman who thinks of herself as not yet married, just as the elderly widow's life is vastly different from many concerns of younger widows with growing families. Black women told us repeatedly that their single status had different meanings in their world than in the mainstream, largely white, society;

Third World women in general (with the growing exception of small groups of middle-class professional women) do not want to submerge their cultural differences in a movement that first appeared to identify and support the priorities of white women. This chapter, therefore, will look more closely at the needs of the elderly women alone and at those of minority women.

There are other kinds of smaller groups as well whose social situations are little known. Rural women alone, for example, are neglected; the "heavy urban bias" in research about family life reflects the difficulty of obtaining data from sparsely populated areas. The little information we have shows that fewer than a quarter of all single women live in rural areas and a disproportionate number of them are elderly widows with little schooling and marginal incomes. Rural farm and nonfarm women tend to marry earlier than their urban counterparts, and the younger single women in rural areas, whether never married, widowed, or divorced, tend to move to larger metropolitan areas in the more populous states, presumably for the improved employment opportunities.[1] However, in many rural states, there are small cities and large towns where single women live, but their needs have not been counted in the social planning and advocacy efforts thus far directed to the needs of single women.

Farm life probably could still support extra single household members as family workers, as it has in the past, but in rural life the prevailing stereotypes may suppress new nontraditional roles for women. True, some rural areas have witnessed the modern phenomenon of collectives and communes, made up largely of young unattached members of both sexes, but the new lifestyles are urban imports usually strenuously rejected by their conservative rural neighbors. Collectives of single women are reportedly scattered here and there around the countryside of northern New England and other locations, but most of these women also come from urban backgrounds and at the moment details of these groups are obscure. More needs to be learned here.

LESBIAN WOMEN

No other group of women has been so isolated, stigmatized, misunderstood, both in and outside the women's movement. Until very recently, gay women have been regarded as psychopathologically deviant—even dangerous—women. Like other low-status minorities, many lesbians have hidden their identities, remaining in marriages or living alone, simply to be able to survive, to preserve their respectability, often to keep their children, for many lesbians are also mothers.

Most lesbians are also working women, subject to the same economic pressures and discriminations faced by all single women, but in addition they often dare not identify themselves and work for their own concerns for fear they will lose their jobs. Lesbian women are white and black, low-income and upper-class, young and old, yet no one is sure just how many American women are gay. The most reliable data still are the Kinsey studies of a generation ago, which estimated between one and two percent of American women were lesbians. Even more striking was the fact that around one-third of all the women interviewed had had some homosexual experience. Some gay activists claim that there are now more lesbians than male homosexuals as a result of the strength of the women's movement.[2] Accurate demographic data on gay women and their dependents are needed to begin realistic social planning, but even the small group presently known can offer some valuable insights into the concerns of single women.

The crucial issue for lesbian women is legitimacy—community acceptance and immunity from harassment. Until very recently such legitimacy was hardly thought possible and consequently most voluntary associations among gay women were refuges rather than activist organizations. Emboldened by the civil rights movement of the early sixties and the parallel rise of feminism, many gay women have "come out" to join alliances and networks which publicly identify their cause. Established organizations like the Daughters of Bilitis have become more visible and more active, helping form hotlines, student groups, social clubs, local clearinghouses, even a lesbian credit union. Lesbian groups have also joined in such national organizations as The Gay Activist Alliance, the Gay Liberation Front, and the Sexual Freedom League, and there are now more than eight hundred gay groups in this country, with goals ranging from sociability to legislative reform.

The relationship of lesbians to the mainstream of feminism, however, remains ambivalent—not because the lesbians do not share feminist goals, but rather because many feminist leaders fear and reject the support of gay women. The most devastating blows aimed at feminist activists have always been attacks on their sexuality, a wholly vulnerable region of self-image and personal identity, and many feminists fear the support of lesbians would jeopardize the movement's appeal to straight women. This uneasy alliance became apparent in the formative years of the new feminism and was a crucial policy matter at the first national Congress to Unite Women in 1969, when lesbians were pointedly excluded from both publicity and participation in basic decision-making.[3]

At the second congress in 1970 the lesbians had organized, first under the name of Radicalesbians, later calling themselves humorously the Lavender Menace. They openly challenged the other feminists (predominantly National Organization of Women leaders) and held workshops and forum discussions on the issues of sexism within feminism. Many straight women accepted the honesty and courage of the gay women and welcomed their support, particularly on the issues of equal opportunity and civil rights which affected them all, and lesbian mothers joined in supporting child care and abortion reform.

At the same time homosexual women and men were actively seeking public support for their particular concerns, and on June 28, 1970, the first Gay Liberation March took place in New York City, and lesbians joined the march in large numbers. Another small step was taken in December 1973, when the American Psychiatric Association issued a press release, stating the association's new position that homosexuality was "to be no longer a disease." In other professional associations gay subgroups had openly formed to explore the implications of sexism in their own professions and colleagues. The first of these, the Social Responsibilities Round Table of the American Library Association, founded in 1970, has been followed by other groups, such as the Association of Gay Psychologists, the Gay Nurses Alliance, and the Gay Teachers Caucus of the National Education Association.[4]

The injection of homosexual issues into the forums of professional associations has been important to the employment of gay women, particularly in certain professions deemed "sensitive," such as teaching, where discrimination based on sexual preference has cost many gay women their livelihood. In 1969, the California Supreme Court ruled that such discrimination was unlawful, as have local courts in San Francisco and Washington, D.C., although the issue is unresolved, even unfaced, in the majority of school districts.[5]

At the state and national level, the struggle for acceptance goes on.[6] The Federal Civil Service Commission has recently reversed its ruling that homosexuals are "unfit for government service." Bella Abzug has introduced an amendment to the 1964 Civil Rights Act to include the phrase "affectional or sexual preference"—but there is little hope for its immediate passage. Some states are considering specific legislation to guarantee the civil rights of homosexuals, sponsored in some cases by publicly avowed homosexuals such as Representative Elaine Noble, elected to the Massachusetts General Court in 1974, the first known lesbian in the country to serve as a state legislator.

The drive toward legitimate community status has pointed up the needs of many gay women (and men) for specialized social services which recognize their individual situations. In spite of the traditional Christian—Judaic proscriptions, many individual clergy and some church groups and councils have begun quietly to offer support services, counseling, and sex education that focus on issues of homosexuality and even gay family lifestyles. The Unitarian-Universalist Association's Department of Education and Social Concern has developed training materials and curricula on gay relationships, the United Methodist Church Council on Youth Ministries has offered services to homosexual youth, and Dignity, a mutual self-help group for Catholic gays, has been developing national objectives to present to the Catholic Bishops' Council in 1976.[7]

Counseling and mental health services have changed their focus from the earlier emphasis on altering sexual preferences to one on successfully functioning in a preferred lifestyle. In Massachusetts the first licensed mental health facility with a gay orientation, the Homophile Community Health Service, serves as a counseling and referral agency for homosexuals, providing counseling, psychotherapy, and educational services to individuals and institutions and information to the public.[8] Its official publications do not, however, appear to address the separate issues faced by lesbians, although counseling for child custody problems is one area of focus.

Much of the gay activism has been dominated by male homosexual leadership, as the September 8, 1975, *Time* magazine cover story amply demonstrates; and many lesbians do not feel a close identification with the needs of male gays, primarily for two reasons. Gay women reject the sexist exploitation they feel characterizes so much of the male homosexual's life. In addition, because many lesbians are also mothers, they must deal with such feminist concerns as legal custody, single-parenting, child care, and the creation of a stable family alternative, issues apt to be ignored or rejected by both the male homosexual community and the radical lesbians.

The Women in Transition Project in Philadelphia, described in the second chapter, has been one of the few organizations to offer specific legal counseling for lesbian mothers. Their advice is concise: "If you can possibly avoid it, stay out of court!" Although lesbian mothers won a significant victory in a Seattle court in 1974 when two gay women, each with children, were allowed to remain together and raise the children, such judicial leniency is rare. Much more typical is a 1975 case in which an eleven-year-old girl was taken from her lesbian mother. The child had lived with her mother and her mother's lover for a year and was returned to her father in another state. The mother was allowed limited visitation rights, in the father's apartment with the father present. The mother's lover was barred from all contact with the child. The decision was based on a writ of habeas corpus, issued in the father's home state and the child's original residence, where the original custody suit had been filed. The legal maneuvers were complex. The parents lived in different states, and testimony from an earlier hearing, including statements from psychiatrists and the girl's teachers affirming the child's health and happiness with her mother, was not considered, although an opposing psychiatrist called the mother's household "highly psychopathological." This testimony was substantiated by a social worker, but neither had ever met the child or the two women involved. The child was forcibly removed, screaming, from her mother and placed in her father's custody.[9]

Legal battles are not the only battles lesbian mothers face, however. Their children are apt to be victims of the rejection society accords their mothers; and even within the gay movement, many lesbians are not sympathetic to gay-parenting, regarding it as irrelevant or as an obstruction to setting up new lesbian lifestyles. Gay mothers who desperately need the support and shared experiences of other single parents thus are turning to such straight networks as MOMMA, the magazine for single parents, and to single mothers' support groups. Some welcome their participation while others feel they will endanger community support.

A basic issue with lesbians at this point is that of surviving their own rhetoric. Can lesbians really claim (and implement) the contention of some radicals that lesbianism is the final solution to the questions and demands of feminism? Jill Johnston's position that men are women's natural enemy, the sole barrier to female supremacy, is so exclusionary that it abandons not only existing lesbian families, but also the crucial support of the mainstream feminists. And, what of those women for whom a separate life with women is seen as one of several options to be selected within the course of one lifetime? The single women we interviewed expressed interest in some of the lesbian alternative family styles, such as collective, female-headed families, which jointly raise the children of their members; and no woman expressed a wholesale rejection of legitimate gay advocacy, although some organizations did. Groups of older widows, for example, found the values and goals of gay women to be antithetical to their own; but most of the women individually were committed to changing *all* social stereotyping, including the reinterpretation of men's roles in the family and workplace.[10]

ELDERLY WOMEN

Dr. Robert Butler says, "The old are people caught in a cultural time lag—suddenly there are large numbers of them, and no one knows quite what to do."

The statistics alone are significant. Today, twenty-two million people, over 10 percent of America's total population, are over sixty-five and three out of every four are women, more than half of them widows. Declining birth rates, advances in medicine, and the extended life expectancy of women beyond the childbearing years make the elderly the fastest growing segment of our population. When many of our parents were born, only 4 percent of Americans were over sixty-five, but it is estimated that by the year 2050 this population will exceed 25 percent of the total.[11]

What kind of image can we project from this huge group of older Americans? And what kind of agenda are elderly persons, particularly older women alone, developing? What kinds of social institutions are responding to the needs and goals of older women—and in what ideological framework? Are social programs for the elderly to be considered welfare, or are they entitlements, rights, national priorities?

One thing is certain—older people as a group are here to stay, no longer a rare phenomenon of longevity providing ancient wisdom, but a sizable proportion of a changing, urbanistic, increasingly complex society. Their experience of that society, spanning a time in which traditional family structures and individual roles have undergone irreversible changes, has been significantly different from that of younger Americans.

Older women were brought up to value the roles of wife and mother first, far ahead of the roles of worker and community member. Most were not expected to learn the kinds of skills needed for survival in modern urban living, which depends so heavily on personal attainment and abilities, and involvememt in voluntary and community associations.

They are less educated, more class- and ethnic-bound women—and they are poorer than younger single women.[12] Small wonder then that not long ago elderly women were invisible. In a highly mobile society, organized around small two-generation family units, the oldest women live alone, survivors in poorer, often unsafe, neighborhoods. Traditional community resources based on village and small-town life-styles, have declined, no longer providing useful links to the resources of a mass society. These fundamental changes have been underscored by what activists now call "agism," the artificial segregation of the generations in family and community life. Elderly persons, especially women, are seen as low-status simply because they are old in a society which values youthful energy, physical beauty. The dignity of old age, the positive values of long life experience, have somehow been lost on a fast-moving, youthful culture.

From the 1930s, the political process has been responding with social planning and legislation directed to the increased number of aged in the country. The cornerstones of entitlement have been the Social Security Acts and Medicare, programs granting certain guarantees of income and health care to older families and their survivors. They are based on traditional assumptions of American family life: that the male is the head of household and principal earner of the family and that marriages remain intact until dissolution by death. These assumptions, valid enough at one time, no longer match the needs and life situations of many older women alone.

The Older Americans Act of 1965, and its subsequent amendments, gave even broader recognition to the needs of the elderly, not only for income security and health care, but for housing, nutrition programs, transportation, and work alternatives, both paid and volunteer. It provided the enabling legislation to systematize and coordinate programs for older persons through the establishment of state agencies, which act as umbrella institutions, to plan service networks and coordinate the activities of all public and private agencies serving the elderly.[13] Other legislation supporting civil rights, subsidized housing, food stamps, and pension reform, to name but a few, has created additional state and federal responses to the needs of the elderly. In short, we have, in the past forty years in this country, created an enormously complex bureaucracy which has the potential for vast resource allocation, expanded services, and a new role for older persons.

Parallel to the growth of this bureaucracy has been the growth of powerful national lobbies, a movement toward formal organization that received its major impetus in the drive for Medicare in the early sixties. The most powerful of these lobbies include the American Association of Retired Persons (7.7 million members) and the National Council of Senior Citizens (3 million members), which is linked to organized labor. In addition, there are the National Association of Federal Employees, the National Caucus on the Black Aged, the National Council on the Aging, and the National Retired Teachers Association. Many of them have experienced legislative staffs, provide newsletters and other publications to their members, and act as lobby coordinators and advocates for the rank and file of the elderly. [14]

These earliest pressure groups for older persons have shown a strong male bias, both in their leadership and in their programs. Historically, they have been focused on the issues of retirement, a focus which presupposes the retirement of the *male* head of the family, not that of his dependent wife. Some of the most successful federal programs reflect the same bias. For example, there are many programs designed to reinvolve retired workers, in volunteer and part-time advisory and service positions and in a variety of enterprises and community organizations. While the programs are by no means exclusively male, they tend to recruit older persons with long work histories and those with demonstrated business and organizational skills. The Service Corps of Retired Executives (SCORE), which functions as an advisory pool through the Small Business Administration, is almost entirely a male volunteer group. In the Boston office, for example, there is one female advisor, the former owner of an employment agency, in the whole program. Other volunteer programs under ACTION, the federal agency for volunteers, or under state sponsorship have difficulty in attracting female participants even when they are designed to use homemaker and parenting skills. The Homemaker Health Aides, for example, administered through state agencies, has trouble finding recruits, even with a stipend of over $4 per hour. [15]

The executive leadership of the national organizations listed above are almost without exception male. It is perhaps not surprising that such groups would turn at first to those with management skills and experience in advocacy, but they further exclude older women from the decision-making and organizational processes they need so badly to learn. Some new and radically different groups have thus come into being, specifically to fill this learning gap, to tap the skills of nontraditional organizers and to form new alliances with other activists.

The Gray Panthers · One of the most widely known of
the new groups is the Gray Panther Movement.[16] Founded in 1970 in
Philadelphia by a remarkable woman, Maggie Kuhn, and some of her
colleagues who had been forced to retire, the organization expanded to
over twenty cities and has recently merged with the Retired Professionals Action Group, an activity sponsored by Ralph Nader. The Gray
Panthers are now partially supported by Nader funds, as well as by
small grants and individual contributions.

Today the Gray Panthers can best be described simply as a rapidly
growing network of people, old and young, drawn together by deeply
felt common concerns for human liberation and social change. The
young and the old live outside the mainstream of society. Agism—discrimination against persons on the basis of chronological age— deprives
both groups of power and influence. The Gray Panthers believe that
the old and the young have much to contribute to make our society
more just and humane, and that each needs to reinforce the other in
goals, strategy and action.

The Gray Panthers emphasize that they are a movement, not an organization. Their encouragement of the membership of young activists
is unique, and the group has both youthful energy and the wisdom and
experience of those over sixty-five. They project an image of radical
militancy quite at variance with more conservative groups of senior citizens. They do not, for instance, emphasize increased government services for older persons so much as they push for action and basic change
in the institutions and service systems themselves. In the case of nursing home problems, an area of concern for all organizations of the elderly, the Panthers are advocating the creation of new and legitimate
living alternatives for older persons, such as collectives and three-gener-
ational communities.

While not a single-sex association, the Gray Panthers are organized
around a concept of shared leadership, and have encouraged women to
take assertive roles in both policy planning and social action. They publish a newsletter, bibliographies, an organizing manual, and other media
materials. The first national conference was held in Chicago in the fall
of 1975, to ratify new articles of agreement and to discuss new agendas
for their membership.

The accomplishments of the movement are as sweeping in scope
as its orientation. They have sponsored legislative support in the fields
of national health care, housing, and nutrition; free banking and transportation networks in some communities; housing coalitions which

encourage the "de-ghettoizing" of housing for the elderly; needs-assessment surveys in many localities on alternatives to nursing homes, consumer issues, mass transportation, and home health care. They opposed the Vietnam war and urge the amnesty of the war resisters. Their current priorities lie in the area of national free health services and alternatives to compulsory retirement.

The Panthers have demonstrated an extraordinary potential of organized talent and capacity for self-directed change among the newly militant elderly. Even more important for older women has been the provision of new roles and new solutions to their needs and problems.

NOW Task Force on Older Women · The Task Force on Older Women developed from a policy resolution at the NOW national convention of May 1974.[17] Its main functions are to initiate legislative change at the national and state levels and to coordinate the efforts of elderly advocacy in local NOW chapters. Major priorities include retirement security, income maintenance, pension reform, health and welfare services, job opportunities, and retraining for older women. The NOW Task Force has sponsored the Displaced Homemakers Bill now before the Congress (H.R. 7003) to set up programs and training for housewives who have been widowed or divorced or whose government benefits have ended. They are currently designing new jobs for older women that use the skills women have employed as housewives and mothers, such as home health technicians, lay advocates to help other women cut through bureaucratic red tape, neighborhood safety specialists, staffers for community outreach vans, and the like.

NOW local groups developing resources for older women are encouraged to link up with other groups with common concerns, especially those working to develop new paid work opportunities for older women to replace their volunteer efforts in the community. One such program has been sponsored by the Jewish Vocational Service.[18] This organization has set up pilot models in three cities (Boston, New York, and Chicago) to help men and women over fifty-five reenter the world of paid work. The programs, funded by the Department of Health, Education, and Welfare, the Department of Manpower Affairs, and the Combined Jewish Philanthropies, are staffed by older workers.

Jobs are also the concern of Project Retain in Boston, which works closely in the local CETA councils to develop retraining and job placement procedures of special benefit to those over fifty-five.[19] Special counseling is offered to help older women make the transition from home to the community and work force. Of equal value are the efforts of these projects to publicize the assets of the older worker to prospective employers.

Educational institutions are also playing a special role in the transition of the elderly from traditional roles to new lifestyles. Community colleges now offer reduced or free tuition to elderly citizens in their continuing education departments, and at some colleges, the community services divisions plan courses in organizational and community planning skills for older citizens—training bases for the new advocates. Five colleges in New Hampshire recently offered on-campus summer programs for senior citizens. They provided comfortable, low-cost accommodations and one-week adult education courses in such subjects as oral history, "survival tactics" for the older person, arts, crafts, and other recreational activities.[20]

One of the most pressing needs for older women has been for information networks which forge links to these burgeoning programs and opportunities. A new publication called *Prime Time*, published in New York and directed to the common issues and problems of older women, has become a clearinghouse for resources for older women that also provides them an alternative, positive image of themselves—their appearance, their roles, their usefulness in a new kind of society.

But what of the older woman alone who needs not activism, not organizational skills, but basic survival—friendship, a warm meal, a winter coat, a place to sleep? Increasingly in our cities we are creating women derelicts, although dereliction has been assumed to be a social ill of men only. These women are "street women," alcoholics, ex-mental patients, the handicapped, the homeless—usually cut off from family and friends. Few programs even recognize the existence of these women though they are numerous in any large city, but one program which does is Rosie's Place. Based on the Catholic Worker philosophy of Dorothy Day, Rosie's Place is more than a drop-in center, less than a "rehabilitative" program.[21] Part of the Christian ministry of a group of Catholic women activists who work out of an inner-city settlement house, Rosie's Place serves women between forty and sixty-five. Many are homeless, sleeping at friends' or in doorways, hungry, lonely, down and out. Rosie's Place feeds them, finds them clothes, provides a home base—and doesn't ask too many questions; it is, as one worker says, "casual, comfortable, compassionate, cool." The women are now involving other neighborhood women in a volunteer mutual self-help effort, to provide cooking and company, particularly over weekends and holidays, when loneliness can be overwhelming. Rosie's Place depends almost solely on contributors who "feel it's a good thing to merely offer free basics to women."

All these activities, programs, groups, and national organizations, it seems to us, are straws in a powerful new wind. Older women today, as Lopata has said, are unique. "These women form only a segment of, at most, two generations of one society; they present an historical instance of people born and brought up under conditions which are not likely to be duplicated in future generations of human beings." [22] It will be critical for the next generation of older women to learn the new ways of reconnecting to a society increasingly complex and voluntary, but older women today or tomorrow must acquire participatory skills. The varied resources reviewed above are valuable training bases for just such learning. Certainly they will expand and change over time to adapt to an increasingly educated and sophisticated population of women—but for now, they represent the cutting edge of the new advocacy.

MINORITY WOMEN

"The next step in understanding among women and between peoples is mutual identification of needs. Many of life's difficulties for Native American women are no different than those of other minority women—blacks, Chicanas, or the Appalachian poor. And then when the commonalities between minority and majority women are recognized . . . we may expect to witness a national movement for the quality of peoples and sexes." [23]

These words of Shirley Hill Witt, an Iroquois Native American, clearly point to the way ahead, but the fact that this "next step" is not imminent and that it may not even occur at all was glaringly evident at the International Women's Year conference in Mexico City, in June 1975. Factions, cliques, alliances, caucuses, merged and dissolved; wholesale walkouts occurred when national ideologies clashed. The priorities of highly articulate white Western women—employment opportunities, legalized abortion, political legitimacy, and individual autonomy—seemed almost heartless next to the stark survival needs of the nonwhite majority from the Third World. A universal "women's agenda" seemed almost impossible to construct, when *The New York Times* urged the conference, in a widely publicized editorial, to resolve these differences by focusing on the overriding needs of women alone. [24]

Certainly in this country, alliances between feminists and minority women have been tenuous, marked by misunderstanding, mistrust, and genuine cultural conflicts while feminist activism in the Third World has been largely among small groups of educated middle-class women whose outlook and lifestyle closely resemble that of their counterparts among white women.[25] Underlying the ambivalence of minority women about joining cause with the white majority is a rhetoric which says that racial discrimination has first priority.

Yet minority women have everything to gain by a coalition with white women, particularly if the issue is the needs of women alone. The 1972 Virginia Slims American Women's Opinion Poll reported that 62 percent of black and other minority women favored changes in the status of women compared with 40 percent of white women, an important response when single women are more numerous in minority populations than in the white majority.[26] They also remain single longer; they take early and continuing responsibilities for the lives of others in their families; and they are at the bottom of any economic scale one might devise.

Making sense of the statistics concerning the population of minority women in this country is not an easy job, but it is an important one. The useful special edition of the *Civil Rights Digest* called "Sexism and Racism: Feminist Perspectives," for example, often considers all minority women under the one category "nonwhite." And figures for the Spanish-speaking population contain serious errors due to language barriers and migration. (It is estimated that in New York City alone 200,000 Puerto Ricans are uncounted.)

A general profile of minority women can be drawn, however, from the 1971/2 figures used in the *Digest.*[27] Loosely speaking, close to half (45.8 percent) the nonwhite females over fourteen are single. Broken into the three subgroups, the smallest is that of divorced women, the largest the unmarried, and the middle group of widows is only half the size of the unmarried group. In a theoretically representative gathering of ten single nonwhite women, six would be unmarried, three widowed, and one divorced.

It is also important to note that minority women are very often heads of household—28.9 percent of all black families and 29 percent of all Puerto Rican families are headed by women. But their incomes are low; 30 percent of minority women workers are employed as domestic service workers or low-level clerical and technical workers and only 12 percent of the Puerto Rican women worked full time all year.

In the Southwest there are large numbers of Native Americans and Chicanos, but there is little data concerning single women in these cultures. Certainly Native American women are on the lowest part of any scale for employment, education, and health. Even their status within the culture has declined since precolonial days, for once many if not most Indian societies were matrifocal and matrilinear, but this has changed under the pressures of the dominant Anglo culture.

Chicana women enjoy high status, as the true center of the home and family, but roles external to those concerns are not sanctioned by the culture. Being a single woman is considered highly undesirable and often goes unreported; girls marry young. Divorce is not seen as an option, being barred by the Church and traditional family values.

This scant outline of the life situation of minority women in a white society makes it clear that single women share needs that cross racial barriers. Poverty, inequality of opportunity, heavy child care responsibilities, culturally defined stereotypes, all impede minority women. Yet few single minority women are turning to mutual self-help associations.

One factor that may help to explain this is family style. The nuclear family as a basic unit has never been especially useful in minority life in this country, where extended family networks have frequently meant the difference between survival and dissolution. Single women in these kinship networks have had important—even crucial—roles to play. (An excellent description of how black families function and maintain themselves under the pressures of urban poverty and discrimination is anthropologist Carol Stack's book, *All Our Kin: Survival Strategies in a Black Community*.[28]

Chicana families, too, depend heavily on their women, to act as links to the white—often hostile—society. It is the women who deal with the schools, the welfare officials, the law, on behalf of other family members.[29] Such "linking pin" roles are common in all minority families, and closely resemble the ways white female-headed families cope in the larger society.

Perhaps it is this very real importance of women in minority life which prevents many from forming alliances with white advocacy. One of the most commonly heard statements of black women is that "black women don't need liberation, they are already liberated." In a certain simplistic sense, that is true. The black women we interviewed felt strongly that they were much further along the road to self-determination than were most white women—and that they saw the pitfalls of that road more realistically. They also resented the luxury of *choice* with which white women seemed to be struggling, choices of entering or leaving the work force, of child care versus home care, of preserving or terminating a marriage. One woman, in a group interview with the staff of an inner-city women's educational center, said this about her responsibilities as a divorced mother and professional woman:

You say, I've got to work, and I'm a mother and I go to school, so you distribute those responsibilities in your time. It's not comfortable. It's not comfortable having to get up and go to work every day. It's not comfortable realizing that if you don't get up and go to school, the rut is going to get deeper. I didn't go to school because it was the nice or the comfortable thing or I thought I was going to enjoy every minute of it. I hated it! I could never sit back and say, I loved getting up to go to school. I didn't even love going to the graduation! But I wanted more mobility than I had where I was.

Another critical point of departure for minority women is the image they feel the feminists project. The director of a project on educational opportunities for inner-city women stressed this difference in a description of her minority staff:

Like many of the middle-class women represented by much of the women's movement literature, women [in this project] express a realization of the futility and wastefulness of preoccupation with household tasks—endless compulsive cleaning and decoration, etc. However, few women expressed resentment of the responsibilities and duties of mothering. On the contrary, the raising of one's children represents the core and the hope of the day-to-day struggle for survival in which these women are engaged.[30]

It is clear that at least the *rhetoric* and media *image* of the women's movement is in bad repute with many minority women. A Puerto Rican woman, writing about the lack of involvement of *Puertorriqueñas* in feminism, said:

For all Puerto Rican women, the movement must concentrate on education concerning the issues involved and the true distinction between the women's rights movement and the negative image of "women's liberation" created by the media. Although we have been mistakenly led to believe that radical feminists advocate doing so, Puerto Rican women are not going to divorce themselves from their cultural heritage or be alienated from their men. . . .
It has been the basic misunderstanding of the movement as anti-male, anti-family, and somehow sexually promiscuous which has made it difficult for more Puerto Rican women—as well as Anglo American women, I might add—to embrace the cause of feminism.[31]

Finally, the difficult and complex issue of black and minority women's relationships to their men, and to the struggle for racial equality, has prevented many women from joining white women on problems of mutual concern. The origins of women's protest in this country lie in the long struggle for black civil rights. Through their long identification with anti-slavery causes, and the civil rights activism of the 1960s, women learned the tactics of activism, the skills necessary for organization and self-directed change. Indeed, this "proxy fight for freedom," as one feminist calls it, brought many white women into public life.[32] At the same time, women of all races were told to submerge their feminist objectives to those of the male-led civil rights movement. This perception that rights and freedom are somehow divisible has created enormous doubt and confusion for minority women. They want to support their men in the struggle for equality, but not at any cost. One of our respondents, a young black woman, expressed this ambivalence this way:

My mother was the head of household, and she was always head of the household even when my father was there. She was the one who was working. He rather enjoyed staying home and taking care of the children. He'd work when he could find a job. He was a very gentle man, very articulate, the top ten percent of his graduating class, and then went into the service. When he came out, who knows what happened? But thinking about those two together, I can see what my father was and why he was the way he was. And my mother was constantly surviving—you've got to work. Kids have to eat, and we have to pay the rent.

There's another thing about being single. There are a lot of things that I feel at this point I wouldn't do because I've never met anybody that hasn't tried to restrict me in some way. "Well, you can't do this now, because you're my wife." Or, "You can't do that because it would be a reflection on me." I don't want that—I need somebody who'll say, "Do what you want to do, and it's all right with me. I love you." And there are very few people like that. And black women are definitely realizing it too. I don't know how many black professional women stay single rather than marry a white man who will accept them for those things. I've resigned myself to the fact that I could stay single, because there are not that many black men who can accept that. Black men tend, when they get to that point, to marry white women, because they don't feel a black woman could appreciate them at that level. That's how a lot of black men feel.

Geraldine Rickman, a black woman writer who feels that black women will become the "linking pins" between black men, white women, and white men, points out the risks they thus will run—loneliness, further alienation from black male leadership, increasing personal burdens.[33]

Few writers really stress this last factor sufficiently. Single women carry many burdens, working, maintaining a family and home, struggling to make connections in an indifferent community. To expect all such women to be activists on their own behalf is unrealistic, in spite of the many, many examples to the contrary in these pages. The tasks of survival in the single life for women, particularly for minority women, are more than heavy enough to account for the lack of many formal voluntary associations among the ghettos and barrios of the cities.

Most feminist advocacy has been among black middle-class professional women, who account for less than 10 percent of all the professional women in the country. It is from their ranks that the new National Black Feminist Organization has recently been formed. And there are new alliances forming between such organizations as the National Organization of Women and the Urban League, who recently joined in a boycott against General Mills; and the National Association for the Advancement of Colored People, the Mexican American Legal Defense and Education Fund, and NOW have joined to protest widespread failure to enforce affirmative action programs.[34]

Such alliances represent tentative detente between essentially centrist groups of both movements, and do not begin to reflect the objectives of the radicals or the rank and file of either faction. Groups fighting for equal rights and social welfare are still fragmented minorities. Unless all women, of all races seek some kind of coalition for common cause, there is no way for them to achieve a majority. It is a formidable task, in which no group has more at stake than single women.

V O I C E S

"What I most wanted was . . . someone I could take care of and love."

The speaker is a middle-aged social-service professional who has never married. She lives in an apartment in a working-class suburb with her daughter whom she adopted several years ago.

It'd been roaming around in the back of my unconscious for some time. But I made a very definite decision in 1970 that I would like to pursue it. I think when you start approaching middle age, you begin to take stock a little bit. I certainly hadn't given up ideas of getting married somewhere along the line, but I began to realize that what I most wanted was a family, somebody who belonged to me, someone I could take care of and love. Since marriage didn't seem to be in the cards, I decided to pursue adoption. I think it was the perfect course for me. . . . I've always had the feeling that if I had gotten married, one of the really big reasons would be to have a family. As I've said to a lot of people, I didn't want to miss the whole show, so I made a very definite decision that I would try to adopt. I think it's perhaps one of the few decisions I've made very, very consciously . . . plotted it very carefully.

I had also been in my old job for several years and it also was very clear to me that it was time for a change, or else I would settle down there and stay until I retired. But the decision to adopt was the paramount issue.

It was a great wrench to leave the locale where I was living—I'd been there many years and had a lot of friends and a good life there. The whole time I lived up here without my daughter was hard. I had a nice apartment, but making friends . . . I think that has something to do with age—as you get older, it's not as easy. When you don't have children, you hardly fit in with the families, and you hardly fit in with the younger singles' groups, so it was difficult.

Well, suddenly everything just meshed right. My child's foster home was closing and the agency had to find homes for these children. I had had my home-study approved and this worker contacted the right people and I was off to the races. I visited my daughter four times, and then we came back here together. It was traumatic! I lost ten pounds. Like so many of life's experiences, you'd almost be afraid to do it again—when you don't know, you do things that you don't think about.

Actually, it worked out fine. Her adjustment wasn't that difficult. She cried at night and she didn't understand what was happening—I don't blame her. I felt completely immersed in the experience—I literally did nothing else that summer. I had a lot of help from my parents. Not a smothering kind of help—they left us alone, but they were there. I discovered what I never knew about children, that the days are long. I found myself plotting endlessly about walking to the mailbox for a little outing, or to the local playground.

My friends were very supportive. Of course I now have a network of friends who are single adoptive parents, but at that time I didn't know very many. Some of those people have had people who were critical of their adopting, but I can't think of a soul except one of my aunts who made a comment to my mother that she thought that women who had children ought to stay home and take care of them—she objected to me being a *working* mother! I think most people thought it was a fascinating idea. They were kind of looking to see how it would work out.

In fact, my parents always said the right things, the right and true things, to me. For example, "It's better to be single than to have the unhappiness of a bad marriage," which I think is true too. And my mother kept emphasizing to me what hard work child-rearing was and I know that now. But I certainly knew they wanted to have grandchildren, which is *not* the reason I adopted. I didn't adopt to give them a grandchild, but it's nice for them, too.

When you change from being a working woman to a working parent, I think you invest a little less in your work. At least I have. I think I give full measure when I'm there, but I don't do the after-hours of thinking or meetings or committees or stuff like that. I just don't feel that I can. You see, I don't think I really understood parenting until I had the experience. I'd been helping people do it for years, but for myself I certainly understand a heck of a lot more now than I ever did before. I certainly don't think I understood the frustrations of being a mother until I was doing it. Parenting is a twenty-four-hour-a-day job, especially when they're little.

Based on this experience, I don't think I attempt . . . any more to comment or pass judgments on people's marriages. I've never been married. I used to think I was an expert on everything. That doesn't mean that I don't talk to people about their marriages and offer them emotional support, but I'm a little more leery—I don't know that experience. Realizing what I know now about parenting, I'm a little more cautious in thinking I can help people with their problems.

I'm still single, but I'm a family person now. I think of ourselves as a family and I very often hear myself saying, "When I was single." My daughter made the difference. It really started when I left my other way of life—I was then somewhat typical of a single professional woman. I was embroiled in more organizations and spent a great deal of time with committees and groups and with community activities. I was well aware of the fact that I was getting very sick of it. It was getting very hollow. When you're alone, you have to fill up your life somehow or other, unless you're a recluse or like to read a lot.

I am at home now more than I ever was then. People wondered how I would adjust to this—after twenty years of being able to go at the drop of a hat, I am now very tied down. But I rather enjoy it. I suppose part of it is that I'm so tired at night, I just throw in the laundry and watch a little TV or read the paper! But I wouldn't have dreamed that it *wouldn't* bother me. . . . I traded what I consider shallow satisfactions. I think that when you have a child, there are the very small, daily types of satisfactions—when you see her happiness, or she's being very affectionate. And, it's fun.

Also, I'm very gregarious. I have a lot of company, and there is my SPACE group for adoptive parents which I helped organize in this area. We work for public support for this lifestyle and the choice to be a single adoptive parent. I think single women who want to do what I did have two options today. They can either work very hard to change legislation, to hope, for example, that more foreign children can be adopted by single parents. Or, they can do as I did, only more thoroughly, and really comb the states and agencies.

There are a lot of people who don't think that single people will make good parents. I frankly can see a lot of married people or divorced people or widows who don't seem to be doing any better job than I'm doing. But I'm awfully aware of the fact that if every child could have two parents, that's preferred. I'm sure, for instance, that my daughter will raise the question at some point in her life, "Why did *you* have to take me? Why didn't you leave me so I could have a daddy?"

As for my neighbors, it helps that I am a verbal, well-educated person who comes across as a solid citizen. Therefore, I think the neighbors respect me and accept my daughter. I live in a very blue-collar neighborhood. There are also some older retired people. I think they look on me as a bit of an oddity. If I was a woman with a child out of wedlock living here, I'm sure I'd be getting the glances and the evil-eye. Unfortunately, what some of my neighbors and the world in general say is, "Wasn't that a grand thing for you to do." They turn it around to say that I was so kind and generous to take this poor little waif, which really disgusts me, because she does more for me, I think. . . . But I think the average person looks on it this way, which of course puts me in a different position than divorced or widowed women with children, or women with children out of wedlock. It's kind of a unique situation.

My church has been very supportive. That's why I decided to go there. My daughter is very well accepted there. She has a nice Sunday school teacher, and there's an older couple that have really become a second set of grandparents. Yes, it's been very nice, but there again, my status is known. Most people know it.

Would it have been the same had she been thought of as my illegitimate child? It would have been impossible. I'm always conflicted about this. Half of me says, "Well, so what! This is my business." The other half of me doesn't want her penalized. I really haven't had to make this an issue, because most people have known about me.

I honestly don't think I've been looked down on because of being a single woman. I don't think I've experienced that. But I think my profession might have something to do with this. I'm very much aware of how important to me it is to be something definite. I've always been aware of that. It has nothing to do with my daughter. I'm proud of being a professional woman. Even before motherhood, it defined me. Now, I could ask myself, has that always been because I've been single that I needed that definition? I just don't think being a parent has been that different for me because I've continued to be a professional.

It extends to other people, too—I have to get people fixed in my mind, in time and space. I don't think it's a snobby thing—I don't care if you're an accountant or a file clerk, or whatever. I found myself . . . even in my twenties and thirties asking people at parties what they did.

As I look around at most of the single parents in our SPACE group, it's very interesting. They are for the most part highly educated and in the helping professions. Really, there are very few who are in the lower echelon, office work or sales or something like that. That's too bad, but they perhaps wouldn't have the money. Child care is very expensive. I think there might be single women who want to adopt who just can't afford it. I think they would find it hard financially to have an independent home, and to finance day care and to be able to live like you want to live.

In some ways, I'm more like the young-matron "Mummy" in my spare time, which I don't necessarily say is true of all the women who are single parents. It just happens to be true of me. What I have missing in my life, and I know a lot of other single women feel the same way, is that I don't have very much heterosexual life with men. I find this very hard to come by, in a format that is acceptable. I work with some men—that's good. I do have a little contact. I do think you can get a little stultified with all women friends, and I know that's a problem for single women parents in general, finding satisfactory outlets. I'm not opposed to dating, I think that would be fine. I don't think that would be bad for my daughter or anything like that. But it's difficult finding the people.

I don't think too far ahead. I would say that the next three to five years won't be too different. I think she needs me as much as possible. One of the real problems is that I've boxed myself in professionally. If I want to move up the ladder, the price of that is moving into a longer work year and more responsibility. It might be longer hours. I'm not sure I want to pay that price right now. And, of course, by the time I decide I want to pay the price, I'll be pushing fifty, and I don't know if the opportunity is going to be available. But as far as making big changes, I'm not sure what price I'm willing to pay. I think I give my job good measure. I think I've got all I can handle now to go along in my present job and to be a mother.

I would certainly like to find somebody who would like to share a family life. I really spend a lot of time thinking about another child. You have to reach your own decision before you jump in to see whether you can make it or not—I have a feeling I could not. I would like to find a husband and, hopefully, he would have a family. Or we could adopt together. I'm getting older and I'm not going to get pregnant at this point. I would like to have a larger family if I could have some help with it. But I'm not sure whether I have the stamina to do it all over again by myself. For everything, there is a price. I think a larger family would be nice for my daughter, but I don't think you can add to your family because it would be good for the other children. I think you have to decide whether it would be good for *you* or not. And that's the part I get hung up on.

I've been working with a group of single mothers, all divorced. I learned very quickly how different the outlook is. I was so fascinated with how much these women had to talk about their ex-husbands. I think the problem is that they went along with the great American dream. You get married and you have a contract—when you have children, you have them together. And then, the contract is broken. It takes a long time and a certain kind of personality to get over this bitterness, and you feel left, holding the bag. (My situation is completely different. I never anticipated any help with the job.) One thing that surprised me was that they had such trouble with everyday things, like getting an apartment. Evidently, the landlords want to know the whole life history, what the support money is going to be and whether it's going to come through or not.

I sat there thinking, "Oh, my God, I can identify with these women from the point of view of child-raising, but these other matters?" When I want to rent an apartment, I tell the landlord that I'm employed. I tell him my income level. People don't have the same feelings about me. My concerns are more with things like loneliness, not being able to share the problems and the joys, too. I am aware of the fact that you trade off. O.K., so I'm alone and lonely at time, I'm lucky to have a lot of friends. I also don't have to accommodate myself to a mate, so that's a trade-off, too. I have fantasies like everyone else of getting married, but I know that it would be something like getting my daughter, a fluke.

part Two

SINGLE WOMEN: MEETING THE CHALLENGE

This society does not make it easy for women to live without husbands, yet an increasing number of single women are transforming their individual struggles for survival into lives enriched by their growing courage, zeal, and compassion. This section begins by looking at single women's lives in personal areas—how they live with their families, their friends, their neighbors, how they meet their desires for companionship and love—and then moves beyond to the steps they take to create full lives in the larger communities—what happens when they seek help from professional counselors, how they are planning their work lives, making their needs known, and influencing the machinery of the institutions that have governed their lives. Finally because each step along this path from the most personal self to the citizen working in the larger society is marked by the courage and strength single women have gained in the organizations they have formed to help themselves and each other, the book ends with a look at women's organizations. We look at past groups that obtained the vote but failed to gain equal rights and those of the present, and the role single women have in the unfinished struggle. For women can never be liberated unless both men and women are free to choose lives together or apart.

Chapter 5

INVISIBLE WOMEN IN
MARRIED COMMUNITIES

*H*OWEVER A woman becomes single—fate, revised plans, or long-term intentions—she must continue to live in a world populated by other people. Some of the most critical influences on her life will be the formal institutions of that world—the church, the schools, the law, and government—and this book will discuss these in later chapters, but the individual single woman is apt to consider the way these institutions relate to her life a secondary question. Her first concerns are for the problems and solutions she finds in the matters of her day-to-day life. How do her family and friends view her singleness? Do her children, if she has them, feel set apart because she is single? What are her social networks? And how does she build or rebuild them? What supports are available to her in her community setting? These informal social networks are where she spends much of her life, where she is hurt or helped by support or its lack, where the effects of the labels "widow," "divorcee," or "old maid" may limit her even more than the large difficulties she faces with the formal institutions that set the rules regulating her life.

This problem was obvious with many of the women we interviewed. One middle-aged woman we talked with said, "I don't use the word divorced in reference to myself and I'm just about at the point where I don't want to use any term to describe myself. I'm even thinking of starting over in another area with a new past."

We asked her what that new past would be. Her answer makes the problem plain: "I don't know—I'd give my own name and so forth, but I'd forget the whole divorced bit. I don't think acquaintances need to know it."

The issue of stigmatization, of feeling branded as someone deviant, incompetent, a somehow discredited member of one's community, is a subtle one. It invades a person's self-image, eats away at her essential femininity. Pressured by pervasive images of the "ideal family," the single woman daily confronts her singleness as it is seen by her relatives and close friends, her children's teachers and babysitters, by the social arrangements and organizations of her community which make her feel like an outsider. Certainly the woman who has never married and is also a mother experiences the effect of one of society's oldest stigmas. Even her closest associates and peers will brand her as "an unwed mother" unless she is an adoptive parent and publicizes that fact. It is encouraging, however, to note that public attitudes toward the unmarried biological mother are changing, albeit slowly, especially if the woman either gives up her baby for adoption or doesn't receive welfare. And attitudes toward divorce are also changing, but divorced women still encounter bias and prejudice, although older or more affluent women who live in a settled neighborhood find divorce matters less, both for the women themselves and their neighbors.[1] Nonetheless, many of the women we spoke with testified to the presence of this stigma, to the sense of not fitting into the community. "I sometimes feel as if I have two heads," one thirty-four-year-old mother living in the suburbs said. "If you're single and you're a parent—well, you don't fit into a studio flat in the city with the kids and you don't fit out here without a husband."

Widows experience the effects of the social stigma in subtler ways. A widow's former role has been abruptly altered; all too frequently her financial status is lower. And widows tend to become invisible women, set aside by a culture that worships youth and fears reminders of death and grief.[2] "You're really on a shelf," as one young suburban widow said. "As a widow, you're put into a little box and that's it. Goodbye. Nobody discusses it with you." On the other hand, another—older— widow pointed out, "The widow doesn't have to prove anything even if she had a rotten marriage. She is simply there and what has gone before is forgotten."

The never-married woman, long stereotyped as an "old maid," has only recently begun to assert her right to decide to be single and have her community accept it. But the social isolation of single, never-married women is one of the greatest barriers she must overcome.[3] One solution to this problem one woman found was to have "no relationship to the community," but she was irritated by our questions about it. "You keep pushing on my relationship to the community as though that were the only thing. So much happened to me regardless of the community because I was able to make communities in conjunction with my own set goals. I was growing and creating so much. So, to hell with the community!" Like the other never-married women we interviewed, she presented a firm view of the *value* of singleness. Yes, she "would have enjoyed relationships with other people, some contact in the community, but at the same time it wasn't crucial." Her strong feeling of self-worth was obvious—"I was meeting the demand to support myself emotionally. I knew where I was going. I wasn't really looking around for contacts. This is the essence of it—different groups bring out different facets of you, different kinds of friendships."

FAMILIES, FRIENDS, AND NEIGHBORS—
SUPPORT THAT SOMETIMES FAILS

Although the strongest supports for single women come from their families and close friends, there are some subtle shadings in that support. Certainly divorced women discover that friendships alter, relatives take sides, and sometimes parents who try to understand still cannot accept their daughter as a divorcee. One young woman likened her friends to a fireman catching her in a net as she jumped out of a burning building. "It really helps to have friends who cared about me—you're a terrible person because you got a divorce and your background is Catholic." Her mother "just assumes that at some point my husband and I will go back together. She's doing better than she used to but I don't think she can quite get the fact that I'm leading a life as a single person."

Another woman, who had been both widowed and divorced, also found her parents unable to provide "what I really needed—somebody to know that, sure, you want to be courageous but there are times when you just can't and you just have to wait." She had gone to them "expecting some moral support but what actually happened? My parents took my ex-husband's side. They had the problem of age, of understanding what was going on—I understand that. Their expectations of my doing the divorced or the widowed bit was giving parties graciously or getting into serious work or getting another degree or something like that."

In other cases families stood by with support while subtle cues came from married friends and neighbors indicating disapproval of the altered status. Where the women lived seemed to make a difference as well; those women in the more affluent suburbs complained of loneliness and isolation, but did not in general feel that their neighbors criticized them consciously, or were passing moral judgments on them. Instead they lived in a sort of tree-lined, ranch-style limbo with few guideposts for their behavior. One newly separated forty-five-year-old woman who lived in comfort in a charming, exurban community far from the city had this to say:

Everything in this community is all couples. I suppose there are political things that I've never been involved in that I could do, but again, the town itself is married—the whole town is married. . . . I feel sometimes as though I had a social disease, as though I don't really belong here *really*. I'm not sure, because I think now almost every family has divorce in it someplace and so for most people it's not that foreign to them. Most people who act cool to you do it out of a sense of not knowing what to say, not knowing what to do, or out of a fear of talking with you because they may see in their marriages some of the things that were in your marriage, which are probably in every marriage. . . . I have talked to several people and I've seen them get kind of nervous because I've mentioned certain things and feelings that I have, and they have said they've had the same kinds of feelings and then, I think, they just back off a little.

The church I go to happens to be a very married church. They do include the single people and I do go to a lot of their functions, but I eventually get tired of it. You know, it was kind of exhilarating to go out on my own at first, and find out I could do it and I could make it alone and I could have a good time going alone, but now—going out alone and coming home alone every time . . . it's not that exhilarating anymore.

And this is a transient community of people on the way up, and they're very interested in moving up. It's quite social. Tennis is the thing to do now, and boating is the thing in the summer and cocktail parties every weekend. And this is not my style. I went out for dinner with some married women in the neighborhood last week, and that's when I realized part of me had been amputated—because of the conversation. Married women are so *married*. I guess I was when I was married, but so much of the conversation revolved around what their husbands were doing, had done and were not doing and wouldn't do and refused to do, you know, all of those things. . . . I just sort of sat there, left out.

In contrast, women alone in working-class urban communities felt they were all too visible, that the community actively disapproved of them and branded their children with the "broken home" label. Anything their kids did wrong was blamed on the absence of a father, an assumption unfortunately encouraged by many professionals in the social sciences.

But this attitude may be changing. One review of the research on "fatherless homes" found that most existing studies are totally inconclusive because most researchers have a strong societal bias and label the father-absent family as deviant and pathological. Not surprisingly, the writers in the field who are challenging the old assumptions are black sociologists and women social scientists. Andrew Billingsley, for example, has worked tirelessly to present a positive view of the strengths of black family life in the American experience. His work is a much-needed alternative to the voluminous problem-centered research on black families. And the Women's Research Center has looked at both the reality of stigmatization of women single heads of families and at these same families as models of effective social units which *do* function, *do* cope, and *do* survive.[4]

The older women alone whom we talked with, for the most part widows living in publicly subsidized housing for the elderly, were both visible and invisible in the larger community. They lived in a world apart from the mainstream of local life and their lowered income reinforced the isolation, for there was little discretionary money for trips and visits. They went, therefore, on group tours to subsidized entertainment and on group-transported shopping trips, visible to the community solely as "an old people's outing club," rather than as individuals going about their daily lives.

THE WAYS FRIENDSHIPS WORK

A closer look at the friendship networks of single women will help us understand their community settings. Women alone are caught in a basic conflict: marriage and the family are still the primary commitments Americans believe women should make, yet women's needs for friendship are important to everyday life, and never more so than when the married state no longer exists. Women who accepted those commitments then turn logically to what remains of their family for support and affection. But the life cycle moves on—children mature, move away, and form new households, other relatives die—and never-married and childless women find the family an even more tenuous resource. Alternative life plans must be found and choices must be made. It is in the category of relationships *by choice* that good friendships occur.

Many writers and social scientists have analyzed the friendships of women alone from a variety of perspectives, but the emphasis is typically on negative, problem-centered strains and themes that suggest single women have more troubled lives and disordered relationships than we actually found. Further, since most social science finds it easiest to assume a static environment, fixed in the quantity and quality of resources, the fact that such networks are dynamic, constantly being changed, molded, and created anew is inevitably ignored. But time and the life cycle are potent variables.

One study of the friendships of divorced women found that while most divorcees kept most of their old friends, strains inevitably developed, especially with friends who were actually friends of the former husband. The women tended to acquire new friends, particularly other divorced women.[5] This was also true of the women we talked with. Obviously such friendships are a positive force in their lives, for other single women not only offer moral support, they also can share child care, meals, and transportation, all important units of currency in the exchange of services in everyday life.

Old friendships, however, present a problem. One psychotherapist warns that it is necessary to understand what divorce *means* to close friends in order to evaluate their reasons.[6] Some will see divorce as a threat to their own marriages, others experience guilt or shame vicariously, while still others find in the divorce the fulfillment of their own secret wishes. The "plot" of a divorce—who was the initiator, who opposed it, the presence of a third party—is also important to the attitudes friends take. It's necessary therefore both to be candid with friends and to allow them to talk out their feelings if the divorced person values these friendships.

Widows, too, find their old friends may be moved by unconscious reactions. Lynn Caine comments that many of her friends found her confrontation with mortality and grief unbearable and avoided her.[7] And Lopata found that friendships that were sustaining and nurturing depended on the widow's situation. Fewer blue-collar widows had had extensive couple-friends; since they instead knew and socialized with a few women friends and relatives, their friendships were not much changed after widowhood, especially if the woman was past sixty at that time of her husband's death. On the other hand, the friendships of upper-class women who'd had many couple-friends, largely initiated by the husband's work and lifestyle, suffered much strain when death changed their status. The older these women were, the more likely they were to be unhappy, angry, and withdrawn from former networks. Finally, Lopata found a few women, mainly educated persons with adequate incomes and a history of community involvement, who were able to move from couple-friends and old neighborhood patterns to new kinds of interests and activities, and consequently, new friends.[8]

Younger women alone now have more positive self-images than was once the case. It is reasonable to hope that as more and more women achieve higher levels of education, more work experience outside the home, and form new voluntary associations, the unhappiness of the present lonely generation of elderly widows will not be repeated—that there will be a new style of woman whose friendships have not been prescribed solely by marital status but are the result of a mutual choice. A woman's extended years of singleness, whether she has chosen that life or has survived a partner or a marriage, can reinforce supportive friendships which enhance everyday living. The younger women we saw, whether widowed, divorced, or never-married, were decidedly more innovative in developing friendships, more skillful in making links with community resources, more at home in the world at large than the older widows Lopata described. These younger women are working and teaching, organizing and politicizing their communities. Their friendships are shaped by their desires to make their own decisions about their own lives and then to make them work.

In summary then, single women often do feel branded and isolated within their communities, but the degree to which they feel that stigma and isolation seems to depend on a variety of factors: age, income, friendships, location of the community, and whether one is widowed, separated, divorced, or never married. Women have always seen themselves through the eyes of others and derive their sense of worth and involvement in the community from the opinions of family and friends. But now we are seeing more and more single women joining together, actively forging new kinds of social supports and networks that are adapted to their new lifestyles and their own needs.

NEW FRIENDSHIPS IN A COMMON CAUSE

A look at two different women's community groups in two cities near the same central city illustrates this new sense of community among women alone. The organizations differ markedly in style, goals, and the population they serve; yet they are alike in that they have been founded by community women in direct response to their needs and provide new kinds of services and supports for women alone.

The Women's Cooperative, Inc. [9] · Located in a settled, affluent, suburban city, seven miles west of the core city, this organization of around three hundred women is housed in a parish hall in a barely heated room rented for fifty dollars a month. The cooperative began as a support group several years ago when some older professional women wanted to identify resources for and needs of women in their suburb. They held a series of meetings that they advertised in the local paper, exploring the implications of the women's movement for women in their city. Their original goal, a multiservice center with a strong counseling component, has not been achieved as it was originally planned, primarily because their city already has the services of a variety of professional agencies, including town-sponsored youth services, family services, an excellent hospital and medical complex, and one of the strongest, most innovative school systems in the country.

The city itself is not a high-need, low-income area. [10] Its population of 91,066 has a median annual family income of $15,381, high by most standards, although that half of the families that earn less than that figure tends to be ignored when community boosters promote the city's image as a center of upper-middle-class affluence. It has a population density of 5,098 people per square mile, distributed among fourteen non-governing "village" units. Some are almost wholly residential, while others are urbanized commercial and industrial centers, with light industries and multiple housing units; but more than half the housing is single-family dwellings, many of them extremely large.

It is a well-educated community—over 79 percent of the adults have completed high school—and the cost per pupil of the public school system is $1,520, one of the highest in the nation for a city of its size. It is also overwhelmingly white, with fewer than 2 percent nonwhites, but 30.5 percent are first-generation Americans and 10.8 percent are foreign born. Once predominantly Protestant, since World War II the city has had an influx of Jewish families, who support five temples, and the Jewish High Holidays are observed on the public school calendar.

The women's original group changed both by necessity and circumstance during the initial period, adding younger women and housewives, many of them new residents who had moved to the community with job-mobile husbands. These were women in transition, looking to each other for support as newcomers to an established city containing many long-term residents. A core of half a dozen or more women formed the new leadership and saw the organization through its tedious process of incorporation as a public, nonprofit, charitable, and educational institution with tax-exempt status. Funding is based primarily on membership fees of six dollars per year. Other activities such as book fairs and the conferences have yielded small additional revenues. The cooperative is currently contemplating a self-supporting food cooperative and additional proposals for support from outside sources.

The original leaders set up a number of task forces in such areas as child care, counseling, and resources for and information about the education of women. Its first conference, Opportunities for Pre-School Children, cosponsored by the city government, the school and library systems, and the local State Office for Children, and resulted in an after-school child-care program that uses school property during non-school hours, primarily for the care of young children of working mothers. The program is a model of the kind of response the cooperative can make to a defined community need. In addition to being the fiscal agent for this program the cooperative serves as an information clearinghouse on child-care resources in the community.

One of the most effective areas of focus for the cooperative has been the task force on divorced and separated women. There were a number of female-headed families and other single women in the city who had little or no status in the community—at the worst, regarded as deviant, at best, invisible. The cooperative held a conference for women alone, again cosponsored by the city, which donated printing and publicity for the event. Workshops explored such issues as widowhood, divorce, finances for the woman alone, alternative living situations, legal issues, single-parenting, and personal growth and change. Follow-up questionnaires generated a new core of members with newly identified needs. The conference successfully provided information and community education concerning a genuine service deficit in the city, a deficit that might be defined as the need of single women to come together with like-minded peers to support each other and, even more important, design styles and directions of action which could improve the quality of their lives. The increased visibility of these women has been in itself an instrument for change and an opportunity for community "consciousness-raising." The cooperative is now considering a crisis line for divorced and separated women or the possibility of a once-a-week resource night for women alone. Farther into the future, some of the women would like to buy a house which would serve as a gathering place where women and their families could dine communally—in general, to provide an alternative to the current family lifestyle of the community.

It is in many ways a radical vision. The city's residents, for the most part, see themselves as nuclear families in single homes, leading private family lives that are to a greater or lesser degree isolated from those of their neighbors. There is, however, some neighborhood identity, probably fostered by the informal village structure and parental involvement in the neighborhood grade schools, and in some parts of the city there are informal and cooperative neighborhood groups that occasionally penetrate the isolation of the nuclear family. But even in these cases the aid neighbors give is limited by the value placed on privacy. On a sunny spring day a newly separated woman working outside on her house will receive help from her neighbors, but if she does the same job inside in the winter and hasn't told her neighbors about the work she's learning to do or about her new situation as a single woman, the chances for neighborly support are very low.

The concepts of privacy and freedom of choice in associations are very powerful influences on the community's life. One study of an adjacent town with similar educational and financial characteristics found its residents had a need to present a positive idealized image of their town. Coexisting with the valued privacy was a darker side—fearfulness, lack of trust, and insulation from the lives of others, not simply separation from lifestyles that differed from the preestablished norm, but a lack of awareness that such lives were being led in the community. When human services are needed, these townspeople go and expect to go to established formal agencies staffed by professionals and supported by substantial fees.[11]

Probably the concept of shelter for women like the one the Women's Cooperative envisions, outside the structures of the family and existing service agencies, will be resisted by many people in the cooperative's community for many of the same reasons found in the adjacent town. The city government has indeed loaned minimal support to the cooperative's conferences and has lent a sense of legitimacy to their projects, but as one of the members said, "They don't come to us. We beg from them." An exception to this city policy is a widows' support group, now supported wholly by the city and housed in one of its facilities. While this is in every way praiseworthy, it is a little disheartening to note that once again, widows command a community sympathy that divorced and separated women do not.

The Women's Cooperative is now weighing its future priorities. It must somehow find additional funds, womanpower, and a need-based agenda if it is to survive. It must offer alternatives for women which the community is not yet providing. It must both interpret and implement the changing roles of women in the community at large. In many ways the cooperative itself is an institution in transition like the women it tries to serve. Its attempts to define priorities and to identify areas of real need for the women of that city seem to be moving the group through a metamorphosis from the earlier projection of a multiservice agency, based on existing models but with a feminist cast, to a more activist stance, as a visible community advocate for a defined population, in effect, a collective spokesperson for women's needs. It is also, in that process, becoming an educational tool for community group learning. Finally, the cooperative is a training ground for its members who are learning to work together cooperatively for common goals—a new and urgent agenda for single women.

The Somerville Women's Health Project · Opened in a storefront on one of the city's busiest downtown streets in November, 1971, this project, founded by a group of women reacting to a severe service deficit in their community, provides health care services to women in what was then a medically indigent city.[12] At that time there were no free clinics for maternal or infant care, no obstetrical services at the local hospital, nor were there any women's service groups working directly on the problems of health care for women in this low-income, working-class city.

It is a mixed residential and industrial city, just north of one of the large metropolitan core cities, with many large manufacturing firms and wholesale distribution centers.[13] Its population, now 88,779, has been steadily declining since 1950, but its 26,044 persons per square mile is still five times the population density of the cooperative's city. Median family income here is just under $10,000 per year, and about 65 percent of the adults over twenty-five have finished high school. This city too is overwhelmingly white, over 98 percent, but almost half the population are first-generation Americans or foreign-born, mostly Italian and Irish, which means that much of the city is at least nominally Catholic, an important factor in issues of pregnancy and birth-control counseling and support of divorced and unwed mothers. Only ten percent of the residents live in single-unit dwellings; it is instead a city of double-decker houses, "Aunt Tobys" as they are called in the area, nine out of ten of them built before 1939. There is a scarcity of service agencies of all kinds.

The project's organizers were working class and middle class, twenty to fifty years old, of differing marital status. Some were "movement women"; others were activists from a neighborhood civic association; all shared the radical goal of providing nonprofit free or low-cost health services to women by women, based on a public-health model of preventive medicine. Funding has always been precarious and each payday is a recurring crisis. Monies come irregularly from federal and state funds and from private sources that support alternative health care, but this latter source is drying up as the recession depletes private philanthropy. Because there are no fees except for ongoing mental-health counseling, the service population has been strictly defined as long-term residents with demonstrable income needs. There is currently a three-month waiting list for medical services.

Staffed by a collective of forty women, including a paid day staff and volunteers recruited from community women who have been served by the project whenever possible, the project provides pediatric and gynecological medical care; counseling in the areas of birth control, venereal disease, pregnancy, abortion, drugs, and mental health; group meetings that focus on single mothers, diet workshop, childbirth, sex education, city health planning, and welfare advocacy; information about and referral to community resources; and a quarterly newsletter.

Every Tuesday morning some of the city's single mothers leave their aging apartment houses and "Aunt Tobys" to meet at the storefront. The women seem to be representative of the city's population in all respects except one—being single mothers—divorced, separated, never-married—in a community that largely disavows such choices. About one-third have come to the group as a result of serious mental-illness referrals; others drift in, perhaps having heard about the group from a neighbor or having read about the center in the local paper. They are all seeking support and social contact from women who share their life situations. The group is led by a staff member of the project, herself a divorced mother of six children and a twenty-seven-year resident of the city. (She is currently completing her degree work in psychology while working three-quarters time at the project as a mental-health counselor and group leader.)

This group is an ongoing program and usually consists of eight to twelve members. Some have been with the group since its inception two years ago, and some are newcomers. The program offers them support and a chance to learn from each other as well as the chance for individual counseling and some follow-up social-work services. Some of the long-term participants have become staff members at the project. And while some group members are working, they all have children and are all recipients of some kind of public family assistance—food stamps, Medicaid, public housing, and Aid to Families with Dependent Children.

For many of the women in the group, their marital status is very much in transition and they are under concomitant stress and emotional strain. Two long-term members who have completed the divorce process are seen as examples of the stability that comes with survival, able to provide visible strength and new perspectives to the newer group members still in the throes of the separation process.

For many this process resembles a veritable battlefield. During one morning's discussion, the women talked about the way their families and friends viewed them from the time of their decision to separate from their husbands. Those who had had prolonged therapy and/or hospitalization were invariably labeled as "crazy," and their every act was now suspect. Further, supposed sources of support, such as parents, expressed dissatisfaction with whatever therapeutic treatment had taken place. The families had expected therapy somehow to "restore" the woman to her former self—docile and obedient, happy in her marriage and "adjusted" to her spouse. They were unprepared for militancy and independence, and frequently "blamed" the mental health professionals for the decision to separate. The realities of many of the marriages, which included alcoholism, repeated infidelities, beatings, and other brutalities, were clearly nonfrivolous reasons for separation, yet one woman was told by her parish priest that since "marriage was forever," she must endure it for the honor and glory of God. And the majority of relatives and in-laws seemed to agree.

The project came in for its share of the blame in the family dissolutions. Many of the husbands (and other local people agreed with them) called their wives' involvement with the project, "going with the libbers" —if not something stronger and less polite. One woman's ex-husband came to the storefront during the morning's session and tried to prevent her from staying at the meeting.

Clearly for these women the project is meeting specific needs of support, shelter, and counseling. Moving actively beyond the meeting of specific needs to actual advocacy for women is seen as the next logical step. Several of the women in the group are already involved in tenant organizing, learning new political and social skills in the process. A new planning group, affiliated with the project, is now developing a multipurpose proposal, called "Respond," to address more directly the shelter needs of community women who are alone. A major component will be a crisis center planned as a refuge for battered women who have no place to escape from brutal husbands and apparently little sympathetic protection from the cop on the beat, who is frequently an old school buddy of the errant husband. The new project will seek funds from local, state, and federal sources, and will also include a youth crisis service; an apartment for young women in transition from home, as an alternative to early marriage; and temporary housing for welfare mothers. The mayor's office has awarded Respond a CETA position, to help with the initial planning and implementation of the project. Its planners see it as having at least as much potential for social change as the alternative health care they are offering through the center. They are modeling the new plan on the British Women's Aid plan in England, where there are at present three such centers offering refuge and alternatives to the violence in women's lives.

Once women begin to take charge of their lives in such vital areas as health care, shelter, and crisis management, community resistance is apt to crystallize. The project women find little overt hostility at the institutional level and, in fact, in their service-needy city many officials want to cooperate, but they are covertly opposed by many forces not unrelated to the lifestyle of a traditional working-class community confronting radical social change. The clergy and law-enforcement officials have been notably apathetic; even more critical opposition comes from the entrenched attitudes of family and friends about issues of women's roles and status, potent attitudes which work in the women's own self-concepts to produce guilt and conflict.

The Women's Health Project has many strengths, however. Working in an area with few services and many needs, the women have been using a low-cost model and offering quality health care to women who desperately need that care. Highly visible to the community, both by their location and in their service, their work in reducing the mystique and the cost of gynecological health care interests many health professionals in the United States and abroad. They have a clear sense of political purpose and direction, and an increasing knowledge of how to implement their goals, especially in the manipulation of public bureaucracies. And finally, because they are serving the very population they are trying to politicize, their services and program are educational models for the community.

Chapter 6

SOCIAL LIFE AND SEXUALITY

*N*OT ALL women are cast in the mold of community leaders and community activists and even the most involved organizers look to other, basically recreational social settings for fun and relaxation, for adult companionship, and relief from the realities of hard work and serious responsibilities. The question, "What about your social life?" leads, however, to answers that are various and complex. It's a confusing question often used to mask an inquiry about relationships with men, although its broader and equally legitimate meaning includes hobbies, vacations, evenings out, and sports —any activity other than work that includes adult companions. But not only is the question itself confusing; many women we asked, who recognized the ambiguity, had simply not yet decided just what "social life" personally meant to them or what potential meaning it was apt to have in their future lives—indeed, whether it could or should include male companionship at any level, whether as friends, lovers, or new husbands.

That the issues of social and sexual activities are intertwined was pointed out to us by one woman who said, "I have a complicated social life. I don't have a fully adequate sexual life. I find that really hard." She told us she had had a lot of short-term relationships with men during one period, but her attitudes toward men had changed so that she no longer dated as much. Her social life still was very real; she has "a lot of women friends that I'm not involved with sexually and I have a good group of people I go out with. I have things that I do on Friday night."

She has not foreclosed the possibility of a social life that includes men, however. In fact, she told us that she felt "more ready for an intimate, long-term, slowly developing relationship" than she had four years before, "but," she added, striking the theme we found with many women we spoke with, "I'm not in any hurry about it."

One factor that plays an important role in the social life of single women is the number of possible companions. In another woman's view the growing numbers of divorced persons made it easier for her to construct a rewarding social life. "If it was a matter of being the only one or one of few," she said, "I think it would have been much more difficult than being one of many." But the process had not been without pain. She said, "When you get divorced, you find your married friends don't have terribly much to do with you." But she found "people in the same boat," other single people in her age group living in her area, were not hard to find. "There were a great many things going on for single people," and she took advantage of them. Nevertheless it is interesting that while this woman's reply never excluded men—that she gave us a view of a rich and full social life—when she talked about the support she'd received from her new friendships, she specified "women who were recently single, had small children, and were trying to cope with the same sort of things that I was. When you're married you don't meet too many people in this category."

Many of the women we talked with felt they were almost too busy to engage in any social life. These women, more active now than they have ever been before, are taking courses, going to college and graduate school; working outside the home; attending support groups, women's conferences, retreat and encounter weekends, consciousness-raising groups; and organizing after-school child-care programs, tenants' meetings, and crisis hot-lines. But these activities represent new social networks of friends and events, although most of them, being outside the social patterns and frameworks of married life, may not be immediately perceived as such. They may not even *feel* like social life, but more like necessities or even substitutes for that which sustained them before.

"I'M BECOMING MY OWN PERSON"

The Women's Research Center studied divorced women who were in the first five years of separation and divorce. They were most involved with community organizations related to issues like housing, single parenting, and the public schools their children attended.[1] Many of these women were constructing a sort of inner timetable for a return to social life, and one priority on this schedule was self-discovery, to find oneself as a human being within this new status and role as an unmarried person. "Right now I'm working at becoming my own person," a divorcee told us. "I think there are some areas in becoming myself that I probably missed by becoming married at twenty-two. I don't think I was a fully developed person." She avoided dating, she said, and sometimes wondered if she had ever really wanted to be married. She wasn't sure; she liked the

feeling of myself—I'm just testing out feelings of myself as a whole human being and not as a nonperson. I was talking to a friend at work yesterday feeling like a whole human adult and that was a very good feeling. That's what I've wanted to feel like and I haven't felt like that for a very long time. . . . I'm not sure enough of myself—I'm very vulnerable. I want to be certain I'm sure of me before I become involved with another person. I think I would lose touch with myself.

And a new widow said it this way: "I feel as though I'd been given a second chance in life almost." She told us, "At first, I thought I'd have to get remarried and I aimed at that and it was a disaster. It really was and I've since turned it around. And now I don't care whether I get married or not. I want to make a life for myself, contentment within myself." She was also wary of the danger of being "tied down to a widow's group for years and years. I want to be able to help, to be called on to be helpful but I don't want to be the leading force and be the professional widow. I think you have to grow and develop, get back into society. By getting back into society I feel much more independent and I like it."

Inner Timetables

The guidelines for divorced Catholic groups include a prohibition against dating during the life of the group, a rule based, in part at least, on the stated belief that dating hampers the personal growth and the support system the groups are designed to enhance.[2] Obviously dating might also lead to the thorny question of remarriage, but, as we have just seen, Catholics are not alone in seeing personal growth as a prerequisite to building a new life. And in addition to this need for growth, most women we talked with felt their first commitment was to their children; their own social needs were to be postponed until the children were "older," until "the little ones are in school," until "my job with the children is finished." How much of this is mixed in with guilt feelings and fear of neighborhood disapproval and how much is addressed to the realities of single-parenting is impossible to determine; some women said they simply didn't want a third party involved with important life decisions concerning the children. In this sense even the younger and more innovative women are clearly following the traditional, sanctioned model of the duties and rights of motherhood. And in that model, motherhood and dating are frequently in conflict.

This conflict is manifested in numerous events, large and small, which mark everyday life for women alone. For example, many mothers are concerned about the lack of male models for their sons who seldom or never see their fathers. The Big Brother organization, designed to meet this concern by providing surrogate big brothers for fatherless boys, has run support sessions for the mothers of boys in the movement; and in the sessions many women expressed a need to talk to the young men who were their sons' companions, who, they felt, should spend more time with them, the parent. While they may have been moved in part by parental concern—who their sons' companions were and how the time was spent—they seemed to be reaching out for adult companionship as much out of their own loneliness as to help their boys.[3] Other women alone have said they feel they couldn't entertain men at their homes because it would be harmful or upsetting to their children; others complain that their children are anxious and disruptive when they go out for an evening, a price too high to pay just for their own pleasure. And finally, some women have said that their only problem with social life was that appropriate male companions were nonexistent—"good men are either married or dead."

Since the expectation of the mainstream society is that any previously married woman wants to and should remarry, social supports for single life, especially for women, have been fragmentary and frequently almost subterranean. Single socializing is viewed with suspicion, a particularly troublesome problem for single women, who must fight the twin public images of promiscuity and home-wrecking. Single men tend to be treated more fairly, being more frequently seen as "carefree bachelors" and desirable "extra men," although if they remain unmarried, by the age of forty they too acquire pejorative labels, such as "Momma's boy" or homosexual. Although data on never-married women, other than the experiential and impressionistic materials we've explored, are, as usual, fragmentary and unreliable, they seem to indicate a tilt toward marriage. In fact, whatever social life women resume or pursue is seen by most observers, both the professional and society at large, as having an ultimate goal of marriage and remarriage. William Goode, for example, the author of a classic treatise on women and divorce, not only sees the resumption of social life as an index of reintegration in divorced women's lives but also as the first step along a continuum toward marriage that begins with ties to friendship networks, especially insofar as they yield potential spouses, and moves through casual dating to steady dating to a full relationship and, finally, marriage.[4] That this "inevitable" progression is drastically changing should be clear.

Authors looking at widows are compelled to admit that far fewer widows remarry, but they offer explanations based on such simplistic variables as age when, in fact, far more complex issues are at work. Since widows experience less overt stigmatizing by friends and families, old established patterns of social life tend to persist, and the lack of money that is characteristic of the situation of older widows is an obvious reason for restricted social activity while yet another factor is the increasing lack of potential mates in each decade after forty.[5] And many widows simply don't want to marry.

Added to the confusion between social life as friendship and as sexual activity is a strong overlay of fear of and aversion to homosexuality. Many of the how-to books written by women to help other women survive their single status, at least until the next man comes along, warn against overtly seeking the company of too many women too often. In the first place, say these "helpful" authors, this practice tends to place one immediately into a competitive disadvantage. One should thus try to avoid sex-segregated jobs, clubs, travel arrangements, and other settings. In the second place, avoiding large aggregates of women protects one from the ever-present threat of lesbians who are constantly on the lookout to victimize both the woman alone and her daughters![6] These authors are obviously not alone in this concern; one woman we talked with told us that men frequently asked her about her involvement with several women's groups and with the women's movement in general, apparently worried that her affiliations indicated a pathological sexual preference. And clearly the women "going with the libbers" in the health project's single mothers' group were being at least implicitly accused of such homosexual contamination.

This use of an identification as an accusation is a formidable weapon and a real obstacle to the new kinds of bonding among women. In the first instance, it further limits the choices and alternatives which already unnecessarily complicate the lives of lesbian women who want to live full lives mainly with other women. And second, because "lesbian" is effectively a pejorative in the society at large, it stigmatizes all women who come together in groups for mutual support and self-help.

She Brings the Casserole, He Brings the Wine

One militantly heterosexual institution certainly cannot be the target of this particular bias. The singles' clubs are dedicated to the proposition that men and women want and need each other's company. Little formal analysis has been devoted to singles' organizations and that little has been denigrated, a puzzling situation since, despite their liberated and even swinging image, most singles' clubs are bent on preserving the traditional male-female role stereotypes in a hundred different ways, some subtle, some blatant. Although it's difficult to collect hard data about singles' clubs, which until recently announced their activities only in the underground press or in church newsletters, small mimeographed mailings, and local bulletin boards, one now can purchase comprehensive guides to singles' activities on most big-city newsstands.

One metropolitan area has a bimonthly magazine called *SAGE, or the Single Adult's Guide to Entertainment*, which contains a bewildering calendar of events for singles ranging from sailing to bridge, from discussion seminars to kite flying, with a special section on dances and dancing.[7] The magazine lists over fifty singles' clubs in the area, specialized along a number of dimensions. Some are age-specific and include, for example, no one over fifty-five or under thirty; some state the religious preference of the membership; others are organized around the pursuit of an activity, such as bridge, or an interest in the arts. There are many dinner clubs, typically requiring women to bring casseroles or desserts while men have the option of bringing a bottle of wine. The basic membership fees for all the clubs averages around $15 with extra expenses for trips, court or green fees, and the like.

The magic formula in many singles' clubs seems to be drink, dance, and divorcees. So many women in fact attend these meetings that many clubs restrict or screen female membership, and youth and an attractive appearance seem to insure acceptance; a fifty-year-old widow who needs to lose fifteen pounds won't always be welcome. Many singles' clubs, however, do make a real effort to reinforce a positive view of single life. Their newsletters and promotional material stress casual friendships, mutual interests, and, most of all, *fun* , time off from the demands of life and from loneliness. They have tried to legitimize single sociability in a larger community which tends to regard them as little better than dating bureaus or singles' bars. Some groups regularly include the children of singles in their programs, thus providing at least temporarily an extended support system for the whole family, and some church-based groups have become serious forums for the single adult where new ideologies of marriage and family can be explored.

The best-known organization for single adults is Parents Without Partners. PWP may have once been regarded as a mate-swapping club, but this organization has for over twenty-five years enjoyed a degree of community acceptance and visibility that no other singles' group can boast. "An international, nonprofit, nonsectarian educational organization devoted to the welfare and interests of single parents and their children" which started in New York City, PWP has over 700 chapters and a membership of more than 95,000. Its magazine, *The Single Parent*, includes commentary from thoughtful and important authors as well as local chapter news, and PWP has acted as an advocate in public forums, focusing public opinions on the interests of single parents.[8]

Of some importance to some members is the fact that many members find new mates in the organization, as almost every single issue of *The Single Parent* attests. Many widows complain that PWP is dominated by divorced persons with whom they share few common interests, although the members we spoke with said their chapters had many male members who were widowers. While technically never-married parents are eligible for membership, few are actively involved.

The many women interviewed for this study found singles' organizations of varying usefulness in developing a new lifestyle. The divorced or separated Catholic women and the older widows did less socializing with mixed groups compared to other divorced women and younger widows. The never-married, the most experienced at dealing with their own loneliness, tended to rely on long-term stable networks of friends of both sexes and on themselves. And, again, more women are finding resources and social supports in women's action groups than many books and articles suggest.

THE "KINSEY" QUESTION

The answer to "How's your social life?" is incomplete, however, without some understanding of how women alone deal with their sexual needs and natures. Very little is known about the sexual behavior of single women; the Kinsey Report, which dealt with a negligible sample of previously married women, did not distinguish between widows and divorcees. One of the original Kinsey researchers, Paul Gebhard, who has completed a study of the sexual activity of some 632 white females who have been widowed, separated, or divorced, has made these distinctions because he felt that social science has ignored postmarital sexuality, particularly that of women. The literature, both serious and popular, stresses the importance of sex in the marriage relationship but finds it hard to abandon a moral stand when it comes to sex for adult women outside of marriage. Gebhard found that 82 percent of the divorced women and 43 percent of the widows engaged in sexual relations and that this basic ratio held true for each age set. He assumed that while religious strictures accounted for some of those women who abstained from sex, an even more influential factor was the past history of extramarital sex—clearly divorcees would tend to have engaged in extramarital sex with more frequency than widows. In addition, the trauma of having had a husband die inhibited the sexual desires of many widows and this was reinforced by pressures to be "loyal" to the deceased. Gebhard also found that most of the women who did have sexual relationships enjoyed them with greater intensity than they had during married life.[9]

Research like this in a delicate, private, almost secret area of social activity is vital to the understanding of lives of single women, and surprisingly, the women we talked to were often open and explicit about their sexual needs and activities. The so-called sexual revolution is having a widespread impact on women of all ages and situations. It is fair to say that most of the women we talked with were increasingly dissatisfied with the institution of marriage and at any rate did not see remarriage as the only option for resuming a sexual life. When we discussed the future of American marriage with a group of black women, conselors in an inner-city agency, one voiced the feelings of her colleagues when she said that America's high remarriage rate represented the white but not the black experience; yet we found many white women as well who thought remarriage was an unattractive proposition. One woman's story is illustrative of many. She is over forty, divorced, and the mother of five teenage children; she works at a demanding professional job and comes from a liberal Protestant background with special training in religious education.

A couple of years ago I started going to a singles' group at the Unitarian Church. There I met a real nice fellow who I've been dating steadily for two years. The group has kind of fallen apart now. It's very small. The original group that was kind of taking the leadership fell away. There weren't very many people who really wanted to put in the time and effort that it takes to keep something like that going.

So I can't complain now—I spend a lot of time on weekends at his place. My kids are old enough so they're just tickled pink that this came along and they can manage by themselves when I go over there. It's a very quiet haven. Decent single or divorced men around are few and far between. Plenty of them are guys with such tremendous problems or just guys on the make or something like that. It's nice to have a steady and easy relaxed relationship. He's really a nice guy. He cares a great deal about me and about people in general.

Marriage is not in the cards at least for now. Neither one of us feels that marriage would be the answer because in a sense we still both want our freedom. Although his marriage was a good one, he also feels that he may want to end up doing something very different. He may want to go away or something like that. And in terms of my kids it's much better I don't get anybody else involved at this time. This is a difficult stage for kids and I think it's much better that the raising of these kids not get involved in our relationship.

I might end up at some point living with this man, I don't know. I think the relationship will continue for a long time the way it's going. I look on marriage in a very different way now. The basic question is "Why get married?" I don't feel that pressuring me. We started sleeping together almost as soon as we started dating and found it was a very beautiful, warm kind of relationship. So there's not that kind of pressure —you know, you've got to get married so you can do that.

In a sense, my mores took a real flip at that point in time—that when I was in that existentialist situation I could look at it and say there was no reason why we shouldn't. It's a very meaningful part of our relationship. To have gotten married so we could do that would have been a foolish thing. In another five or six years when the kids are all up and away at school, I might decide to do something very different, do some traveling. It'll be kind of fun to be footloose and fancy free. It's only been in these last couple of years that I've had the freedom to go away overnight or weekends. At the time I didn't find it chafing, but I'm certainly glad now for that kind of freedom.

We were interested particularly in the feelings and relationships of the women over forty; most of them have not enjoyed the same open dialogue and sympathy of their peers that younger women have enjoyed. For many, the coming to terms with one's own sexuality has been an ambivalent, lonesome, even painful experience. One woman we talked to expressed her conflicts to us. She is almost fifty, comes from a conservative upper-class-family background, and lives alone in a wealthy, highly traditional, even hidebound, suburb. Her children are now grown and are experimenting, sometimes to her distress, with lifestyles which diverge widely from her own upbringing and the values her present townspeople hold sacred.

I have a friend now, so that there's his place in the country, someone with whom I can take a bicycle ride or a walk in the woods. And we're beginning to make friends, as a couple. It's easier to make friends when you have someone you're used to interacting with. This doesn't put the whole onus on you when you're with another couple. I feel like joining in more things. But I don't think I've made it strong enough, to say how hard it is to have a boyfriend, vis-à-vis your parents, your community.

My children have been the most understanding. They're not thrilled with the friend I have now, but they at least realize I need someone who is fun to be with. The big problem is that *I'm* just so conscious of what ideals and values are—that a full relationship with any man is going to be "wrong" or "bad" or "ugly" or "dirty" to some people . . . particularly some of my family.

It seems to be true that many more women, including older, tradition-minded single women, are thinking about and discussing sexuality as a valid and negotiable issue in their own lives and that of their families and friends. Even more important, they are talking to each other, sharing experience, and supporting feelings. But we only know this about women *who want to discuss* this formerly private area. The sex researcher, as Kinsey said, must make do with the informants available. We know little about those women for whom sex is a forbidden topic, who can't or won't discuss sexual concerns, or who, for some reason, have never been asked. We suspect this is a very large number of women still. Lopata's widows, for example, when questioned about their sexual life, both in the past marriage and in widowhood, gave answers, as we pointed out before, that were hard to accept at their face value; they tended to idealize the dead partner, and to say they felt they should remain chaste in widowhood. It is perhaps wise to use the information on sexuality that the single women we talked with offered as indicators of new trends, and as statements of newly perceived social options, rather than as values universal to all women's lives today. [10]

Secondly, to assume the acceleration of the "sexual revolution" is a risky business. While more candid explorations of sexual issues and increased sexual choices are part of a healthy social trend, history repeatedly has demonstrated that sexual myths and values change slowly, in a cyclical rather than a straight-line pattern. We are very probably not headed for a brave new world of unlimited sexual options, as some moralists fear, and indeed, it is doubtful if that world would best serve the needs of most single women.

The one trend which does seem to emerge solidly from the issues examined in these last two chapters is that single women themselves are making public concerted efforts to become change-agents. They are outlining a new agenda of personal concerns: social roles that have no stigma and need not be hidden; the right to make sexual choices; health and child care which is designed by women for women's needs. They are implementing this agenda through their own agencies and organizations which bring pressures to bear on friends, neighborhoods, and local community planners. They are demanding visibility for themselves and for their formerly hidden, private needs—and are insisting that those needs be considered as a part of the public debate.

There is a new courage here, a courage that challenges adversaries once all-powerful in women's lives—public opinion and social conformity—a courage that arises from mutually perceived interests and collective action.

V O I C E S

"And in our generation we all just got up and moved out."

The speakers are two young women, each twenty-four years old, talking about their own experience as single persons—with family, friends, fellow workers. *Sandy* is a retail department manager with a major corporation. She started her three years' work experience in a management training program. A college graduate, she lives alone and is self-supporting. *Karimah* works as a counselor and administrative assistant in an inner-city community agency. In the five years since her high school graduation, she has worked for several community organizations. She shares an apartment with relatives and sends part of her earnings to her mother.

On the Family

Sandy: All my aunts and uncles and cousins and parents are in Springfield. They all grew up in Springfield. They all got married, and they all stayed in Springfield. And in our generation, we all just got up and moved out. I've got a cousin in Canada—another in New York, my sister in Colorado, and I'm up here. All this happened within maybe the past two or three years. The whole family is kind of flabbergasted. Where did they go? Why? None of the older generation of women ever even had their own apartments. They got out of school and they got married.

They all think I'm more liberated than I am really. My mother worked all the time she was married, but she worked as a teacher, which is sort of a traditional thing. And she was a nurse for a while. My other aunts don't work at all. They were housewives, and raised their kids, the whole bit. And here I am with the crazy hours, working nights, going to meetings with men, business administration major—kind of far out for them.

My mother worries about me, I'm sure. She tries not to say anything because she knows it irritates me. We don't get to talk that often these days, so we'd rather not argue when we do get a chance to get together. She thinks I like my job, and that I'm going to be a success at it. I think she's proud of me. But it's things like, "Aren't you dating?" and "Barbie's pregnant again." And, I know she'd like some grandchildren.

Karimah: Most of the girls I went to school with are married. You know, it's funny, when I go home, all the girls I went to school with there are married and have families. I don't feel bad about it. They all ask the same question—"Why aren't you married?" And I just laugh it off. I'm not ready yet and that's the truth. My mother kids me about it. She'll say something like, "It's time to have some grand-kids." I'm the oldest, and it's like everybody is sitting around waiting for me to get married. It's that whole thing, that I'm twenty-four years old, and you're supposed to be married at least by your middle or late twenties. Every time I talk to my mother, she will say, "You're not getting married yet? You're not going to change your plans?" And then she'll say, "If that's what you want, fine." My mother never worked. She was a wife, stayed home with the soaps, and our dinner was cooked when my father came home. I still believe in that. But I don't think that's all there is. I just don't see how you can keep a marriage alive and interesting if the woman is just a homebody. I'm not even saying a woman has to go to school, but she has to have an outside interest; she has to grow. The whole myth about growing up, getting married, having babies, that's changing.

I know I'm unrealistic because nothing lasts forever. I think it stems from the fact that I was hurt so badly when my parents broke up. I'd be at a friend's house, and her father would come home from work and grab her—and I didn't have anybody. My mother, my uncles, but it wasn't the same. If I get married, I'm going to do everything in my power to make it work, I really am. I would like to think that I could be such a fantastic wife that everything is going to work out fine.

On Getting Married

Sandy: I get very aggravated with the pressures from everybody. I don't think I want to get married. I don't think I have the personality for it. I get impatient, and irritable. Maybe if I were married and still working, it would be better. But I've seen so many of my friends get married right away, to young guys who have about the same kind of job that I do, and they're sitting at home with nothing to do. I go crazy with two days off from work in a row; I'm climbing the walls of my apartment!

We went through the weddings right after graduation, and now the baby showers are starting. One girl is a part-time teacher. Only one girl I know has a career—my college roommate. She and her husband are both in the service. Right now, he's stationed in Europe, and she's here in the States, both going their own way. For most of them, that's not what they wanted to do. They wanted to get married and be housewives, and they love it. But I'm the only person I know who's doing what I'm doing; I don't have any idea why I'm different from those girls.

Karimah: I love being single. Although I do ultimately want to get married and have a family, there are so many things I want to do—especially as far as my education is concerned, marriage cannot possibly fit into my present plans. I have this burning desire to be a career woman, and this is something I have to accomplish before I say I do, I will, or whatever it is you're supposed to say. If I got married now I'd feel so incomplete, because there would be this nagging desire to fulfill my career goals. If I don't accomplish this, I would be a very miserable person, even though I want to be a wife and mother. I think I'll be a very good wife, and a good mother; I love kids. I'm not a woman's libber at all, but I know that when I do get married, I'd want to have a part-time career. I think it's important for a woman to have outside interests, because she's a better wife. I don't want to be one of those soap-opera buffs, and when my husband comes home, all I have to tell him is what I did that day, which would be nothing. I think he'd probably find me a very uninteresting, unstimulating kind of person.

I just read a book called *Open Marriage*. The only part of that book that I disagreed with is the author's statement that you should expect your husband to possibly engage in extramarital affairs, and you might ultimately consider the same. Maybe it's to be expected, but I totally disagree. I'm going to try to live up to my part as a wife so that it won't have to happen. I don't feel I'd be a *wife* if I had an affair—I don't even want to think about looking for anybody else.

I think there should be a lot of flexibility in a marriage. You're two different people so you're going to have other interests. You shouldn't have to give up your friends just because you two decided to get married. Most of the people that I know have those old traditional kind of views. They want their husbands on a chain and don't want to give him any leeway.

I know the track record of marriage is very poor, and more couples are just living together. I'm not against living together, but I want to be married; I want to stand up before a judge and hear him say, "I pronounce you man and wife." I know that doesn't really guarantee that it'll be a marriage and will last forever, but maybe I feel this way because that's the traditional way. I might live with someone, I don't know. I'm not against it, but if I do, I'd like to think this is the man I'm going to marry. And, as for my husband, this is definitely going to be a together thing. He'll probably even have to babysit some times when I go away on my escapades. It's going to be hard, I don't know, just because of the position that men are placed in society, as man, as breadwinner, as the strong one. It could change, but it's been drummed into them for a long time. The black fellows my age, take care of kids? They would never think of it! Or, working part time while the wife goes out making more money? Oh, never!

On Education

Sandy: I went to a really big high school, over a thousand kids just in my graduating class. But I was with the same small group in the advanced program from seventh grade on. I was in lots of activities in high school, and I worked, too, because we went to school on split shifts, so I had an afternoon job. The guidance counselor recommended that I go to River City College because it's small, and for a private college, quite inexpensive; it receives a lot of support from the Presbyterian Church. And it was far enough away so that I was living in the dorm, but still close enough to home.

I might have been happier at a bigger school. River City is a very conservative college. Like that show on TV, it stopped sometime around the 1950s. The women had dorms on one side of the campus and the men had dorms on the other side. We had required chapel, and the big issue my senior year was, could we actually have coed meals? Sunday afternoons our senior year, we could visit, but during the week the men weren't allowed beyond the lobby. The men could be in the library until eleven, but the women had to be back in dorms by ten. Men could live off campus, women couldn't. Men could have cars their freshman year, women couldn't. And a funny thing happened there recently. Someone instigated a suit, claiming discrimination against women, so they set up hours for men, and men could not live off campus anymore. Instead of letting up on the women, they have clamped down on the men to keep it equal.

I was the only girl in the entire department of business administration. About two years previously, another girl tried, and the department chairman gave her such a hard time that she finally changed to secretarial science. As it was, he recommended that I go into retailing, stay out of manufacturing, stay out of the industrial end of it. It turned out he was right. It *is* easier for a woman to get into retailing—and I like it. I started out as a secretarial major, and did typing on the side for the whole four years I was in college. But I had to take some administration courses to meet requirements, and I got interested. All of a sudden, there I was, just a few credits away from completing a major in business, so I kind of hustled, taking nothing but administration courses, and I graduated. I think I kind of snuck it in on them. They didn't know what I was doing until it was too late!

Karimah: There are some very specific reasons for my not going to college. When I got out of high school, my mother got sick, and she wasn't able to work anymore, so I had to take on some of the responsibilities for the family. I used to live in Ohio; for a long time I went to school there. Things were beautiful and I was a straight A student. It was an elementary school, but the learning environment was very, very stimulating. I loved it. Then my parents broke up and we got carted off to Alabama where I had to go to a fourth-rate school for the "colored." It was awful. There were just barely enough books to go around; plus it was a rural school, no bigger than a matchbox. Although my grades went from A to B, my mother didn't say anything because she was busy trying to get our life in order. I got to the place where I didn't even study. I was very hurt and upset because my parents broke up and I was mad because I had to be in that school. So, in 1968 when everybody in our county got the letters which said that you could go to whatever school you want to now, I chose to go this all-white high school in the town where I lived. That was a rotten experience. I was the only black child in the whole high school—this was ninth grade. I had to go through the whole racial slur kind of thing, being rejected by everybody else. It was terrible. The last period of the day I didn't have any class, so the principal told me I didn't have to stay at school and that I could go home. I didn't even go to school very much that first semester because the busdriver refused to pick me up, and she had to drive right by my house. My grandfather and I went to the superintendent's office, who said, "I know it is her job to take you to school and to take you home in the evening, but if she doesn't want to, there's nothing I can do about it"; and he was the top man. My mother was in no position to take it to court. Actually, I don't think the thought entered her mind. It did mine, but I didn't say anything. So, I didn't go to school. I'd go here and there. Finally, I came north to live with my grandmother, and went to school at Girls' High, here in the city. *That* was a trip. We had one teacher for three classes. She'd sit in front of the class and tell us to open our books and read while she did other things. I'm not exaggerating. There was only one black teacher in the whole building while I was there.

When I first enrolled there, I told my guidance counselor I really didn't know what I want to do when I finished school. I think I want to go to college, but I'm not really sure. She told me not to worry about going to college. "Why don't you get into a business course? You can probably get a nice secretarial job after high school." I didn't like it, but I went into the business course, and then I went back later and said, "Isn't it possible that I could take some college entrance courses?" She said, "No, your schedule is such that you wouldn't be able to fit it in."

Then my mother got sick, and I got a job. And see, the thing is, the whole idea of going to school nights didn't enter my mind. Nobody told me that you can work days and go to school at night. So, I wound up in community organizations that taught me a lot. But I do wish things could have been a little different, because I think I could be someplace by now. I've had a very, very hard time doing the things I want to do simply because I don't have a college education—trying to convince people, employers, that I'm worth it, to give me a chance.

No one knows better than I the worth of a college education. But I also believe that it doesn't take a college degree to do everything. However, employers don't ask you, "What can you do, and how well can you do it?" They want to know what kind of college degree you have. It's exasperating! I am a capable and qualified individual. I know my job and I perform well—no college taught me what I know. I acquired these skills by actually doing, being exposed to intense real-life experiences that no textbook could have taught me.

Here's a good example of what I mean. The organization I work for held a symposium for our clients, and administrators from the various colleges and universities were present. I was having a conversation with the director of continuing education at one of the schools, telling her my views on adult education. She evidently was very impressed with me, and said, "What school did you attend?" I said, "You mean what college?" She agreed, and I said, "I haven't attended any college." Then she said, "That's too bad, because I was going to offer you a job in my continuing education program!"

I've started college at night as an undergraduate student, but I'm presently trying for admission into two nontraditional masters' programs. I would like to get my doctorate in education, get a top-notch administrative position in adult education, and make some definite and needed changes in this area, particularly for adult women.

On Work

Sandy: I really didn't have any concrete plans when I got out of school, just some foggy notion of making a big success, conquering the world; but it hasn't happened like that.

I started out in this training program which was kind of crazy. There were twenty-one of us, six women and the rest men. Most of the guys didn't expect to see women in the training program at all. One fellow, who started the same day with me, said he thought it was so nice that the store manager included the secretaries in the opening-day meeting with the trainees! And he was very embarrassed when I told him I was a trainee too. He thought it was to be all men. Well, we ended up going out a few times.

The training program was very thorough, and you get responsibility early. The whole idea of the program was to get you early into high-level jobs. When you make that jump, there's a difference in pay, in status, in the hours you work. Right now, I'm overdue for that promotion, and I'm getting a little edgy. You see, they started the training program when the economy was brewing. They got real enthusiastic and hired too many trainees; now they're left with all these talented people sitting there. The government's been all over them to implement affirmative action, so they have to promote women, and I'm the only woman left from my group. All the rest got married, and they're all pregnant. Yet the economy's so slow, and they're not opening new branches, so that there is a backlog of people before me who haven't been promoted either. They just can't promote me. But I feel that I can't stay where I am too much longer, either.

It's a touchy situation in another way, too. I have a lot of responsibility for my age. There are two kinds of people at work—the young kids in their twenties who are getting started, and the middle-aged men in the store, family men of forty or fifty, who have made being a division manager the peak of their career. And there's resentment. I wouldn't have a department as large as I do if it wasn't for affirmative action. They had the opening, and they had to fill it, and I was the only woman there.

The resentment is really obvious at meetings. The men sit on one side of the room, and the new ones sit on the other, and we look at each other. And at a party, one guy said, after a couple of drinks, "Look at her, she's just a kid. Why, I have a daughter her age, and she's married." It made me feel kind of funny. Not that they can really affect my career or my promotion, but it's awkward. I'm doing a good job. I got my job mainly because I'm a woman, but it's worked out well. I'm running a sound operation, and everything's all right, knock on wood! But there is no one at work that I can really ask for an honest appraisal because my boss isn't about to tell me why I'm not being promoted. It's a very delicate situation. And with the economy the way it is, and two million experienced people with families to support, looking for jobs, I just can't get up the nerve to risk pushing the issue or looking around somewhere else. My big problem is, I don't dislike the job. There are frustrations, and sometimes I get really fed up, but I don't hate it enough to walk out on it. I have to get a little more emotional, either good and angry so I'll really look for a new deal, or else I'll really have to get going and push someone to get that promotion.

Karimah: I love working with people, I really do. Sometimes I think I'm working myself crazy here, but I don't mind, I enjoy it. In community organizations you do so many things; you wear a lot of hats. I don't mean to give the impression that I'm a super-duper person, but I'm very intelligent; I pick things up very quickly. I've worked as an employment counselor, as an administrative assistant, a lot of things. I made it my business to get into everything. I learned a lot of administrative techniques being right next to the boss. Now I need to be able to use what I know. To put it simply, now *I* want to be the boss, I want to be in charge.

You know what I'd really like to be right now? I'd like to be the president of a university, so I could rework that whole educational-institutional theme. I would keep the programs for traditional college students, the kids, but in some way incorporate a college for adults. Adults, particularly women, are having a tremendous impact on the campuses of today's colleges and universities. You're going to have to change the curriculum, develop a program for the woman who's been working in accounting for fifteen years, so she can get a bachelor's degree in accounting without going to school for four years. When you're thirty-five and have six kids, you don't have time to go to school for the rest of your life. You've got to be programmed to the older woman. Some of them can't even put a sentence together, but they know how to express themselves orally. The colleges, the admissions offices, the counselors, they're just not sensitive enough, especially with inner-city women, who are not as articulate as middle-class suburban women, because their lifestyles are so completely different. But this is the woman I know, and know how to help, and I didn't learn how in any college course.

On Living Alone

Sandy: This job, and the first move, was <u>really a big shock</u>, especially to some of the other women in the training program who had never been away from home before. You know, all of a sudden, <u>the first apartment, the first car,</u> just <u>handling the finances.</u> I was sure that first year that I was going to be flat broke at the end of every month, and not be able to pay the rent. I'd never had any of that before. I think I was afraid, and I didn't have to be, because it all worked out. I've never missed a rent payment or a car payment, and I've never had to call home for money. But at the time, I was terrified. I'd never signed a lease before, or bought insurance; but Daddy wasn't there to go to, so I did it. And I had no trouble getting housing, as a single woman.

In a big apartment complex, it was all kind of impersonal. If you didn't look like you were going to destroy the place, the agent couldn't have cared less whether you were single or not. And I felt perfectly safe, until last week when my apartment was broken into. I came home and everything was dumped out all over the place. That really upset me, the shock of knowing that some guy was going through all my things.

Karimah: I would love to have my own apartment, I really would. I have even attempted it several times, but every time I would hear something awful that happened to a single woman, and I'd say, oh no, I'm not moving. It's really a fear with me. My uncles are not even in the apartment most of the time. But I'm at peace with myself, because I know that they're going to come home at some point, eventually somebody's going to come in at any given time. If I lived alone, I would be afraid of getting out of my car, getting hit on my head, or having somebody burst in on me while I sleep. The only problem that I have with my uncles in the apartment I share with them is the housekeeping. Their mother spoiled them terribly, but we get along fine except for that.

On Social Life

Sandy: I don't do too much. I'm tired, and I like to go home. On Sunday, I do the laundry, and clean the place up. And I make myself a big breakfast, and sit around and relax. Besides, I work crazy hours, especially at Christmas. By the time you lock up and come home some nights, you're exhausted. My day off keeps changing, so I can't really sign up for a course or anything. I'm too tired for hobbies . . . usually I see a lot of the people I work with, because their hours are crazy, too, and it's easier to be in touch with them. They're mostly older than I am, some married, some single.

I used to be very self-conscious about going to a married friend's home by myself, but now that they don't try to get a date for me, we're very relaxed about it. If I want to go for a drink or for dinner, I'll go by myself, or I'll go with a group of girls. I don't make a habit of going to a bar by myself, because you get stared at, and people try to pick you up. And that's not what I was looking for. I know the student hangouts don't mind if you're alone, but I'm kind of out of the bluejean stage now. I want something just a little more sophisticated, and an older crowd.

But the whole thing of social life is kind of crazy. There are no rules. You never know how to handle it. When I was first in the training program, I dated some of the guys. We'd go out for dinner, and I'd know that he couldn't afford to pay for me, because we made exactly the same pay. But it was always very touchy, you could never suggest paying your own way, because he would be offended, or he'd think I was trying to be a libber, and you can't let them call you that! Even with married friends, the husband always has to buy me a drink.

Karimah: My social life? Well, there is someone I go out with who would like very much to get married, but as I've said, I don't want to get married right now. I like to go out sometimes—you know, get dressed up and go dancing, but my ideal evening right now is to stay home, with a few friends, and listen to music. Besides, I expend a lot of my energies, a lot of myself in this job—too much, my boyfriend says— and I don't always want or need to have very much social life. I really get tired, and also, I'm going to school one night a week. But, as a single woman, I'd be afraid to go out alone. You're just asking for trouble, especially at night in this city. Whether you mean to or not, you're sending out messages when you go out alone, and you have to recognize that.

Chapter 7

THE ECONOMICS OF SINGLENESS

"It's shocking how little a lot of women know about money. There are women who are married, who've always been married, who have never had to buy a bobbypin. But the thing that shocked me more than those women, is the women alone, never married, divorced, or whatever, who are handling their own affairs. They don't know what's going on."—The treasurer of a feminist credit union.

*O*UR SOCIETY is organized on the assumption that most women are financially dependent on men for housing, food, and support of the children, and in exchange women provide unpaid domestic labor and child-rearing. But the growing number of single women and female-headed families is straining our economic institutions and practices while economic alternatives for women are increasing. Indeed, some people believe that women's increased opportunities for work outside marriage place greater pressures on family stability while others turn the same argument around: the rising number of families headed by divorced, widowed, or never-married women, they say, generates the pressures that create the new economic opportunities.

A few economists have recently begun to explore the implications of large numbers of single women in an economy that assumes the universality of the nuclear family and the sexual division of labor. While the greatest interest has been focused on female-headed families and the shocking poverty of elderly widows, the increasing number of young women remaining single throughout their twenties is also beginning to interest some to study the impact of this on the labor market.[1]

Single women do have more alternatives for support outside marriage than did their grandmothers. An unmarried woman, given some reasonably effective level of training, education, and household stability, can earn her own living. She has little hope of earning as much as a man in a comparable job or profession, but she can support herself and her dependents if she has them. And should she be less fortunate in education or social situation, she can turn to the courts and the government for some protection—for welfare, child support, alimony, or Social Security, or some combination of public assistance and private benefaction.

None of these alternatives even approaches the income level or economic security of most married women; the loss or absence of a husband means the loss of the principal financial support of the family. The government effectively subsidizes the married; the benefits of joint income-tax filing and laws concerning inheritance and property combine with the absence of government scrutiny into private marital life to act as powerful incentives to stay married. Of all adults with no income at all in this country, almost 85 percent are women, usually nonworking married women.[2] Yet one-third of the adult women in this country over the age of eighteen are single at any given point of time. More than nine million children are dependents of single women, and some eight million widows are surviving alone on fixed incomes from Social Security, pensions, insurance, or Old Age Assistance, in a period of spiraling inflation.

Neither the choice nor the happenstance of singleness is economically rewarding. The prevailing social policy, insofar as one can say that we have a family policy in the United States, is to reward those who have stable marriages in a legal rather than an emotional sense and to penalize those persons who for any reason are unmarried. As a group, single women are especially vulnerable to poverty. Very little is known about the working poor, but obviously the twenty-seven-year-old unwed mother working at a $400-a-month clerical job who does not request public assitance has at least as precarious a situation as a welfare family. The young single woman sharing a substandard apartment with three other women and supporting herself as a waitress cannot be faulted for regarding marriage as her best economic option. Yet the proportion of women living alone or with roommates rose 50 percent in the decade of the sixties; the rate is 10 percent in the twenty to twenty-four age group. And although the level of education women achieve has risen steadily over the past fifty years, 19 percent of all female college graduates work as clerical, sales, factory, or service workers; and 69 percent of all women with at least one year of college are similarly employed.[3]

At the other end of the life span, the elderly widows and other women alone constitute a poverty culture which is a disgrace to an egalitarian society. Project Retain, an agency of the Jewish Vocational Service, which acts as mediator and advocate for persons over fifty-five seeking jobs, has found that in Massachusetts the majority of female-headed households in all age decades have incomes under $10,000; and except for the forty-five to fifty-four age category, most households also fell below the $7,500 level. The majority of women living alone or with unrelated individuals had incomes under $6,000; many of the youngest and oldest single women had incomes less than $2,000. The federally funded Old Age Assistance program has 2.1 million elderly recipients who make up 24 percent of the nation's welfare budget, a steadily rising figure undoubtedly much lower than the level of existing need.[4]

In more general terms 36 percent of all female-headed families were living in poverty in 1970, although the proportion of all families in poverty declined from 20 percent to 10 percent during the period from 1959 to 1968. Male-headed families in poverty represent only 7 percent of the total. And 18 percent of college-educated female-headed families live in poverty while 3 percent of the families with male heads having the same educational level are poor.[5]

Clearly for women to be single is to be poor. And fortunate circumstances such as a reasonably high level of education, a secure social status, even affluent relatives, are at best only partially successful in preventing poverty for single women and their dependents. Except for a few widows, the women we talked with—women who were exceptionally resourceful, competent adults—saw themselves as having financial problems. Some were on partial or total public assistance, many more had been welfare recipients at some time, and most worried about their financial future, particularly their economic security in old age.

WELFARE: THE BOTTOM LINE

"All women are only a husband away from welfare." This old saying, like most folk wisdom, is founded on bitter reality. Yet no institution in our country is more criticized or misunderstood than the national welfare program. There are a number of prevailing myths about welfare that must be examined to understand the complex role welfare plays in the lives of single women.

One is the "culture of poverty" assumption, based on a monolithic view of welfare recipients as uniformly beset with insoluble problems of personal failure, semiliterate, members of a racial minority. Welfare women, this myth declares, are always promiscuous, spawning enormous families in order to remain on the dole. One comprehensive study, Louis Kriesberg's *Mothers in Poverty*, attacking this idea of a single culture of poverty, found that not only was it untrue; it also affected the way in which social services were delivered to the poor.[6] When human service workers see poor people as deficient—poor because of some personal failing—services are punitive and judgmental, rather than fair and compassionate. Kriesberg saw a variety of life's problems, social classes, and family structures in the low-income housing projects he surveyed and found that many of the mothers had suffered downward economic status as a result of desertion or divorce, leading him to suggest use of the term "situational poverty" as a more accurate and objective description than the deficit concept underlying much social service.

Situational poverty has forced many single women onto welfare rolls. In an analysis of Aid For Dependent Children data from eleven cities, covering the years 1961 to 1968, there were enough educated, middle-class women receiving aid to raise substantially the overall average of the educational and occupational attainment of all recipients. Many of these women were college-trained, with extremely young or sick children, or were themselves handicapped. Many would have worked if adequate child care had been available. Such women were rated as "high potential" because they managed to drop out of welfare programs at twice the rate of their proportion in the caseload. And another part of the myth is also easily demolished; the average welfare family size is around 2.7 children, as compared to the national average of 2.4, hardly indicative of rampant promiscuity.[7]

Nor are welfare recipients exclusively persons of color. As one welfare-rights activist said, "Too many people are saying welfare's a black problem, when it's really a green problem. Why don't we have decent food, clothing or shelter? It's simple. We don't have enough money." In fact, the majority, 55 percent of all welfare recipients, are white, 39 percent are black, and 6 percent are American Indians or other minorities.[8]

Another myth is that welfare recipients refuse to work; this is coupled with the notion that a little hard work would be extremely beneficial to such shiftless people. But official data from the Department of Health, Education, and Welfare show the country's caseload breaks down as 24 percent on Old Age Assistance; 8 percent permanently disabled; 1 percent blind; 50.3 percent children under eighteeen; 2.9 percent incapacitated parents in homes; 13 percent mothers; 0.8 percent able-bodied men. Thus the essential targets of the "won't work" myth are the 13 percent who are mothers, but over one-fifth of them are either in job training or are already employed, earning so little money they are still eligible for aid. The Work Incentive program (WIN) found that only 7.6 percent of all adult AFDC recipients were suited for training. Of these, only 17 percent of all WIN trainees were ultimately placed in jobs, and only 4 percent remained employed after six months. An enormous amount of money is spent on WIN training programs (estimated at $6,000 per trainee), yet child care supports for mothers are so fragile and the eventual job placements so poorly paid, that most programs are ineffective. Hundreds of thousands in research money have been spent to evaluate WIN program failures; the principal conclusion: the program was aimed at male household heads who in fact do not exist; the majority of potential trainees are single mothers.[9]

Another myth is that women on welfare are living the good life. Here is what one woman, the mother of three young children, told us:

Last year, I was living on straight welfare. I wasn't doing anything on the outside and it was impossible. . . . I got to the point where money was on my mind all the time. There were no food stamps at the time. To feed three kids and myself on the sixty-five dollars a week—well, it was impossible. At that time, my husband was around here, and every month I'd go ask him for fifteen dollars and he'd give it to me. But since I'm doing the typing, I'm not finding it that difficult right now. I can buy a pack of cigarettes and put some gas in the car so we can go to the beach or something. It's O.K.

According to a study by the National Welfare Rights Organization, the average monthly welfare payment to AFDC families is $49.50 per month per person, or $198 for a family of four. Even with food stamps, Medicaid, and subsidized housing, this is far below subsistence level. In New York City, where welfare benefits are the highest in the country, as are the living costs, the annual total welfare package came to about $7,800 for a family of four.[10] The only women we talked with whose finances improved on welfare were those whose prior marital situations had been so unstable, the family income so low, that welfare represented a more reliable support than their ex-husbands.

Still another common belief about welfare is that the very existence of welfare contributes to family instability; that is, that welfare is an attractive option to many women. Certainly there is an unquestioned relation between poverty and divorce; more poor families dissolve than do those that are financially stable. A major study sponsored by the New School of Social Research in New York phrased the problem this

way: "To what extent has a wife come to regard welfare as an acceptable alternative to the standard of living provided by a low-wage earner
husband whom she no longer cares for, or whose behavior she no longer
wishes to tolerate?" [11] The *New York Times* headline, "New Study
Says Relief System Penalizes Intact Families Here," was somewhat mis-
leading, but the study showed that around 21 percent of all welfare
mothers did separate from their men in order to increase family income
through welfare payments although the income realized thereby was at
a bare subsistence leve. Their families were in need of massive social
services, and the study stressed the utter lack of strong supportive services for both intact and female-headed families in poverty. [12]

In the few places where some effort has been made to provide supportive services for single mothers, the results have been positive. In the
Alameda County (California) Welfare Department a social worker started a mother's support group, focusing on mothers who were the sole
heads of a family with at least one child in trouble at school. [13] The program aimed to improve the mother's ability to cope, and to relate such
improvement to the child's improved adjustment. The group leader, a
man, found himself in an atmosphere of despair and hostility, but surprisingly, the group persevered and began to move away from personal
grievances toward practical issues. The mothers requested, and received,
special training in money management, home economics, practical con-
sumerism. They began to make friends. They showed a growing sense
that they could master their hostile environment to some extent
through collective sharing and learning. That the mothers thoroughly
enjoyed getting out of the house, in spite of problems with both child
care and transportation, came as a surprise to the welfare workers. Few
apparently had realized the extent to which shame, loneliness, and isolation marked the lives of poor women.

The quality of welfare life is oppressive. One sacrifices one's privacy
and freedom of action to public, often judgmental, scrutiny. The isolation often leads single women to behave on impulse, acting out fantasies which have no goals, no basis in reality. A single welfare mother
told us:

I did a crazy thing. I had this idea that I was going to find this other
place, like I was on my search for Utopia. I wasn't thinking of how it
was really going to be. And I packed up all my kids and a tent and everything in the car and took off. And we camped on the beach in Connecticut for a couple of days, which was really nice. We went to New
York to visit some friends. And we went down through the Blue Ridge

Mountains. And by that time they were getting really antsy. They'd had enough—no more camping. If there was a place to swim, they were really happy. They didn't want any more of this tramping through the woods, they wanted a television set and a swimming pool. I went to visit my sister who lives in a commune. They are really strict with the kids there. After about three days I left. It was the kid thing that was upsetting me—everything else was really nice.

The older welfare mother presents a special case of hardship. An inner-city counselor from a community agency told us of seeing "women who are single heads of households, some of whom have never been married, and have children that are grown now." Their total income might have come from state welfare, and "now that their kids are older, they're going to be taken off because their kids have been taken off." At an earlier time, the counselor pointed out, "The mothers really couldn't look for something for themselves because they had the responsibility of the children. But you have to make them feel as if they are worth while when they come in, over a certain age, and they haven't done anything. Now they want to do something, so you just talk and build them up. I don't say, 'You're not going to get a job because you're forty-eight.' I say, 'They're looking for very mature women to run child care centers.'"

The welfare role in single women's lives is potent, acting as threat, deterrent, regulator, or accomplice, depending on the situation. Advocacy groups now forming among welfare recipients, most of them single mothers, are militant, well organized, and chronically unfunded. The most prominent, most criticized, and most successful has been the National Welfare Rights Organization. Established as a national network and lobby in 1966, the NWRO has started groups in most major cities and has had enormous impact on the size of welfare caseloads and on the recipients themselves. Offering its services to all low-income people and to senior citizens, the organization urges all the poor who are eligible for aid to apply for it, since it is their *right* to receive aid for their families. Its leaders have compiled formidable resources on the law and the delivery system of welfare and encourage welfare mothers to activism. Local chapters have frequently been harassed, often severely enough to drive local leaders underground. The handbook published by NWRO, *Welfare Mothers Speak Out*, has been distributed nationally, providing more fuel for the "welfare debate." Yet an opinion poll on attitudes toward welfare, published in California, showed that most people are not anti-welfare. The public's major concern is for children;

programs for child welfare are universally endorsed and most people polled believed that social welfare is a legitimate function of the government. A single mothers' advocacy group, MOMMA, suggests that welfare's principal critics are the politicians and the media, who find the search for "welfare fraud" newsworthy. [14]

COURT-ORDERED INCOME

Closely related to any discussion of welfare and single women is the "dank and murky region" of alimony.[15] The law holds men responsible for the support of their children; in some cases they are also accountable for their wife's support, and most alimony payers are convinced that the courts discriminate against men in making awards to wives and children. Yet a study in a low-income urban area reported that the average yearly award of court-ordered income due from the husband was only $1,638, and an American Bar Association survey found 61 percent of judges responding usually awarded less than 35 percent of the husband's income to both wife and children. [16]

The only nationwide study of alimony and support found alimony was awarded in only a small percentage of all divorce suits; nearly 90 percent of the plaintiffs waive alimony, and in only 2 percent of the cases is it a permanent award. As for child support, only 38 percent of the fathers are still paying the full amount after one year, and by the end of the tenth year, 79 percent are making no support payments at all. [17]

There are several reasons for this abysmal record of alimony and child support. First, as Congressman Robert F. Drinan, a former law school dean, points out, divorce places the ultimate economic stress on the nuclear family, which is in itself already undercapitalized.[18] In other words, two households cost more than one. Not only does the sexual division of family tasks preclude any notion of dividing family property equally between economic peers; in addition, the wife's earning potential is lower than that of the husband, and small children needing care will make further cuts in her income. Most wives receive one-third to one-half the economic assets of the family unit, yet the woman almost invariably has the children to maintain as well.[19] Some divorced women, particularly if they have been awarded the family house in the settlement, have tried to share housing with other women, but such arrangements present some difficulties. One woman told us she'd done this "to ease my money situation," though "it was in part to ease my living situation—mostly, it's been friends who've been living here." Most of the arrangements lasted a short time: "The longest term was a year and a half with a woman who had a child my son's age, a girl. It was good for the first year. It was not good for the next six months. It got very bad. . . . It was very complicated. You each turn into the person you don't want to be." Who's in charge can be a problem: "It's my house, there's no way to get around that. You can't pretend communality when she's paying rent and board." After this woman left, "another woman moved in and overstayed her visit—she had said she'd be here for a month and it went on for three." As a result of these experiences the woman we were talking with had decided she would "consult with my children, much more than before, and make rules."

The courts and the legal profession, as most feminist writers hasten to point out, are singularly uninterested in pursuing nonsupport actions.[20] Since the law is heavily dominated by males, such an aversion may be predictable, but it is also grossly discriminatory. Another woman we talked with had quite reasonably decided that "divorced mothers of minor children should be granted at least as much child support as they would get if the father of their children would be dead." So she asked Social Security, "If my ex-husband would be dead, what would I get per child?" The answer she received, $228, $456 a month for her two children, was disregarded by the judge who granted her $70. His attitude, she said, was "What's that about? Oh, I don't want to know. That's enough child support. I want to go out. Who is coming with me? I'm going to lunch." She told us that "the probate officer was very nice and he said, 'But, Judge, that man owes her almost ten thousand dollars—for the last few years he doesn't pay.'" The judge's reply was, "Oh, that doesn't concern me. I can't do anything about that—that's another matter. Seventy dollars. That's enough."

As a result of this, this woman had concluded that widows, "as sorry as I am for them, they're much better off. They have the guarantee to have that money coming in until their children are out of college or are twenty-one or twenty-two."

"No-fault" divorce may further complicate the question of alimony and child support. The Citizens' Advisory Council on the Status of Women has been concerned with the issue because "no-fault" divorce can deprive the dependent spouse of the leverage she needs to secure better economic arrangements. The council feels that homemakers and children have *rights* which must be protected and that some monetary value must be placed on women's contribution to the home so that more equitable judgments can be made.[21]

That contribution, the Women's Research Center says, is not limited to housework and child care, but also includes other less tangible tasks —the socialization of the children; the maintenance of the family wage earner; serving as the liaison between the community and the home; and being the custodian of the sick and disabled and the principal creator of leisure-time activities.[22]

Lastly, yet another factor in the poor record of child support is the fact that default on court-ordered awards is not confined to low-income husbands. A California study has pointed out that most noncontributing fathers remained in the state, often in the same county as their children. Many of the fathers were earning twenty-five to thirty thousand dollars per year, yet contributed token payments or nothing at all. Many were professional men who concealed their assets, others were military personnel or federal employees who are immune from collection suits by statute.[23] If their families are on welfare, the state has an obvious financial interest, and many states are trying to stiffen enforcement procedures. An additional prod is a new federal law requiring all states to establish an "effective support program" by July 1977 or lose at least 5 percent of their federal welfare monies. California has saved more than one hundred million dollars in welfare funds by enforcing support orders, and New York State has recently passed a law, sponsored by feminists, that requires full disclosure of all financial assets prior to a divorce action, in order to determine fair awards.[24]

The New York law is one example of women bending their own efforts to change this dismal scene. NOW has proposed that court-awarded support payments be deducted from an ex-husband's paycheck as a routine procedure. Another group, the National Organization to Insure Support Enforcement (NOISE), headed by New York attorney Diane DuBroff, advocates the institution of "divorce insurance" by which couples would save an adequate fund to be used, in the event of divorce, for child support. If there were no children (and four out of ten divorces now involve only adults) the fund could be used to "rehabilitate" the dependent spouse by paying for vocational training and guidance.[25] There are some obvious problems with the concept of divorce insurance. Most young couples do not anticipate divorce; planning for such an event may seem abhorrent and unnecessary. Were it voluntary saving, only the prudent would benefit, but mandatory savings would be very difficult to legislate.

Other approaches are also being explored. The Older Women's League, in New York, is working to combat the "alimony drone'" image which has been unfairly perpetuated in the media.[26] And organizations like the Women in Transition project feel that there is a real need to support women and their families especially during the transition from marriage to single life. Given the handicaps most women will face in earning a living, some kinds of institutional supports and "bridges" will be needed for women until they can enjoy full equality in the labor market. Those "bridges" must be designed by women themselves, not male legislators.

The reform recommendations of the Citizens' Advisory Council on the Status of Women are based on two premises: that the economic welfare of children must be protected in divorce law and practice; and that some recognition, as we have noted, of the economic contribution of homemakers must be incorporated into equitable settlements. The council has urged that the family home be routinely awarded to the spouse who has custody of the children; that insurance policies which benefit the children be made mandatory; that equity in such funds as pensions and annuities be considered as community property in any division of assets; and that divorce settlements be evaluated by some standard criteria such as duration of the marriage, the family standard of living prior to divorce, and the economic situation of the spouse seeking maintenance.[27]

SURVIVOR BENEFITS FOR
ELDERLY WOMEN

At the other end of the life span too there are questions. How well does society, its individuals, and institutions, take care of economic needs of elderly women who have survived either a marriage or a husband or who have never married? Unfortunately, most women do not plan for their own retirement, old age, and death. The implicit assumptions of female dependency work through both individuals and institutions to effect widespread poverty among elderly women. Listen to what one thirty-five-year-old woman, never married, says:

It hasn't yet sunk in, actually, that I may have to be responsible for my old age—indeed, I probably *will* have to. I'm still going to give myself a few more years of free rein and look for the skills and the environment I can really enjoy. I'm not ready to sacrifice much at this moment for social security or pension or whatever. I've never been dependent on public agencies for my support, and I suppose if I ever really had to be, I'd become unstrung, I'd lose my dignity. . . . I've never really taken the problem of personal income and future security as a real thing. I never went through college thinking, I've got to learn a marketable skill.

Another index of this attitude is the fact that most single women never make wills, leaving the matter to their ex-husbands or their parents. Even the majority of never-married women—a group we found to be planners—die intestate, often to the detriment of surviving dependents.[28] And widows who inherit from their husbands often need extensive education in the management of their finances; their financial ignorance represents an enormous opportunity for fraudulent schemers.

The main sources of income for most widows are pension plans and Social Security, but these funds are so inadequate that many elderly women depend on such supplements as food stamps, subsidized housing, Medicare, and Old Age Assistance. The special irony of elderly poverty lies in the fact that both Social Security and private pension plans were designed with the male wage earner in mind, yet the majority of persons over sixty-five are women.

Private pension plans present a case in point. Ralph Nader has made the inadequacies of the present system plain.[29] Using 1967 figures, he found that one-half of the unmarried women who received pension benefits were eligible for $664 per month or less—$200 below the median benefits for unmarried men, and $305 less than couples. Most women work in jobs in industries that employ large numbers of low-earning women, jobs having the weakest pension arrangements or no pensions at all. In addition, the discontinuous work histories that characterize the work lives of women also effectively bar many women from full pension benefits.

The situation for widows is worse. Half of all pension plans provide no widow or survivor benefits at all, and the remainder seldom pay full benefits to the widow, providing instead limited periods of payment or lump-sum payments averaging around $1,000 to $3,000. Neither working husbands nor their unions have made much effort to remedy these discriminatory practices, and Nader points out that voluntary associations concerned with the elderly have done little constructive work in pension reform. Yet despite the obvious failures of private pension plans, their existence tends to keep Social Security benefits down even though only a small percentage of the total work force is included in private plans.

Social Security was designed to supplement the private pensions and savings of wage earners to provide an adequate income in the retirement years. The complex legislation was developed on some critical assumptions which are no longer valid; that most marriages are stable, that most women work intermittently at low-paying jobs, that a man is responsible for the support of his wife and children, and that women are generally three years younger than their husbands (the reason for the lower retirement age provision for women). The average monthly Social Security payment to widows in 1971 was $113 per month, and direct benefits accruing to never-married women, even if they have worked for most of their adult lives, are substantially less than for men and for couples. No Social Security credits accrue to a woman in her own name for homemaker tasks, so that upon divorce, unless she has been married twenty years, her stake is lost. Even then, she can become eligible for benefits only when her ex-spouse draws benefits—if they are both fifty at the time of the divorce, this can mean years of nonsupport!

Women's organizations, notably NOW's Task Force on Older Women, have begun to analyze the inequities of Social Security legislation, especially in the areas of tax reform and credit for unpaid homemaker services. While Social Security was originally a small part of total taxes, it has become the heaviest tax burden for low-income wage earners, a large percentage of whom are women over forty-five. Even the Federal Commissioner told a recent Senate hearing that the law was discriminatory and was becoming more so as a woman's status in the society was changing. And the Supreme Court has declared those provisions unconstitutional that treat men and women differently, even though resolution of these differences can add some $450 million a year to the cost of Social Security.[30]

Other institutional forms of aid are doled out grudgingly. The food stamp program is constantly threatened in Washington, and federal housing programs lag far behind need in many urban centers. Those who marvel at the new militancy of elderly groups need look to no further cause than the financial plight of elderly women: six out of ten older women live in poverty, in the richest nation in the world.

WOMEN'S WORK, LIMITED OPTIONS

As sociologist Jessie Bernard says, "The true revolution in motherhood is taking place among female-headed households. Here we are faced with the basic issue: what do we really want women to do?"[31] And what we want a woman to do depends largely on her situation. If she is married and middle-class, she can and "should" stay home and care for her children and home. If she has the misfortune to be both single and indigent, then she must go to work, whether or not she has children. The formula is simple; as one of the women we talked with pointed out, " 'No marriage' equals 'working.' " While most single women do work, working can hardly be viewed as the *solution* to their economic problems, for the consistently depressed level of earnings of most working women, the lack of equal opportunity in the labor market, and substantial conflicts with homemaking and child-rearing tasks make employment at best a partial answer to single women's economic needs.

The level of women's full-time earnings in our present labor market averages three-fifths that of men working full time and the gap is widening. (See Chart I at end of book.) Even if the figures are adjusted for such factors as education, continuous work experience, skill level, and the demand for the particular occupation, there is an estimated differential of 20 percent between the earnings of women and men. Yet 56 percent of all single women work as do 62 percent of all those separated and divorced. Only widows (25 percent) participate less in the work force than married women, primarily because of age factors.[32]

Seven out of ten women workers in 1973 had at least a high school education, one out of eight was a college graduate; yet their occupational distribution in the work force was very different from that of men. Women are heavily clustered in the service professions: nursing, teaching, social work, paramedical services, and secretarial and clerical jobs are predominantly female—and low paid (see Chart II at end of book).[33] Even the high-earnings professions, where women are a small minority, show a differential. The median salary of women scientists, for example, when adjusted for equal educational attainment, is about $3,000 per year lower than the median annual salary of all scientists of both sexes.[34]

Some efforts are being made to encourage the entry of women into nontraditional work areas. The skilled trades and crafts offer perhaps the best opportunity for women to improve their earning power. Traditionally excluded from these jobs, except in time of national emergency, women have regularly shown their abilities in this area. In World War II, during the period from 1941 to 1944, some 2.9 million women entered the skilled trades, but Rosie the Riveter retired after the war to make room for returning veterans. The trend is reversing, however, and women craft workers now make up some 4 percent of the total in that occupational category.[35]

The Women's Bureau and women's own advocacy efforts have been largely responsible for this increase. Some projects have been funded to work with potential employers and women on such critical issues as new apprenticeship slots, new job definitions in the crafts, sensitivity training for supervisory personnel, and new approaches to on-the-job training. The three-year Women in Apprenticeship project at the University of Wisconsin has worked directly with the state labor department to analyze discriminatory practices in the skilled trades and to develop entry plans for women. Other programs, funded by federal, state, and local manpower funds, include Better Jobs for Women in Denver; WAGES (Women and Girls Employment Enabling Program), Chatanooga; Advocates for Women, San Francisco. In addition, the federal government's Manpower Administration changed the thrust of its Apprenticeship Outreach Program in 1974 to include the recruitment and training of young women. [36]

In the professions women are researching and planning new strategies to equalize opportunities. For some years the Radcliffe Institute sponsored a program to assist women physicians through medical school and internship programs, structures that excluded most women. And at the Center for Women in the Professions and Academia at Wellesley College a research and action project is focusing on the occupational segregation of women in all areas of the labor market.

The effects of such action on a variety of work opportunities must eventually modify workplace discrimination. But many observers feel that women themselves exhibit profound ambivalence in their attitudes toward paid work. Roslyn Willett, who is a top executive, writes, "The trouble with working women lies in themselves, in their definition of themselves and each other." Women have all too often absorbed the myths which adhere to working women. If most men believe that women cannot handle leadership and responsibility, and that the few who do succeed are manipulative, castrating bitches, so also do many women. Margaret Adams notes that most women extend their self-image as caregivers and nurturers into low-paying jobs in social service or office housekeeping, out of the mistaken belief that they are "needed." [37]

Such arguments are essential features of feminist rhetoric, and the focus of much consciousness-raising, but they smack strongly of "blaming the victim." As long as this economy depends on a large, flexible labor pool of low-paid women, almost any justification will serve. It seems to us that institutional reform and restructuring of the workplace can do at least as much to change attitudes about working women. Such solutions as Flex-time and part-time job opportunities, ad hoc project designs rather than rigid bureaucracies, creative approaches to on-the-job training and vocational guidance, and the full participation of women in labor unions would go far toward changing the working alternatives for women and men. Certainly, the universal enforcement of equal opportunity laws, which will be considered in Chapter Eleven, will alter behaviors, whether or not the feminist imperative is accepted. What is needed is advocacy and practical demonstration, especially for those single women who live by their own earnings.

CHILD CARE: MONEY OR MOTHERHOOD

Child care is crucial to the economics of singleness. Since single women are both the principal clients and workers in child care services, it is an extremely pivotal issue. No single subject reflects more accurately our society's view of the family and the roles of women and children, both in the family and in the larger society. The inadequacy of child care resources, the fragmentation of existing programs, and the lack of funding serve to define a public policy that says, in effect, child care is an undesirable alternative that should be provided for a few deviant families. The policy is based on the concept that child-rearing is a personal responsibility, one in which the state has no real concern except in the case of family breakdown. When President Nixon vetoed the Comprehensive Child Care Bill in 1971, he noted that there were already sufficient funds for the needs of welfare mothers; "normal" families did not require such aids. Even the Women's Bureau, long an important advocate of the expansion of child care facilities, lists the following as the reasons children need child care services: employment of the mother, especially welfare mothers; illness or death of the mother; mental and physical handicaps; poor family relationships; and inadequate living conditions. [38]

The subject is basic to the economic planning of single mothers, since they must provide care for around 9 million children. Nearly 26 million children under eighteen had mothers in the work force in 1972; more than 5.5 million were under six years of age. Yet today there is space for only 905,000 children in licensed centers throughout the country, and only 3 percent of that space is available for children from welfare families. [39]

Most child care arrangements have been informal and makeshift. Around half of all preschool children are cared for in their homes; another third, in someone else's home; only around 5 percent in group care centers, and a substantial number of the remainder care for themselves or are watched by older siblings. A study of Massachusetts child care alternatives found that at least 10 percent of all children under fourteen are left alone at least part of the day, many of them "latch key" children whose parents' working hours do not coincide with regular school hours.[40]

How much does good, programmatic child care cost? Reliable estimates vary widely due to questions of data collection and definitions of quality care, but there are some standard formulas. The Children's Bureau puts the average cost of "desirable" care at $2,300 to $2,400 per child-year. Care in most commercial centers costs from $1,000 to $2,000 per child-year, while nonprofit centers cost close to $2,000. A survey by the Westinghouse Learning Corporation puts "custodial" care at $354 per child-year, and "developmental" care at $1,368 per child-year. Child care study groups estimate that quality care with strong educational and developmental components costs a minimum of $55 per week per child for eight and a half hours of daily care. Since only about 1 percent of the working mothers can afford this price tag, alternatives—government funds, business subsidies, volunteers, including senior citizens and youth groups—must be employed if adequate services are to be provided. Low-earning mothers who must work must give out substantial portions of their paycheck in order to provide care for their children while working; small wonder that for many low-income earners welfare becomes the only feasible option.[41]

A healthy expanding child care program in this country requires that public support be combined with private initiatives. Most women's groups are committed to parent-controlled, community-based child care available to all families at equitable fees, and they recognize the need for a coordinated effort "to respond to, to analyze, and create multiple and divers solutions to the need for child care in America." Thirteen independent child care resource and coordinative centers under the leadership of the Child Care Resource Center in Cambridge, Massachusetts, and the Day Care Consultation Service of New York City have prepared a joint model proposal to set up a comprehensive nationwide communications network, to insure systematic child care policy development with grassroots consensus, by expanding communications and information about programs and services."[42] In a policy area where there are few standard procedures and much conflict, such a network is virtually a necessity. The participating centers, all presently regional clearinghouses and resource centers to the child care providers in their geographical areas, also seek to form a significant lobby which can articulate local and regional concerns at the level of national policy. All the participating groups are nonprofit women's mutual aid associations which together represent thousands of local services and grassroots parents' groups.

One of the centers, The Child Care Switchboard, in San Francisco focuses specifically on the child care needs of single mothers. The Switchboard has instituted single mothers' support groups, a bimonthly newsletter, a toy library, and information and referral services for informal day care programs such as play groups and babysitting exchanges. Their service area includes the city and county of San Francisco, which has 36.7 thousand children under the age of five.

Another center in the network, the Child Care Task Force in Chicago, has set up a loan guarantee fund with local banks to provide loans of $10,000 to $15,000 to local groups who need help in starting child care programs. Still another center runs a storefront resource center in a high-need neighborhood, to provide accessible, nonthreatening service to low-income mothers. Several of the resource centers offer services and coverage to widely scattered programs in rural areas, where child care for single mothers is especially inadequate.

The proposal of the child care network has a special merit in its thrust to "break the barriers between families and political process." The involvement of single mothers is an essential component of any such consensus. A major antifeminist criticism, frequently voiced but never substantiated, is that women's liberation will push all mothers of small children out of the home. Yet it is apparent from any study of the child care movement that feminists are the only people really concerned about *genuine options* for child care for working mothers or for indigent homemakers. Such issues as child care cooperatives, homemakers' allowances, and part-time working hours are pushed by women, not legislators. Industries and businesses needing low-wage women workers grudgingly provide minimal facilities and supports, government welfare training programs force single mothers into day care jobs with less than minimum wages, paying some women to care for their own and other children for sixty-five cents per hour. But the protection of women and children from exploitation and abandonment has been left to women themselves, through a wholesale default of society. Only now that single mothers are forming an influential mass in that society have the issues become clear-cut and the future hopeful.

CAPITAL GAINS: WOMEN, BANKING, AND
THE CREDIT UNION MOVEMENT

The new ways economic institutions and practices discriminate against single women and their dependents are many and various. The examples presented have illustrated the economic downward mobility of single women as they turn to alternative means of support. The solutions that women have been exploring in their voluntary associations have been largely of a *political* nature—welfare rights organizations and child care study groups seek to change institutions and reform public policy—but relatively few efforts have been directed to *economic* innovation. Few women have felt that they could gain control of capital and thereby improve their life situations.

One of the prevailing myths of our society has been that women control most of the capital investment in the country. It is literally true that many women own stocks and real property; it is not so clear that they control these assets. Few women sit on corporate boards, banking trusts, and other fiscal decision-making bodies. Banks are blatantly male-dominated institutions and have discriminated against women both in services and in employment opportunities. Despite recent legislation forbiding discriminatory practices in granting credit, women are still second-class citizens in the world of finance. [43]

The picture, however, is slowly changing. The First Women's Bank and Trust Company has recently been formed in New York City with a governing board of prominent men and women. NOW has just published a manual on women's problems with credit, and community colleges and adult education programs now routinely include courses in money management for women in an effort to close the information gap. It is no longer considered fashionable for women to remain ignorant of money matters. The widows' conference we attended had two sessions devoted to the mysteries of estate planning and the job market, sessions conducted by women lawyers and job counselors.

An even more direct attack on the problem has been designed by the National Association of Banking Women through their educational foundation. The NABW has long been sensitive to the limited job mobility of women in banking. The support workers in most banks—the clerks, tellers, junior accountants—are usually low-salaried women. But only 12 percent of all NABW members are four-year college graduates, although there are some thirteen thousand women bank officers, usually in the junior rank of any organization.

The NABS has funded a pilot training program to provide women an accelerated financial education. The innovative curriculum includes work-related study, skills enrichment, and an emphasis on managerial courses; it also includes a training seminar for male banking managers, to sensitize them to the career needs of women.

The most effective economic approach to women's money problems to date has undoubtedly been the feminist credit union movement. There are now at least seventeen feminist-run credit unions throughout the country. They are nonprofit savings and loan cooperatives, chartered by the federal government and supervised by the National Credit Union Administration, a federal agency. In the spring of 1975 thirty-two women representing some 5,000 credit union members met in New Haven and established the Feminist Economic Network, with combined assets of almost $2 million.

The credit unions offer women the chance both to obtain bias-free, low-interest loans and to save money in a way that supports feminist goals. In addition most of the unions are developing public education programs with an emphasis on money management skills. The typical operating structure includes one or two salaried full-time workers and an advisory board of interested members from various women's organizations. This cooperative governance has been surprisingly successful. The Massachusetts Feminist Credit Union has already become the fastest growing credit union in that state, in spite of the recession, and other unions are also succeeding.[44] A further surprise came when we interviewed the staff of a feminist credit union: *none* of the women had had professional training in fiscal management, yet they had been able to learn to run a successful operation in less than six months. Such experiences should go far to demystify the world of finance for women.

One woman summed up the credit union movement's goals this way:

The main reason for having a feminist credit union, aside from the issue of discrimination, is the whole thing about banks and what banks do with their money. They take your money and do whatever they please with it, like investing it in nice large corporations that you may very well not want to support. The money that we have on deposit here is that much money that the banks don't have and that the corporations don't have. The more money it gets to be, the more influence it has. And no amount of writing letters to congressmen is going to have the kind of effect that just collecting pools of money of our own will have.

A more subtle issue that arises when feminists go into the loan business is one in which rhetoric and practicality conflict. Several unions have made loans to women for abortions, but since these women are usually young and poor, referred by welfare offices and other social agencies, they represent high-risk loans in comparison to loans for automobile purchases. As one member said, "We're not a charity organization and the fact that we're all sisters doesn't mean we're all wonderful people." The debate between political theory and practical functioning is long overdue; out of necessity the credit union movement is beginning to address itself to that debate.

Chapter 8

UP AGAINST THE STATUS QUO:
COUNSELING INPUT

"When I was widowed, it was very sudden and unexpected. At the time I can remember feeling, well, just numb by the shock and then coming to with the feeling, 'Well, this is my challenge. This is great and I want to do it.' This lasted about three weeks and I sort of went to pieces. At that time there was even less help than I'm finding now in this area as far as couples' groups, singles' groups, this widows' conference, psychiatric or counseling help, which I really think I secretly longed for to help me find some bearings."

*T*HERE IS a pressing need for useful and appropriate counseling services for single women. As more women move into the work force or seek retraining and as more women find themselves facing periods of single adulthood, they are turning to counselors for help in surviving transitional periods, making sound choices, and setting new goals for earning a living and making a life. And under the stimulus of the women's movement, these women are gaining a new awareness of their needs for service and support and the kinds of institutions which will best meet them. As pressures for change in women's roles and status accelerate, women are increasingly demanding that they share in the public debate and that they help determine its outcome.

In the next two chapters we will be looking at the issues of counselling women from several perspectives. The whole profession of human services is in the process of reevaluation both by theorists and practitioners, many of them feminists seeking to impose a radical analysis on existing notions of practice. And the clients who are the consumers of human services are changing, both in class and composition and in their own sense of involvement in the process of counseling; these new clienteles typically are developing their own counseling sites, procedures, and service workers to meet new needs and concerns of women. Finally we will examine the models and curricula of new kinds of counseling that have been designed by women to help single women, whether in crises of transition or in the implementation of long-term life-planning goals.

It is difficult, even painful, to examine one's own profession critically, but counselors and mental health workers are themselves subject to the same processes of social change as are their clientele. Men and women members of the helping professions confront in their own lives the same fragility of marriage and family ties, the same conflicts of careers and parenting, the same cumulative pressures of future shock, as do the single women who are the focus of this study. Most counselors are not male chauvinists and most are trying to recognize the traditional stereotypes implicit in the socializing process we all have experienced. But levels of awareness differ in different people; while young, well-educated, upper-middle-class professional women may easily recognize these stereotypes, older male practitioners in traditional specialties in psychoanalysis or vocational rehabilitation, for example, may well be bewildered at the pace and direction of criticism and change. And counselors work for the most part within the framework of entrenched bureaucratic structures which, like their counterparts in government or industry, resist and lag behind the cutting edge of social change. Human service workers like all other workers must make a living and survive in a less than ideal world. Such constraints hinder attempts at reform, discourage innovation, and make radical dissent difficult if not impossible. Social experiments are costly, but the long-range costs to society are greater if new approaches are not tried. Those who want most to break the traditional ways of counseling, however, are often overworked caseworkers caught in the "compassion trap" Margaret Adams has described, and have neither the time nor the power to innovate.[1]

THE CRITICS WITHIN

The professional community has had a rising concern for the special issues of counseling women, a concern originating in the self-criticism and reevaluation of the entire mental health profession which has been evident since the early sixties. The social values embodied in the War on Poverty and the civil rights movement had an impact on this process of reevaluation; clinicians and social service workers began to sense that the locus of human problems might lie outside the individual, in the community and the larger society. Questioning the individual psychoanalytic approach to such persistent problems as poverty, family disorganization, and violent crime, they moved from the hospitals, clinics, and small private offices to alternative settings in the community at large, a move that involved considerable risk-taking for professionals who felt safer in traditional institutions. The increase in community service aides and nontraditional mental health workers came out of these changing events, and the Community Mental Health Act of 1963 was the formal response to this new recognition of community resources and the responsibility of mental health professionals to address unmet needs and unserved clients.[2]

Vocal critics like Erving Goffman and Thomas Szasz have attacked some basic premises of the disciplines by suggesting that the whole concept of mental health and illness is linked to an inappropriate "medical model" in which mental illness is a disease curable by highly trained specialists with or without medication, hospitalization, and specific courses of treatment. Radical therapists, including such men as R.D. Laing and Seymour Halleck, have added to the debate by charging that a political investment in maintaining the status quo keeps the helping professions in general, and psychotherapy in particular, from participating in advocacy and social change, and several studies have demonstrated that most practitioners view mental health as an adjustment to existing community norms based on traditional concepts of male and female roles and the nuclear family. Kenneth Keniston says many mental health workers regard those who seek counseling services and the aid of public agencies as inadequate persons, and Gettleman and Markowitz, who are clinical social workers, have argued convincingly that most family counselors have a pronounced bias for "normal family patterns" and equate single marital status with pathology and failure. There is, they note, a "universal preference of the mental health professions for marriage."[3]

Increasingly, this criticism is taking notice of the specific life experiences of disadvantaged populations such as minorities and women, welfare mothers, and the elderly. Both the reformers and the radical mental health professionals are especially concerned with the relation of the doctrine of "adjustment" to the counseling of families in a period when it is clear that families are changing both in composition and in functions. Women therapists, counselors, and social scientists, strengthened by the rising expectations of the woman's movement, are subjecting the helping professions to a new feminist analysis.

The Woman's Research Center of Boston, for example, whose research into divorced and separated women's new family styles was noted earlier, is characteristic of the new self-consciousness and advocacy among women social scientists and practitioners. The women in this group, all working professionals—social workers, teachers of college sociology, counselors—earning their living in various large, established institutions, formed an autonomous, nonprofit, tax-exempt organization in 1971 for the purpose of social science research linked to action. Because their work is independent of the institutional constraints imposed by their jobs, they are able to work cooperatively, sharing equally in the research and routine tasks. They are also freer to pursue feminist commitments and goals than they are with their employers. They have published a study of Massachusetts government examining its male domination and inadequate female participation, as well as a number of papers which proceed from their study of divorced and separated women heads of families.[4]

Other feminist theorists and practitioners are now insisting that both research and practice be reevaluated for the anti-female bias that has been found across the board, both in therapeutic services to women and in vocational and educational guidance to girls and women.[5] The bias not only works to women's disadvantage but its presence blinds professionals to the realities of modern family life. For if large numbers of women are living as heads of households and families and if more and more young women are choosing singleness for considerable periods of time into their twenties, they are ill served by counsel to aspire to, adjust to, and maintain traditional roles either as homemakers or in the workforce.

CLIENT-CENTERED CHANGE

In addition, more and more women who are clients rather than professionals in the field are engaging in a critical redefinition of their own lives. A striking number of the women we talked with were consciously examining themselves and their lives, whether or not they were seeking or previously had sought "professional help." (Our somewhat broader definition of this term includes women's self-help groups as therapeutic supports, if in fact they do just that, help a woman who needs help to move toward more confidence, self-esteem, and independence.) The newly separated and divorced women clearly felt that it was critical either to seek professional support or at least to sort out the events and issues of the marriage just passed. One divorcee told us about the process:

You know, it was one of those marriages that couldn't fail. We grew up with the same cardboard in our shoes, the same Depression-type things, same fathers who were Legionnaires—nobody's a Legionnaire—same value systems, and went to the same high school. I've read some of our old letters. We started out with all the same values which I thought was the kind of thing that would make a marriage, the basic values, but I think it's all the travel that changed him.

I don't think I stopped growing, but I think my values have not changed as much as his values. I hadn't thought, for example, of living closer to the city. Now I know that's the kind of thing I would have liked, but I didn't know it then. I thought I would always be married and it would be nice to rear my children in this pleasant rural atmosphere. I think it was ambivalence on both our parts, a long relationship to end. There are a lot of reasons, a lot of psychological reasons. The job isn't the only thing. The fact that we met in high school was a negative thing. Neither of us had a chance to be people on our own.

We had some counseling but then I went back to the psychiatrist and he told me I don't need any help. I'm sad and I'm lonely, I'm not sick. I need to find other outlets. He said he'd be glad to be a gigolo and have me come in there and have lovely conversations for thirty-five dollars apiece but he thought I could do it cheaper by finding my own outlets.

Another divorcee, who attends a women's support group, had anticipated trouble. "I know that losses and separations are particularly difficult to live with," she told us, "so I really expected a terrible time emotionally." She had had marital counseling for two years. "I think in terms of real problems, they're probably okay, but my husband wasn't interested in counseling. He'd say, 'Let me ask you something,' or, 'This is how things are done'—a good legal approach. So I hired a therapist, someone recommended to me by a friend in the support group." Divorce has been so plainly labeled as a "terrible time" by society that these women felt almost obliged to seek counseling even though the woman quoted above said repeatedly in her interview that her woman's group was her main emotional support.

The period of separation prior to divorce was the most traumatic for many women we talked to and was inevitably a period in which self-blame was dominant. Sorting out the issues did not typically occur until later. This newly separated woman said:

I can't help but think about the past, my whole marriage and what was happening through the years to me, losing all my self-confidence. Both of us lost an awful lot. We weren't boosting each other at all. We weren't able to boost each other in the right directions. I'd been bringing up kids, not much else—reading, reading to escape. Sometimes I'd read four or five mysteries a week. And he was having troubles at work. I didn't pay enough attention to them. I was running scared there for a long time but I'm not running scared anymore. But he's running scared, still.

A young widow has set therapeutic goals for herself, or rather her clergyman had warned her that "if I was going to pull myself together, it was going to be in from two to six months, and if I didn't make it then, I really needed help; this should be the optimum time to see some something happening." It is interesting to note that this widow's recovery timetable was set by a professional, not by her own inner need.

This kind of inner dialogue seemed to have occurred much earlier in life for single women who had never married. Characteristically it did not arise out of the crises of separation and loss. The self-confessed "crotchety" woman who in the first chapter told us of her early decision to avoid marriage because "the way to have a good marriage was for the woman to be able to just give, give, give," explained further that "I felt that if I were going to get married, I would want to focus on my husband's happiness, and children would intrude. On the other hand, sometimes I'm very irrational and irritable, and I didn't want to do that to the kids. Everybody's irrational and irritable, and yet most people risk it." At forty-six, looking back, she said, "You can interpret it as, what a wonderful decision I made, or that I copped out. And I choose to define it as my own point of view."

These women are changing their relations to the helping professions and are beginning to seek public, collective solutions to problems which the profession has tended to view as private, personal, and subject to solution in isolation from other women's lives. Such issues as the anxieties of separation, loneliness, grief, and depression; the problems of job discrimination, single-parenting, and legal expertise; sexuality and social roles in new lifestyles—all are now becoming items of public debate among women, particularly young, middle-class, well-educated women who were the first recruits to the women's movement. But many low-income and blue-collar women as well are becoming proactive in seeking counseling supports. They too are forming support groups, growing and changing within them, and then in turn becoming peer counselors to other women in their communities.

The mental health profession is thus beginning to redefine the term "counseling" in a new and very flexible framework, but unfortunately, most communities still view counselors as agents for crisis intervention, and counseling as the adjustment of deviants to established community norms. The medical model of sick clients and healthy professionals continues to be incorporated into the new community mental health agencies, which are thus simply new custodians charged with preserving such traditional community values as the nuclear family and sex-role segregation, and professionals remain largely male, middle-class, and white.[6] While specialites have proliferated, especially in the areas of family and marital counseling, credentials are increasingly prized, the families of clients isolate the individual being counseled, perceiving him/her as aberrant and destructive to family security; and the media elevate psychiatry to a new religion with hallowed rites conducted by a few anointed patriarchs.

Counseling and counseling institutions are not yet viewed as resource bases for ongoing life-support needs to broad populations of legitimate consumers. Clients, particularly those women clients who seek aid at critical points of life transitions such as widowhood or divorce, are all too often labeled "patients" at the point of help-seeking, and are frequently referred to inappropriate specialists who treat them for one or another mental illness. The professional caregiver in time of normal life transitions like separation or death is often more invested to his or her role as caregiver than the client is to hers as a patient, leading the caregiver to encourage a dependency not in the self-interest of the client, particularly if she is a woman. Thus the goals of self-directed change often conflict with traditional therapeutic goals.[7] Finally, the educative role of counseling, both for practitioners and clients, has certainly been neglected in the mental health movement, as has the building of support networks where people can identify sources of help and new skills without the stigma of being a "mental patient" or a "failure."

The status of all-purpose helpers such as clergymen and village elders has eroded under the pressures of an urban, industrialized, pluralistic society. The helping professions, increasingly specialized, offer counseling within the range of the broader term of "mental health services," commonly viewed as a continuum of human services extending from extreme disorder or mental illness to occupational, vocational, and educational guidance. At one end of the continuum consumers are the insane or deviant while at the other end they might be normal persons such as students or professionals, seeking advice for mid-career change. This continuum concept poses questions for single women. What place does family counseling or the counseling of widows, for example, occupy on this continuum? Where can women go without being labeled as patients for help with such transitions as death or divorce, or with the choices and alternatives of new feminist lifestyles? Are the awareness of survival needs and the drive toward autonomy that many single women experience symptoms of internal pathology or matters of public concern and entitlement?

FROM CRISIS THROUGH COPING
TO PLANNING

These questions suggest counseling for women is being redefined along more generally inclusive lines closely tied to an understanding of women's life spans, changing family roles, community resources, and a developmental model of adult life. Women clients are experimenting with new models of counseling that recognize the changing status and roles of women, their increasing control over fertility and general health, their growing numbers in the workforce for longer periods of time, their newly defined legal status. Counseling designs ideally should include both *support* for personal crises of self-esteem, separation, and emotional stress, and *education* for concrete survival skills, training for job-seeking, single-parenting, home management and integration into a new life in the community. New counselors to women are becoming generalists, able to deal with the realities which underlie the crises of transition. They are increasingly women, likely to be members of the same community as their clients, peers and role models to their clients, able to look from short-term coping and crisis issues to long-term planning goals which reinforce successful attempts at establishing independent lives.

Counseling services for women today are often now located at alternative, informal institutions, such as women's centers on campuses, community self-help organizations, church-sponsored rap sessions, and educational resource centers independent of any one college or school. Career-awareness training for women and their bosses at business and industrial sites can often be justifiably called counseling as well. Team approaches and mutual self-help designs will more often deal with normal life transitions, so that clients will increasingly determine their own counseling modes and will shift from consumer to service-deliverer and back again in a fluid pattern.

The new services and clients we will examine have been selected for certain common criteria. All are groups which have been planned, developed, and staffed by women to provide counseling and support services to women. Although they represent a variety of approaches and clienteles, their programs all combine both *support* for personal needs and the *education* necessary to function effectively as workers, parents, and independent autonomous adults. These programs share a general integrative approach to counseling rather than dealing in specialized services solely to treat mental illness, situational crisis, or vocational need. They tend to view the client as a total person and they utilize peer counselors, group dynamics, and the resources of the general community to provide life-management skills, build information networks, and encourage women to advocacy and self-directed change.

These descriptions are not all-inclusive, but are rather guideposts to innovation that also document the rapid growth of women's self-help service programs that meet the needs of single women. Many of these services can be described as responses to specific issues or populations, such as health care of the newly widowed, and many existing and valid programs designed to meet pressing current needs of women in transition will undoubtedly be replaced by more formal structures or will cease to exist, just as special counseling units to serve the continuing-education needs of older women students can be expected eventually to merge with general student services on most campuses as the number of nontraditional students using the university in patterns of lifelong education increases. Other models, such as small residential units which are now replacing halfway houses for persons who've been hospitalized, will be expected to increase. A few such facilities already exist, and are useful to examine as examples of a new kind of supportive resource for women.

A Sane Asylum

The Elizabeth Stone House is a therapeutic residential community for women, a mental health facility, certified by its state Department of Mental Health, receiving public funding.[8] Elizabeth Stone, a Massachusetts woman committed by her family in 1840 to an insane asylum for her religious beliefs, kept a journal of her two years' commitment, later wrote and spoke publicly about her terrible experiences, and was silenced only when her family threatened to recommit her. This project bearing her name was founded in 1973 by a group of movement women who were all ex-mental patients with long histories of emotional disorder.

Many feminist writers have emphasized that existing services to emotionally disturbed women help maintain essentially patriarchal and in some cases positively destructive norms of health and deviance. In "Patient and Patriarch" Phyllis Chesler demonstrated the distinction between women patients, major consumers of services, and the male caregivers and therapists who constitute over 95 percent of all psychiatrists and psychologists; another writer argues that "psychology constructed the female" and that this construct was reflected in the design of mental health environments and treatment programs. As women began to speak out against ill-advised shock treatments, drug therapies that rendered one numb to the point of minimal functioning, or commitments that are punitive nontreatments, advocacy and support groups were formed; and the Elizabeth Stone House was a response to these new pressures for change in services to women. At present eight women, all single, live in this autonomous community and share the home management and therapeutic responsibilities. Everyone is expected to pay $120 a month to the House for room and board, and each woman shares in the work, which can include crisis support, regular weekly meetings, preparation of meals, and general housework. Individuals typically have outside therapists or belong to other support groups as well, and they are expected to inform other community members of their own acute emotional problems before an actual crisis occurs. There are no staff-resident distinctions, since it is based on the self-help approach with a peer-counseling emphasis.

As an alternative to mental hospitalization for women with emotional disorders the Elizabeth Stone program goes far beyond traditional custodial or even therapeutic goals of most facilities. Education for self-sufficiency takes very tangible directions; everyday life-maintenance skills are critically important to single women who have been in and out of treatment much of their lives, and freedom from dependency on repressive or confused families is another important community achievement.

The development of advocacy and service programs in which the residents are now involved is even more striking. For example, when the state turned down their original request for certification and funds, Stone House residents planned and executed a carefully designed strategy ending in an unprogramed demonstration at a statewide conference of mental health planners. The conference participants, who greeted the women enthusiastically, listened to their project plans, and at the end of the evening the state commissioner came to announce that funds had been "found" for their new program, the Women's Refuge Center.[9]

This recently opened center is a place where women facing emotional crises, often precipitated by environmental pressures, can come and stay for a few days to deal with their problems within a new kind of therapeutic setting. Such crises as marital conflicts, child abuse, or being abused by a husband, are treated as temporary experiences rather than as a permanent disabling sickness; clients are not labeled sick patients here. The Refuge Center does have a staff providing follow-up to short-term services that also works cooperatively with clients to share in the major policy decisions of the center. Services will be from three days to two weeks, based on a contract mutually devised by client and staff. Client advocates will work with the women to establish appropriate resources in the community at large and to maintain contacts for at least four weeks following a stay at the center.

Another project which the Stone House residents are planning, in conjunction with an advocacy group, the Mental Patients' Liberation Front, is setting up a mental patients' storefront clearinghouse for information and resource referral for all mental patients, especially the newly discharged women in need of survival information and support. As the Stone House residents grow in personal confidence and in knowledge and skills, they will surely find the funding for this project. The Stone House program is already being studied as a model alternative institution, not only by feminists and radical therapists but by service planners who recognize its effectiveness in terms of both cost and treatment. As a rehabilitative resource for single women with serious emotional difficulties, the Elizabeth Stone House is a milestone project.

Counselors, Not Gatekeepers

A prevailing assumption in the mental health profession has been that certain populations are extremely resistant to help. Low-income persons with limited education have been commonly considered poor candidates for sustained treatment, yet we have seen the success of both the support programs for welfare mothers in the Alameda County welfare department group and the Somerville Health Project's long-term, open-ended support program for working-class single mothers in that blue-collar community. Another argument against the old assumption is being made by the many low-income women, particularly black urban women with continuous work histories and long involvement with community organizations, who have recently become the newest students on many campuses. Many of these women have been single, and have long held responsibility for the lives of others—children, younger brothers and sisters, and the elderly. Returning to school after years of working is in many cases a major life transition; at school they have to rely on counseling services geared to youthful, middle-class students, focusing almost exclusively on personal adjustment and individual psychological issues. Even off the campus, counseling services typically have not met the defined needs of older nontraditional students who need to discover ways to adjust to academic processes to survive in an unknown, untried environment, to preserve their adult identity within the new role of student. In addition, factors of class, age, and race have isolated these women from access to traditional academic skills, information networks, and the basic assumptions of a liberal arts education.[10]

When one group of urban women students formed a study group to share such educational and counseling concerns, a new kind of counseling resource for women was created, one in which urban women with special training and experience help their peers to new goals that provide an escape from the cycle of poverty and welfare. Originally funded with a planning grant from the John Hay Whitney Foundation, this group of inner-city women, incorporated in 1973 under the auspicious name of WINNERS, wrote a proposal with the help of some women professional friends for an autonomous educational resource center for urban women to be located in the inner-city and staffed by community women who were also going through the process and experience of higher education.[11] They were subsequently funded by the Fund for the Improvement of Post-Secondary Education of the Department of Health, Education, and Welfare for three years, the largest grant ever received by an organization of black women. They opened their doors in August 1973, with a staff of ten, most of whom had participated in the original planning study. Their basic organizational assumption is the logical answer to a reasonable question:

Who does the black urban inner-city woman who walks in that door need for a counselor? She needs people like us, someone who understands her day-to-day situation—because she's black, for one thing, because of where she lives, and because she might be poor. And, because there are a gang of assumptions that are put on her *because* she is black that have nothing to do with anything else in her lifestyle. The counselor needs to be aware of those things, and she is, because she's dealt with professional counselors herself who have completely turned her off.

WINNERS, or more formally, the Women's Inner-city Educational Resource Service, provides counseling and advocacy for women, twenty-five years and older, who are interested in continuing their education or are actively doing so. While the Center is open to anyone seeking educational counseling and resources, the target population is black, low-income, inner-city women. Since 1973 WINNERS has seen over a thousand clients, some of them women who have been receiving counseling services since its inception. WINNERS has placed nearly all these women in postsecondary programs of study and training, supporting them through complexities of admissions and scholarship applications and remaining as a resource to them throughout the first difficult year on campus. In addition, WINNERS acts as an advocate for urban women through continuous liaison work with colleges, universities, and other educational sites and has also been a guiding force in the formation of an educational consortium, the Council on Higher Education for Urban Women, which hopes to influence new programs and supports for urban women at many New England schools. WINNERS has supported student groups of women on many campuses through regional conferences and seminars.

WINNERS' counselors are not concerned with "single women" as a special category, possibly because black women are accustomed to the autonomy of singleness. They are used to balancing the demands of family responsibility and jobs. Nor do these counselors employ such terms as "special needs" or "problems." They are committed to a pragmatic, supportive model which avoids the problem-centered approach to counseling, as one counselor pointed out in a description of her work:

We have to look at the total person. I can't just look at the "academic monster." I have to look at a woman who has social responsibilities to herself, her family, her community. She may have economic concerns, too, or psychological. I don't think it's important to know whether she's married or single. I think the issue is—how many people are depending on her for whatever.

Another counselor, who was an adult student for years and has just received a combined B.A./M.A. degree in counseling, said this about her clients:

They say to me, "I've been looking for so long for some place like this that I could just come in, feel relaxed, and sit down and talk about what my educational goals are. I just didn't know that a place like this was available, that didn't cost anything." Another counseling need of a lot of the women we see is some sense of self-worth, some sense of self-actualization—that you make them feel like they're capable, that they can do something besides houseclean and take care of children. Not that I'm putting that down because I think that's a very worthwhile thing you have to do, too. But they haven't been allowed to feel they can accomplish anything in life.

While the WINNERS counselors are themselves urban women and recent students, they are also increasingly credentialed professionals—career women in every sense, but career women who are concerned that they do not unconsciously assume the role of "gatekeepers," putting distance and their own expertise between themselves and the community women who come to them. As one older counselor said:

As a counselor, I'm a guide. I help the woman to make her own decisions, rather than making all the decisions for her. I try to show her some strategies, some alternative, how she can become the decision-maker so I'm not the decision-maker because, in the long run, I could put her into any program or convince her, and that's not what it should be about. It should be about moving the person from one place to another, not necessarily where *you* think the person ought to be, but where that person has decided for herself realistically where it is she wants to go.

WINNERS' future is uncertain; the three-year federal grant is running out. The counselors, who have no doubts about the needs and effectiveness of their service, feel they have much unfinished work to be done, especially in the area of advocacy and liaison with the larger world beyond the inner-city. But they are equally convinced they cannot and will not charge fees to poor women whose educational needs are so critical to the survival of both their families and their community.

It is worth special note that WINNERS had its earliest origins in a support group of women students, but the organization moved from problem-identification to action-oriented goals within a year. WINNERS women do not see themselves primarily as feminists nor have they adopted the techniques and style of the largely middle-class women's movement.

Support Groups: Rapping Is Not Enough

One of the most characteristic features of the movement has in fact been its emphasis on support groups, which is based on the early and enduring interest of feminists in the process called "consciousness-raising" when women, usually educated young middle-class and working women, form small groups to share their awareness of women's condition *as* women, and to start breaking down barriers *between* women through this process of sharing. The agenda for discussion began in the sharing of intimate personal experience and, as historian William O'Neill points out, ended by critiquing the whole institution of marriage and the family in America.[12] These groups rapidly became the basic design for a whole new approach to group counseling for and by women. Femininst consciousness-raising, which was once definitely antitherapy, has been moving from the identification and sharing of problems toward action brought to bear on these problems,[13] and other more formal feminist organizations focusing specifically on the problems and needs of women in separation and divorce, like Philadelphia's Women in Transition, are using the support group as their basic counseling unit. Women in Transition, for example, first offers four weeks of orientation and group support, in which newly separated and divorced women share the life experiences, feelings, and anxieties of this transitional period, after which group members who are still considering divorce move on to more permanent support groups led by "group sisters" who have been specially trained by the project as facilitators.

Many women's groups have been formed along these lines, sometimes through women's centers, churches, women's advocacy programs, sometimes autonomously, among neighbors and groups of friends; but some of the groups have found that the leaderless format and unstructured discussions have been confusing and unproductive. Differences in lifestyles, class backgrounds, and levels of ability to verbalize can add to the dissatisfaction; rapping is not enough. The women we spoke with, who belonged to many such groups, were now reevaluating and redesigning both agenda and goals. One whose support group had been operating for over two years told us they had

found that we have to structure things more. There isn't this whole backlog of things that people need to discuss, and we know each other well enough so that it takes much less time to deal with something when it comes up. And now, in order to keep it from dissolving into a bunch of chitchat, it's been necessary to focus on a particular problem or use a piece of particular written material as a basis for discussion.

We took several weeks to reorient ourselves—verbalizing what our initial reactions were to various members of the group, who we felt they were now, what we felt has happened. That took several weeks. Then we've used a couple of articles. Several of them had to do with sexual behavior.

Many support groups are in similar stages of transition and innovation. They tend now to combine problem-sharing, feminist analysis, and therapy, frequently moving from individual therapeutic sessions to general group discussions and back again. The most striking feature is still that the participant in the group process is also her own goal-setter. It is basically an attempt to achieve egalitarian goals within a supportive setting.

The effectiveness of these new models of therapy for women has not yet been examined in rigorous, long-term evaluation, in large part because women's groups lack both the funds and expertise needed to research and evaluate such programs systematically. Another problem is that counseling practice is subject to fads and fashion just as are other American institutions. Support groups are trendy at present; there is a danger that they will become superficial as well.

Chapter 9

LIFE PLANNING THAT WORKS

"As for careers, or even just plain jobs, the women today have to play catch-up ball."—Public administrator, occupational education programs

*B*EYOND THE issues of personal support and reintegration following crises is another emerging area of concern. Career and vocational counseling for women has acquired both a new vogue and a new approach in both educational and vocational services to women, but career counseling, like all new disciplines, is in a state of transition, ill defined and fragmentary, with conflicting approaches, few clear policy imperatives, and newly identified clients and practitioners.

The general counseling trends noted in the last chapter are of importance here. New models of self-determination, group supports, peer counseling, and an awareness of feminist needs and concerns are profoundly affecting the practice of vocational guidance, which until recently seldom addressed the realities of women's changing life histories; and new theoretical perspectives are reshaping the kinds of career counseling women receive. There are new kinds of clients and newly trained counselors changing old approaches to service. These are changes in areas extremely important to public policy and lead to the question: Is there indeed a public consensus on career and life planning for all women?

In the absence of organized support and guidelines, most single women today typically confront a crisis of decisions—decisions so difficult and intractable that consideration of singleness as a real-life option is avoided at almost any cost. In the past these women, ill-prepared in terms of training, work histories, and job readiness, have had to some-how find their way into an indifferent, unknown workplace, arrange for child care, and weigh the few options for retraining at the same time that they were coping with increased responsibilities at home and their own pressing needs for emotional support. Lacking useful communications with other single women and any knowledge of successful single lifestyles, single women have made critical planning decisions in virtual isolation, without the advice of peers or trained counselors.

Betsy Hogan, a specialist in women and employment, and coordinator of the Association of Feminist Consultants, sums up the need for counseling and support services for women who are suddenly single:

Special attention is desperately needed for the plight of the woman who must support herself and often her family after years of working in the home. As a nation, we have too long lived under the improbable assumption that the men of the country are immortal and divorce is nonexistent. We pay the price of our fantasies in expanding welfare rolls which must accommodate the families that fall prey to reality, the rise of divorce statistics, or the death of the man of the house. How can a woman, suddenly alone, find a job with income enough to support herself and children, when she is unprepared for the job market, inex-perienced in the skills valued by employers, faced by employers who have had no practice in translating homemaking skills into office lan-guage? What of the woman who interrupted even her education, let alone a career, in order to get married, have children, and raise them in that precarious position pinpointed by the cliche, "Every woman is one man away from welfare"? [1]

In contrast, women who survive their teens and twenties without ever marrying seem to have more freedom and leeway in making ration-al decisions about work and life planning. The absence of crises is nota-ble in the interviews we had with older, never-married women; one of them made this reasoned comparison between her past and the present:

There was this formula when I was growing up. Marriage meant con-forming. "Marriage" equals "conformity" equals "not having to work." "No marriage" equals "doing your own thing" equals "working." The conformity issue was always putting somebody ahead of yourself and having to think about another person. Among the young people, cer-tainly working seems to be the big thing. They don't know what they're going to get into. I keep telling them, it's terrible out there. They take work for granted and the problem is where to fit a baby into that, not where to fit marriage into it. Marriage is like an independent decision. They seem to be thinking a lot the way I did—that marriage has its ad-vantages and disadvantages and is not inevitable. As I said, "no mar-riage" meant "working" and one of the things I decided was that since work is such an enormous part of one's life . . . I was only going to work at things that were fun.

In the past decade the number of women perceiving a need for more orderly support in making career and life decisions has drastically increased, for a variety of reasons, but the pervasive force which articulates all other elements has been the women's movement. While both supporters and detractors alike attribute the rising divorce rate, the increase in female-headed families, and the declining fertility of young married women to the direct intervention of "women's liberation," it seems more reasonable to see the main role of the movement as an interpretive, legitimizing force that has provided both the cutting edge and the clarification women are seeking in a time of rapid social change. Although the causal factors are intricate and hard to isolate, it is certain that more and more women are entering the workforce, staying in it for longer periods of time, and truly need the income, whether it's the primary or a second income for the family. Worklife patterns for women are changing, a fact that's been documented by the Women's Bureau; typically, women will work for a few years at their first jobs, leaving at the time of marriage or the birth of the first child, but fewer women now leave the labor force permanently at this time than in former years. Nonetheless most women still have discontinuous work histories during their child-rearing years, although 40 percent of all married women aged twenty-five to thirty-four years were workers in March 1973, and 45 percent of all women over sixteen were workers.[2]

Women spend at least 23.8 years of their lives in the workforce; never-married women spend an average of 45.3 years.[3] Most women thus have nearly 25 years of working life ahead of them, regardless of marital status or life plan. And the rising divorce rate, accompanied by frequent remarriages and extended step-families, plus the *encouragement* for women to enter the workforce that the women's movement offers—all are reinforcing these trends. The falling birth rate is also a factor, although there is some statistical evidence now that these decisions have been postponed, rather than canceled, as many women decide in their thirties to have children.[4] While a woman's age, marital status, number of children, and husband's income directly affect labor force participation, the most potent variables are education level and race. The higher a woman's educational level, the more likely she is to work for longer periods in her life. If she is black, there is even more likelihood that she will be working even during the child-rearing period of twenty-five to thirty-four.[5]

What do these figures mean? It seems that, for better or worse, work is becoming more central to women's lives, not only as a necessary evil, nor simply as a contingency plan for disaster, but as a positive goal for most women for at least part of their lives. The choice is no longer between marriage and motherhood or a career. As divorce rates rise, as single parents and nonparents become accepted as unexceptional, as alternatives to child care and housework increase, the options for women multiply. As these options expand, work becomes less a choice, increasingly an imperative. Women and the communities they live in must begin to plan for life decisions about work, marriage, parenting, and singleness within new, more rational frameworks.

The single women we spoke with were giving first priority to the search for a life plan, one that included a decent income and job satisfactions as well; and they felt they had been ill equipped by both early social training and formal education to make sound plans and set definite goals. One divorced woman expressed her earlier problem with planning in a rhetorical question: "Where did you go after high school in the fifties when your parents were first-generation immigrants with no money to spare for a daughter's education? You got married, right?" Another young mother now on welfare with her three children told us:

I grew up with my mother telling me what to do all the time and I did it. And I got to be twenty-one years of age, having gone through high school and college, and I didn't know what I wanted to do. And it seemed like I wandered around and fell into situations and maybe reacted to that situation and got myself into another one. And I wound up married, with three children, and living here because my husband was going to school here. And then we started having problems and he left and there I was. . . . I think these things happened to me because I didn't take personal responsibility for my life and I think it's about time I did.

A black woman who was working full time and going to school evenings, taking "a couple of courses to get back into it because I've been out for a while, about three years," told us she "was really too young" when she'd been in school before. "I was introduced to school not necessarily as a learning experience or gaining an education or any of that. I didn't really understand why I was in school—I wasn't really motivated. I didn't want to be there so I left. I was in my junior year and I said, "This is not what I want.""

THE LIFE CYCLE OF WOMEN

Another way of looking at career and life planning needs of women is to relate them to the life cycles of women, placing the issues within a framework of adult development. Probably the most complete attempt to integrate counseling issues with the life cycles of women is Dr. Esther Matthews's excellent brochure, *Counseling Girls and Women Over the Life Span*; she stresses the point that "we know infinitely more about the periods of life from birth through adolescence than we know about the whole balance of the life cycle. We also know more about incompetence than about competence, more about failure than achievement, and more about aggression than about love."[6]

More importantly, girls and women themselves have tended to identify strongly with their life situations and marital status rather than with work plans, career expectations, and achievements. This is changing, however, especially for younger women. One authority, writing in a special issue of the *Counseling Psychologist* on counseling women, noted the force of changing social and economic factors that compel women to tie life planning to goals other than marriage; Dr. Esther Westervelt says that for young women today "marriage is a fundamental element in life planning, but it is not as it was for many of their mothers a life plan in itself." She feels that the women's movement is mediating the traditional home-versus-work conflicts, allowing women to plan more effectively, to separate interpersonal issues from those of achievement and work.[7]

The life-stage theory that lies behind the emphasis on the life cycle has its roots in the work of Erik Erikson, who used biological and psychological perspectives to formulate the eight stages of man and thereby laid the groundwork for interpreting people's lives from a dynamic, evolutionary stance.[8] He sees the eight stages as infancy, early childhood, play age, school age, adolescence, young adulthood, mature age, and old age, each with its specific crisis of transition requiring some resolution of that crisis that can use both personal and situational alternatives. And each stage in life has its own task. The adult must come to grips with the basic tasks of intimacy, generativity, and integrity in order to achieve healthy and continuing growth. Challenge and resolution continue in an evolutionary life cycle throughout one's life, rather than just within the limits of childhood and adolescence. Since his work is much more applicable to the lives of men than to those of women, Erikson invited other social scientists to flesh out his framework.

Many of the writers we have reviewed have based their work on the relationship between gender, roles, and life stages of women. Both Lopata and Silverman in their studies and work with widows note the compelling force of the changing years and life situations on women's roles. Widowhood coupled with young motherhood, for example, *has* to carry different meanings and decisions than the situation of the elderly widow. But writers on women in divorce have not yet focused on the changing roles of postdivorce life as a time for learning and growth, one of several normal life transitions for women. A clue to this difference in viewpoint may be that because we all expect aging and death, the fact that it is expected for us all makes us regard widowhood as an integral part of the life cycle while divorce is still seen as an unusual personal disruption in a few people's lives. As one writer on the subject says, "We habitually measure ourselves against the instructions and permissions given to our particular generation."[9]

The life histories of divorced and separated women which are being prepared by the Women's Research Center will certainly be a useful addition to life-stage theory in postdivorce families. The women who talked with us, both widowed and divorced, so universally stressed they were learning and growing in the single life that it seems there must be some kind of predictable theme of development at work here, some basic drive toward redefinition and autonomy that characterizes transitions in adulthood.

A systematic theory of this sort, recognizing human development in the stages of adulthood, will be a change. In the past, the literature of social science seemed to suggest that all developmental events took place before the age of twenty-one and that adult life thereafter assumed a static pattern, dependent for change upon adventitious influences. This assumption has had a critical effect on women. Because marriage was seen as inevitable and long lasting, women were penalized for the events of both death and divorce while lifelong singleness was ridiculed. Since this was the case, life plans were formed at best on a contingency basis and at worst in crisis. Dr. Roger Gould and Dr. Daniel Levinson, pioneers in the new theory, are just beginning to relate an adult life-stage theory to individual marital histories. While Gould focuses on the inner experiences of each time phase, Levinson has constructed an elaborate scheme which articulates the developmental tasks of adulthood.[10] Refining Erikson, he relates themes of marital achievement and conflict, issues of intimacy, power, and the establishment of an individual identity to seven specific time stages in adulthood. There is now some evidence that men and women experience these transitions at different points in the life cycle. For example, the commitment to an occupational identity is frequently postponed in women's lives by tasks of childbearing and rearing. When this identity is sought later, there can be special difficulties; if sought within the crisis of divorce or widowhood, the relative success of the search can be critical to the woman's life.

As career and life planning services for girls and women begin to strengthen and expand, many of these insights may be better understood and better resolved. It's important to note that all of these theories are still based on an assumption that marriage and family life are not only important but inevitable stages for women. We must remember, however, that an increased awareness of singleness as a real choice for women, either for part or all of the life span, alters the life options for women. As Matthews has warned, we have been "stating over and over and avidly studying meanings assigned by society." She suggests that many women have a dual identity, the external, socially conforming self, and a shadow self, the internal, private self of hopes, plans, and wishes.[11] Levinson feels that many men also enter young adulthood with "The Dream," some vision of their personal future, frequently within an occupational context. In mid-life, the individual must then deal with The Dream, examining his life plan with regard to "the goodness of fit between the life structure and the self."[12] Glimpses of this shadow self can be seen in many of the "Voices" and quotations, a reminder that women and their counselors should not ignore the force of that inner self just because they are women.

Search for the Shadow Self

A more complete source of data on these career concepts is found in the records of clients of a private career counseling service for women, New Environments for Women, Associates. [13] A consulting and training organization established in 1973 by a group of women trained in educational counseling and research, it is a fine example of the new kinds of entrepreneurial services being set up and staffed by professional women. To meet its goal of providing specialized services in education, career development, and equal employment opportunities for women, NEW Associates offers direct services and programs for women and consultations to other groups, workplaces, schools, and institutions that serve or employ women. In the past two years there have been some 250 private clients on a fee-for-service basis, clients who range in age from twenty to fifty-seven and come for guidance and skills assessment, job opportunities, training options, and help with setting personal and career goals.

Fifty-six women were single at the time, mainly divorced or never married, and many of the clients who were married had also had periods of singleness in the past, through divorce or widowhood. Others who were married patently would rather *not* have been, and saw counseling and training opportunities as a way of resolving pressing marital issues. The life situations of these women should preclude their classification along traditional class lines since, as we have noted, women acquire status through their husbands and through income sources other than their own, and formerly married women lose social status when their marital status changes, especially if that change results in a lesser income. Nonetheless, were the class distinction made, most of the clients in this sample would fall into a broad spectrum of middle-American suburban women. Again, the life-stage concept offers a more useful description. It is inaccurate to label a woman as upper-middle-class because her former husband was a professional man if she is over forty, some twenty years out of the workforce, and a graduate of a commercial high school program, for she may be living on food stamps, subsidized housing, and the income from a job as a clerical aide to the local library.

All NEW Associates' clients are put through a routine initial interview procedure to gather background information that always asks, "Can you recall, when you were young, what you really wanted to be when you grew up?" The question is potent. While it enables the counselor to help a woman tap her own early fantasies and begin to build new goals from a real base, it also offers some valuable clues to that shadow self to which Matthews refers. A large number wanted to be wives and mothers, first and foremost; those who could state specific vocational goals wanted to be doctors, teachers, scientists, nurses, artists, and ballet dancers (it was surprising how often the last came up). A few had wanted to be veterinarians or lawyers. Some of those who wanted to be wives and mothers had also had a secondary contingency goal—one of the vocations listed above. Most striking, however, is the almost total absence of everyday career choices from this sample—no one had wanted to be a shopkeeper, a secretary, or an accountant although some of them were just that now, and no one saw herself as an engineer, a carpenter, or a police officer, although many of their fathers had held those jobs.

Although these women recalled their pre-adolescent occupational dreams with great clarity, they were less clear about the way in which in adolescence these goals were somehow submerged to the more traditional feminine identities of wife and homemaker, the time when, as Matthews has said, "the girl begins to hear the arbitrary dictates to reduce and foreclose the powerful dual life commitment to marriage and career." [14]

Another background question asks clients who had helped them with critical guidance decisions at either school or college. Except for references to a few charismatic women teachers, their answers are almost completely negative; no one, as they saw it, either offered help or acted as an effective resource in decision-making. Parents, particularly fathers or working mothers who liked their work, were much more influential, but even the most encouraging parent saw career preparation for their daughter as a contingency, "just in case."

The price for this inexorable adjustment process was thus paid in adulthood when death, divorce, or the flight of children from the home deprived many of the women of vocational identities and occupations, leaving them anxious, confused, and in need of informed help. One woman we talked with told us about finding her way through this process:

I do not have a single focus. That's been a problem all my life. I have no great professional designs. I don't want to be a professional in that way. I feel like I have a lot of skills that I can help people with. I'm still torn between seeking recognition and certain elements of service that I'm good at and that help other people. Some things are easier to negotiate and I feel that part of me needs to give those things to other people. There's still a large area of my own creativity that I'm not sure has had a chance to develop, so that in the future that will be a big issue. I'm increasingly aware of personal and emotional blocks, and things like that, that are there. For me, divorce has been really a liberating experience, and I'd like to encourage others to feel that way too.

Old Girls and Queen Bees

Some original assumptions about career counseling for women stem from the word "career" and its association with upper-class, white males who have "careers" in our society. Thus the first women career-counseling clients were also apt to be upper-class, college-trained women, seeking to resume careers interrupted by marriage and child-rearing; they were often in stable marriages to professional men supporting their occupational goals. The Radcliffe Institute at Radcliffe College, for example, was created to support such aspirations, providing opportunities for advanced study, suitable work environments, stipends for homemaker services and child care expenses, and the opportunity to reintegrate with professional networks.

A not dissimilar organization is Catalyst, Inc., founded in the late sixties by a group of professional women in New York City, as a nonprofit corporation to further the cause of educated women in employment. The focus has been particularly on part-time and job-sharing work opportunities. Many of the private groups, both nonprofit and entrepreneurial, that began to spring up to help women reach newfound vocational goals became part of the national Catalyst network of women's resource centers. The approaches varied considerably from presenting career options in such formats as expositions, career fairs, and women's "opportunity nights" to small-group, intensive workshops focusing on personal barriers to career achievement. Many of the centers started resource libraries, and trained their own part-time paraprofessional counselors.

As one might expect, these first women's centers were best able to help the most competent, best-trained women in their clienteles. The increased presence of these new and reentry professional women in the colleges, research institutes, and service agencies has in fact created an "old girl" network, which for a small number of women each year has proved surprisingly effective. The "old girls," however, have been criticized for elitism, for behaving, in general, like their male counterparts, and for exhibiting the "queen bee" syndrome, best summed up by the cliche, "I made it, why can't you?"

Supportive guidance services for a wider group of women in training programs began to expand in the sixties also, as more women began to return to campus and enroll in continuing-education programs. These programs frequently included special counseling workshops to ease the transition from home to college and help the new students make course and career choices. These women were also from middle-class backgrounds, typically with an educational level beyond high school. Many, however, were also widowed or divorced, sometimes with just enough money to finish their schooling and enough foresight to know the money would run out. Their average age was forty-two; their children were usually adolescents, in school full time. The counseling emphasis was on personal enrichment and the pursuit of traditional career goals such as teaching, social service, and health care. The pace of these programs was leisurely. Many schools offered part-time study opportunities, sometimes not allowing the entering older student in full-time programs with youthful students. Those women for whom education was an urgent priority chafed under these and other constraints. Traditional liberal arts curricula, language requirements, difficulties in obtaining credit for off-campus experiences were barriers to quick completion of a course of study which would lead to job placement and career advancement. Even more critical to these women was the fact that the schools had no experience counseling older women for vocational goals and long participation in the workforce.[15]

New Woman on Campus

With the expansion of poverty programs and the simultaneous increase in low-cost community college programs, other women began to think about and seek out occupational and vocational guidance—women who were housewives, young mothers, and low-income urban women, secretaries, retail workers, and other low-salaried women workers searching for new career options. For the first time, blue-collar women began to eye the good wages and work opportunities of the apprenticed and skilled crafts, occupations controlled by guilds and unions that had rigidly excluded women and minorities in the past, but special programs were set up, often in conjunction with community colleges, to prepare women for crafts jobs.[16]

Dissatisfied with campus and off-campus services geared to traditional students and career-seekers, women from all these groups began to set up women's centers that became clearinghouses for the specific needs of career information, labor markets, resources, job and training opportunities. Women's advocacy groups began to publish guidelines and "cookbooks" to help women establish such centers. The manuals spelled out the details of such issues as shared leadership, record-keeping, resource collection, and setting organizational goals.

The community colleges have had a special role to play in the development of women's centers.[17] Under the impetus of massive federal entitlements, new two-year public colleges have appeared on the scene at unbelievable rates. Massachusetts, already heavily endowed with educational institutions, now has fifteen community colleges, New York State has forty-two, most built since 1965. Adult part-time enrollments typically equal or surpass youthful full-time students at these new institutions. Because community-based service and training programs were part of the original mandate of the colleges to provide

the local communities what they wanted and needed in educational resources and services, programming is flexible, responsive to changing
community and labor market needs. The new faculty is equally important; while there are some permanent teachers, others have been recruited from business, industry, and the community at large to set up and
teach specific programs. Field-work practicums and work-study courses
are specially designed for adult students. And the fees are low—bargains
in the educational marketplace.

Many community colleges have set up women's centers in response
to pressures from local women's groups and the needs of local employers to implement their affirmative action programs. Most have started
on shoestring budgets, staffed largely by volunteers. The pool of volunteer women in a community college regional area is in fact critical to
the success of many centers; women once active in PTA's, political
campaigns, service clubs, and crafts guilds are using their skills, staffing
and planning programs.

The programs vary widely. Many are characterized by the supermar-
ket approach—something for everybody: peer-counseling groups, career-
opportunities workshops, study and job-finding skills, and courses in
greenhouse management, weaving, self-defense, secretarial science, para-
legal studies, and automotive repairs. All appear in their pamphlets and
brochures.

Some few centers have tried a more integrated approach, focusing on
one or more real-world needs of women. A specially funded two-year
program at Rockland County Community College in New York State
focused on career guidance and life-planning. Working on programing
and outreach with community leaders in business, government, and
human services, they tailored programs and support to local needs. A
complete evaluation by an outside team of educational specialists was
made possible by the excellent records kept by the program counselors. [18]

WORC · A similar program in Massachusetts at Middlesex Community College uses a large staff of competent volunteers who
have been vital to the growth of the Women's Opportunity Research
Center. [19] In addition to integrated counseling and vocational services
for women, WORC has a job bank, with participants from many local
industries, and also works through the State Employment Service job
bank to make job placement networks accessible to suburban women.

At least one community college women's center has focused programming on the "woman alone." In the winter of 1975, Bristol Community College in Fall River, Massachusetts, sponsored a regional conference for "The Woman Alone," funded by Title I money awarded to a consortium of eleven schools for the purpose of reaching new student populations in the southeastern region of the state. The aim was to assess the educational and vocational goals of single women in that officially economically depressed area. The two-day, low-fee conference was attempting to identify and consolidate a national Women Alone movement and to lay plans for a national conference in 1976. Some 400 women from all over the state attended, 85 percent of them small-town residents who had never attended a conference of any kind. Half were women who had never married, most in their twenties; 20 percent were widows, the same number were separated and divorced, and 10 percent were married women, mostly professionals interested in the subject.

The Women's Center at Bristol now has a model of training and service programs to help single women. They have a comprehensive Widows' Exchange, led by a paid coordinator. They have also set up a series of skills-acquisition courses called "Labs in Independent Living" to help women alone become women "on their own." The labs deal with such issues as concerns of working mothers, legal rights of women, credit and continuing education, and preparing for job promotion. They also offer eight-week workshops for working mothers, the newly divorced, and the widowed. Bristol's programs do not exclude married women, but rather stress the need for all women to move toward self-sufficiency. It's important to note that a public educational institution has taken on the responsibility to implement that goal. [20]

Some advocacy groups would like to move the public commitment into one of entitlement for all single women. A California-based group, the Alliance for Displaced Homemakers, has introduced bills in Congress and in the California state legislature that would insure that homemakers "displaced" from their jobs by divorce or death of a spouse would be included as a needs category in unemployment insurance programs and in public employment programs such as CETA. The bills call for the nationwide development of multipurpose service centers to provide job training, counseling, placement, health care, money management courses, and other support services for displaced homemakers.

Such groups argue that fees-for-service organizations perpetuate class distinctions among women, benefiting most those who need help least, and consider even the low community college fees discriminatory. The

WINNERS program, as we noted in the preceding chapter, charges no fees at all to a clientele requiring massive financial aid if they are to get any educational services. Advocates for free guidance services point out that women as a group are not yet designated as a high-needs category by such public programs as CETA, in spite of the efforts of the Women's Bureau to secure such classification.

This is a period of transition for all women. It seems reasonable and necessary that both the public and the private sector be involved in the innovation and experimentation required to develop sound guidance programs for women. The many conferences, task forces, and research groups currently focusing on these issues need to draw on the experience of all kinds of projects dealing with all kinds of clienteles. Women of all races and income levels need to be heard in this debate. The debate has only begun, and public entitlement programs may face a premature death if national networks of support and a consensus about the needs of women are not first established.

Starting Early

Another approach to the question of *who* provides career guidance may be the current emphasis on upgrading career guidance services to high school girls through the public school systems. Federal legislation has made such programs mandatory, and the Career Guidance and Counseling Act of 1975 was to have provided the funds. At this writing, the fate of this bill is unknown, but many states are presently going ahead, planning and implementing new guidance models for girls based on a theory of prevention—prevention of the mid-life crisis of single women through early programing not tied to marital expectations.

One such pilot program carries special meaning for single women. In 1971, Jeanne Scott and Maureen Rabin started the Vocational Readiness Program at the Los Angeles YWCA. The target group was to be high school girls in the general, noncollege course. Jeanne Scott, a former welfare worker, had seen many of her clients go on welfare because they had married shortly after high school, had children, and were in a crisis when their husbands had left them, died, or could not pay child support. Scott says, "I call them losers in the Miss America contest. They believed so strongly in the myth—the dream of getting married and living happily ever after—that when the dream failed, they fell apart. They were at the end of the rope because they had received no help or vocational guidance earlier in their lives." [21]

Scott and Rabin see their week-long program as a way of giving grim statistics the real-life meaning that can prepare high school girls for some of the realities they face later in life. Rabin, a drama teacher, plays a game with the girls which has them fantasize about marriage for a mythical heroine. They then draw cards which help to predict the future life of their dream girl. A card might read "widowed at 29" or "husband deserts you and three kids." The girls form teams to act out these scenarios. In them they become aware of their own vocational identities and make use of the program's other elements, planning skills and occupational resources that help the girls use their educational environment with an eye to a real future.

Clearly, such preventive training makes life planning for women a more rational process, less dependent on social roles, marital status, and ability to respond to crisis. Counseling for divorce and widowhood at present is asked to do too many things: to provide emotional support in a time of loss and separation and to somehow shore up the woman's occupational readiness while also providing basic family and life management skills. Because of the overwhelming nature of the task, programs for career and life planning for women have been somewhat haphazard, although they are rapidly strengthening as experimentation and research continue to expand. It seems to us that *all* women need basic training in the everyday issues of financial and legal management, parenting and family management, vocational awareness, and concrete job skills. They need a life plan—for contingencies, for life support, and for personal self-enrichment.

V O I C E S

"You go to school and you go to college and you learn all this stuff . . . and you end with a house full of kids."

The speaker is a thirty-four-year-old mother of three children, living in a small house in an affluent suburban community.

Being a married mother and being a single person *are* very different, and I guess I find it frustrating. The thing is, things just don't fit together because even though I've tried to raise my children to be very independent from the time they were small, they all watch the television, they all read their basic reader at school, and they have this image of what mothers are and what mothers do. Now, this does *not* include having a mother who works.

This does not include a mother who needs any kind of social life at all, and the working bit is where it gets you because I think there are very few single parents who don't have to work. I'm only working part time. I've been very fortunate that I've been able to find a half-time job where I only work three days one week, two days the next. Even though I've been working almost a year, they still get me for it. I call up at three and I say, "Remember, you're supposed to" such-and-such, and they say, "Sure, sure, sure," and I walk in the door, and absolutely nothing has been done, and I'm really starting to think that they're saying, "Well, well, one way or another, we'll get you for it."

In a year or so, I have to start working full time because the amount of money that I have coming in will be going down, and I'm also committed then to start putting money aside for their education. But I think they resent very much that I can't do all of this, that I can't *do for them* all the time. My career is going to be of necessity important because I'm not going to have any support once they get out of college, and I don't want to be a little old lady starving on a park bench. I really don't fancy going out to find someone to marry on the basis that I better find someone to support me or I don't eat.

People haven't been what you might call helpful in this town. But if I can just be accepted as not being immoral, peculiar, or something, that'll do. But the fact is basically that the community that I live in and the world in general has never really offered any support of any kind whatsoever, especially in the first year or so that I was separated. What the world has required is an incredible, superhuman effort from me to prove that I was twice as productive and twice as normal and twice as everything as everybody else before it wouldn't be assumed that there was something very peculiar about me.

If the Women's Center hadn't started up when it did and I hadn't gotten involved in that, I think things would be very, very different for me. We lived in a neighborhood previously where we all lived in big houses and everyone minds his own business, prior to divorce. Since the divorce, we live in this doll house in a neighborhood which was formerly the veterans' housing project. But it's a fairly close community and it's geographically isolated.

I've been out with guys in Parents Without Partners who would explain to me very carefully how, of course, *they* don't find me threatening but I should understand that most men would. It's very difficult to deal with this kind of thing without insulting people because when someone comes up to you and starts going on about what a wonderful body I have, they mean to be complimentary and they're trying to be helpful and all this. They don't understand that I'm standing there sort of appalled. I don't want to be treated like meat on the hook.

My former husband and I are where we are because a good education was something our parents were able to give us. All right, now I'm working part time. If I had the job I have full time, I would be making eight thousand dollars a year. Now, supporting a family of three on eight thousand a year . . . of course, it can be done but there's a difference between survival and what you want to be able to do for your children. I guess I really don't see an education as that much of a luxury because that's basically all they can be given to make it possible for them to make it on their own.

The whole work thing is just so bad because you go to school and you go to college and you learn all this stuff and you just start getting somewhere professionally (well, maybe it's not so true now as it was ten or eleven years ago) but for so many of us, you end with a house full of kids. I realized that all the stuff I was learning to do around the house, all this stuff that I hadn't been trained for, I had to learn. Well, I forgot everything I ever learned about doing anything else. And then one day, you find yourself out on the street and you have to start all over again. You don't have the work experience during that time that would qualify you for anything that someone half your age with half a brain ought to be doing. They really don't want to hire you for something stupid, because they say you're too bright, you're overqualified, you're this, you're that, but you're not qualified for what you ought to be doing.

What about money? Well, it depends on how you look at it. Now I spend half my days saying how lucky we are, and half the days saying how unlucky we are. So far we're still being paid what we're supposed to be paid although I know many women who aren't. I can accept it without feeling that my ex-husband is having to live in a little room somewhere, because we can live quite comfortably on less than half his gross income and he is married to someone with a career also.

But it's a very dodgy business. It's a very dodgy business and if he feels that I am not polite enough to him or his family, or if I don't listen attentively enough to his tirades about what he thinks about the changing morals of adolescents, and this, that and the other, I get his threats of nonsupport. Every once in a while he talks about moving away from New England, and he says that if I don't move the children out, too, he will no longer support us. As he put it, he is paying me to raise his children and that the least he could expect was that I would make it convenient for him to see them. Now this kind of thing does make one a little insecure.

I think that the counseling we got was a very good idea. The psychiatrist was really good because he did not feel that his job was keeping marriages together. And I think that's the only way that anything like this can work. He helps you explore the roots of the problems and helps you explore the alternatives. I don't know—in a way I guess having counseling certainly did contribute to the fact that we ended up divorced. But I think the reason that so often happens is that so long as you can avoid looking at things, maybe you can continue for a little longer pretending they're not there. But you get to a point where you take a really good look at the realities and you take a look at the destructive potential and you take a look at what the mess is doing to everybody, and you can't pretend anymore that you haven't seen it. There are a lot of people who don't realize or who don't want to remember the fact that there is nowhere that you are as alone as you are in a bad marriage. That's the height of isolation as far as I'm concerned.

It's a lonely business. I've gotten to the point where I've got places I can go, people I can see. Most of the friends that I've had, I've met through the Women's Center. Now that does mean that they're very likely to be women. If I knew a bunch of men half as nice as the women that I knew of, it would be fantastic. Well, I don't.

I really don't want to stay the way I am, extending myself as much as I am because, frankly, I'm tired. I am not really at this point staying single on principle either. But I've been developing a lot of skills, a lot of competencies, and I think when you're single again, there are a lot of things you understand about marriage a bit better—not marriage as we wish it were, but marriage as it is in this country at this time. I guess I've gotten to the point where there are a lot of things that I would not give up. I would not give up being seen as a competent human being. I would not get into a situation where all of the scutwork was considered my legacy because of my sex. But whether or not I could find a marital situation in which that kind of thing could really work out—well, you know, it's a little difficult—I don't know. I guess I'm planning to live my life as if I never expected to remarry and if it happens, well then, it will be a pleasant surprise. Having the chance to just live by myself with the children and just do the things I've come to do has been fantastically good for me.

Chapter 10

WOMEN ALONE IN THE SIGHT OF GOD

"It takes everything I've got to stand up to Father."—divorced
Catholic woman

*T*HE LIMITED scope of women's roles has con-
fined them to the conservative institutions in the society—the home,
the schools, the church; and churches have traditionally been the principal sources of support and shelter for single women. It has been to
the church that women have naturally turned for sanctuary, solace, renewed faith, and hope. Often the church has served women as the one
legitimate bridge between the home and the larger society, providing
socially sanctioned opportunities for work and community involvement, opportunities tacitly limited, however, to such tasks as church
housekeeping, direct acts of charity, and the teaching of young children. Thus, women's church roles have been consistent with their positions both in the home and in the community; if, for example, their
auxiliaries and sodalities have raised considerable sums of money, wom-
en nonetheless have had little say in the decisions to spend it.

Having been both the supporters and the supported within the
church—the most numerous clients of its services, the transmitters of
religion to children, the rank and file of congregations and committees
—women are beginning to reexamine their relationship to the church,
asking new questions about how it meets their needs for support, advocacy, and personal growth. The single women we talked to were
eager, even insistent, about telling us of their own changing relationship to the church and formal religion. Most of them came from

conventional religious backgrounds and had at one time looked to their church and their faith for guidance and comfort. For many, religion was still important, if only because it so failed to meet their needs. Still others had become activists within their churches, seeking to share their own learning experiences with both clergy and their fellow church members. These women were questioning in some cases the right and in others the ability of the clergy to be caregivers in crisis, but they were also rejecting the idea that formal religion could be the sole moral arbiter of family life.

Not unexpectedly, many of the women who were separated or divorced expressed essentially negative feelings, feelings notably strong among women from Catholic backgrounds. One of them who had attended a parochial high school told us, "I pretty much reject most of my background. I guess I was always taught that religion was there when you needed it, but whenever I needed it, it never seemed to serve the function. So I think either, somewhere along the line, I had the wrong teachers or I counted on it too heavily." The voids in her life had never been filled by religion. "I mean, when I needed someone, my religion didn't fill those holes. It didn't fill those gaps. At one time in my life it cost me a relationship that was really very important to me. And I think after that any faith I had in it just went."

Another divorced woman had "decided ten years ago that the church wasn't for me. They sort of came into conflict with the kinds of ideas they really preached and didn't practice. I just couldn't put up with the hypocrisy. There are certain kinds of people that go to one church, and really love to go to that church, because it has an ethnic base, and I think this is perfectly ridiculous." Another issue that troubled her was birth control. "I didn't want to have more than two children then, and the forms of birth control that were allowable to me were the kinds of birth control by which I had had two children. And I thought it was terrible that these men could sit there in their carved antique chairs and say to me, 'Well, you go ahead and have babies and we won't support you—just go ahead and have a lot of little Catholics.' It made me furious. And that's how I decided to leave."

One woman who has remained close to her religion, but on new, more challenging terms, is a former nun, who left an active Catholic community to find her own life as a single woman. She told us:

I find that I had to regenerate energies and decision-making apparatus that I wasn't using when I was with a community where everything was pretty much provided for me. So, in a sense, I had to leave that support in order to get myself going. I think that's a healthy situation. It is for me anyway. I sometimes could function extremely independently within religious life, but I let it rob me of too much that was essential to me in terms of personal commitment, like the power to decide, to maintain my own opinion. If I lose myself *now*, I'm lost, utterly lost. Nobody's going to pick me up, you know. I really just have to look out for myself. I think that's a vital thing, to be always aware of the fact that you can disappear or that people aren't always going to be there just to pick you up and keep you from harm.

Other Catholic women we met have joined together in small groups and larger networks to support each other in the experience of divorce, often within an environment that is hostile to such bonding.

The many Protestant women we talked with did not feel the need for such drastic severance from their early religious background in order to accommodate their new life experience. Two of them had been professionally trained in religious education, and a third was a minister. These women were involved at several levels with their churches, in such activities as a teen drop-in center, singles' discussion groups, and family life education for both children and adults. Other Protestant women remained peripherally connected to their church community, often for the sake of their children.

The Jewish women we talked with varied in their attitudes. The divorced women without exception maintained little or no contact with their religion unless it was to send their children to Hebrew school. On the other hand, some of the widows had remained close to their congregations and worked with their rabbis both on personal and community concerns.

LESS THAN FULL MEMBERSHIP

The singleness of women is an issue somehow connected with broadly held moral values about the structure and permanence of the family. But while being divorced is an undesirable status, an even greater stigma is attached to single mothers, and unwed mothers are not received gladly, as one woman pointed out:

I'm a member of a Baptist Church, and when my daughter was about four months old, I wanted to have her christened in the church. I was a member, baptized and everything. And I called the pastor and I told him and he said, "Well, I'm sorry but I will be glad to do it in your home but I will not do it in the church." I said, "You're kidding, what's the problem?" Because at first he had said, "Fine, in the church," but

I said, "I should probably tell you, I'm not married." And he said, "Oh, wow, that really changes it." I said, "This is incredible. I don't believe it!" So what I did was call up the National Association of Baptist Ministers and reported him. I talked to another minister, and he said, "I don't understand where his ideas are coming from, but, personally, I have no problems with that. If you want to have her christened in the church, that's your privilege." So as far as church, I will have nothing to do with it now, especially my church. I'll visit other churches. At this point, I find little comfort or support.

In contrast, the claim of widows seems more legitimate to the church and clergy; that they are now single is patently *not their fault.* Consequently, widows, more than other single women, tend to remain closer to the support and socializing which church membership offers them and their families. In addition, because they are often older than other single women, they're more oriented to traditional supports. One forty-year-old widow felt that not only did her faith support her through the ordeal of her husband's illness, but it also gave her children some sense of continuity with their father and their former lives which "was important for them at the time of the death because he was a very important man in the building of this new church, very well respected. This gave the kids a good feeling about their father." She told us:

I think the church is necessary for support, in the ritual of it, particularly. I was a Lutheran, but I had through a Church Women United group been participating in a prayer group, a Bible study group, for five or six years before my husband became ill. And this is where I gained a lot of my insight and support rather than from the church. It was an interdenominational group also. And I really got a lot of insights and strengths to go through the downhill 'til death and then to pick up again. And it was good for my children. They always knew where I was Monday mornings and they liked it, even though they did not want to participate in any young people's church groups or Sunday School or anything like that. . . . There was no forced religion on them, ever. We still go to church.

What does the experience of single women tell us about the position of religious institutions in our society? Can the church remain a useful resource in a society in which the entire family structure is undergoing radical transformation? Or will it retreat into a citadel, admitting only the orthodox and excluding the growing numbers who no longer conform to earlier, time-honored precepts? How is the historical position of the church toward single women being influenced by women who are seeking new leadership roles and opportunities for self-determination within churches? And finally, what new kinds of voluntary approaches within formal church institutions address themselves to the concerns of single women?

Origins of Exclusion

Modern attitudes of the churches and clergy in America toward both women and family patterns have been formed by many traditions, many historical forces, and the sectarian diversity of this country makes religious consensus on matrimonial issues virtually impossible.[1] The three major religious groups today hold significantly different positions and moral attitudes about women who live as single adults, and much depends on what kinds of choices and circumstances account for their single marital status.

Yet through all the variations of dogma and doctrine, there are some common themes. Essentially, our modern secular concepts of marriage, the family, and women's roles in those institutions derive from Old Testament patriarchal values and New Testament hostility to divorce. Americans have inherited, almost intact, a conservative tradition persisting into modern times, which has "rested on the subordination of married women, a guilt-innocence approach to divorce, and the state's interest in preserving marriages."[2]

In earlier times, these harsh and rigid attitudes toward divorce reflected the narrow alternatives life offered. Marriage was essential to survival because the family was the basic unit of production and woman's roles in that unit as both worker and mother were critical. Since early adult death was common, especially for women, "until death do us part" had real immediacy and tended to make the question of divorce moot. In addition, the Catholic Church had since early Christian times presented women with the honorable option of single life in religious communities; virginity was an esteemed, even privileged, status in the church.

By the end of the nineteenth century the three major American religious groups had varying positions on the shape and permanence of family life. The Catholic clergy, led by Cardinal Gibbons of Baltimore, formed the core of conservative opposition to divorce, supported by many Protestant fundamentalist sects. The promulgation of the Third Council of Baltimore declared that since marriage was a sacrament, it lasted until death; those who did not choose to marry could enter religious life. Happiness in marriage was of secondary importance to the preservation of the family.[3]

The Episcopalians and other liberal Protestant groups were meanwhile vacillating on a hard stand against marital dissolution and began to permit divorce, and even remarriage in certain cases, provided the person was the "innocent party" to desertion or adultery. This practice thus replicated that of the European Protestants who had introduced the notions of "guilt" and "innocence" to matrimonial concerns during the Reformation. Most Protestant denominations now do not prohibit divorce; many also offer programs for the support and rehabilitation of newly bereaved widows, as we have seen. In Lopata's group of widows in Chicago, the Protestants were the most likely to have church-connected associatons and activities.[4] But the single women, particularly the single mothers, who responded to this study, nonetheless felt themselves outside the mainstreams of their churches, rejected because they were single, unable to have a sense of full membership and acceptance. That this sense of feeling marginal is part of one's self-image only makes the situation more complex. One middle-aged woman, a divorced Protestant, reported that she hadn't "felt much encouragement. It's part of coming into a strange town as a single person and divorced. Maybe it's me being supersensitive. As a sort of identity, I joined the church, and it has given me people whom I know by name, and they know me. I know the church is *there*, and there are resources. But it took the utmost courage."

The Jewish congregations that maintain centuries-old biases against single women in the community have allied themselves with conservative Catholics on the need to reinforce the strengths of family life. Divorce in particular is seen as one of the major "afflictions" of the Jewish community and was so identified at the 1968 conference of the Commission on Synagogue Relations, part of the Federation of Jewish Philanthropies, along with alcoholism, out-of-wedlock pregnancy, and drug addiction! And, in spite of the ancient Biblical injunction to comfort the widow, most Jewish widows in two major studies made a special point of saying how inadequate their clergy were to the crisis of loss and bereavement.[5]

We are dealing here with generalizations, it must be borne in mind, and there are an increasing number of voluntary approaches which are transforming tradition-bound attitudes in religion toward single women. But one cannot help but be struck by the insistence among all faiths and sects that single life not in a religious order is somehow deviant, especially for women. Singleness is viewed at best as a disaster, at worst a sin. Helping in the sometimes very painful adjustments which single women and their families must endure is simply not part of most churches' ministries. One must conform, and often repent, if one is to be comforted.

The situation is particularly poignant, given the expectations of both women and the clergy. Many of the women we interviewed had turned first to their church for support, whether in the crisis of bereavement, the transition to divorce, or the problems of single parenting. In an age of instant recourse to expertise the clergy, under considerable pressure to deliver services which have few guidelines and cause considerable doctrinal confusion, tend to refer single women to professionals in one or another specialty. Helping single women involves tasks which the clergy feel unable to define or address.[6]

For both widows and the newly separated, these tasks include coming to terms with a new identity and learning to make autonomous decisions, often for the first time in their adult lives. They are looking for caregivers who can deal realistically with their new situation, who will support them, without moral judgments, through a difficult time of transitions, but churches often are unequal to this need. One woman expressed her sense of frustration with her church this way:

This is what my kids have gotten from the adults in the church: "Pray that your father will come to Christ. Pray that your mother will come to Christ." Well, neither one of us is going to come to Christ. So that's an unrealistic prayer. I finally went down to my daughter's youth leader because I was getting signals, especially the day we signed the financial agreement. It was a terrible day for her. I was getting signals that she felt this marriage was going to get back together. . . . I went in to her youth leader and said, "Would you please not pray with her that her mother and father are going to be together again? Pray that things will turn out for the best, and that life will go on and be better."

Ministering to the Healthy

On the other hand, the clergy feel that most people come for help too late, especially if the problems seem to center around separation and divorce. The Marriage Encounter Movement, which has now reached all three major religious groups, is a voluntary approach to family counseling that aims primarily at reinforcing happy, "normal" marriages, a situation in which most clergymen feel more comfortable. The movement, begun seventeen years ago in Spain, reached this country about six years ago and has spread to more than forty states. The movement currently claims to have served 175,000 couples of all faiths, the majority of them Catholics. Marriage Encounter, Jewish Marriage Experience, Episcopal Expression, to name some prominent groups, have designed a weekend program to help happily married couples to learn new techniques of communication. Leadership is provided through teams of clergy and laypersons, the latter usually recent participants in the program. Religious services are part of the weekend agenda, though attendance is not always mandatory.[7]

Information on the durability of families that have participated is not easy to find. However debatable the outcomes may be, one can safely say that those families that reflect the idealized norm of American life, those least vulnerable to the effects of aging, poverty, racial segregation, and other societal pressures, are the most likely to join the Encounter Movement. And an important part of its success has been the overwhelming preference of clergymen to preserve the status quo rather than to deal with emerging and more controversial alternatives.

TOWARD THE RIGHT TO MINISTER

One such alternative has its origins in repeated attempts to gain equal opportunities for women in the ministries of the churches. Many advocates of this goal feel that until women share equally in the decisions and governance of the churches they will remain powerless, second-class members. Today feminist pressures are building behind larger trends toward humanizing and democratizing churchly structures. As yet, however, the role of women in church leadership is minimal; there are a few token Protestant ministers, one or two Jewish women seminarians, and a handful of Episcopalian women priests whose status is both controversial and unstable. And women who hold lay positions in church hierarchies, such as directors of religious education or other administrative posts, are typically underpaid in comparison with comparable male appointments. Seldom do women hold positions of influence on either local church boards or regional councils. A task force of NOW is currently documenting the exact extent of sexist discrimination in the church leadership of all major faiths.[8]

Mary Daly, a professor of theology at Boston College and a prominent Catholic feminist, argues that

In liturgical affairs, as participation of the laity becomes more active, equally active participation of both sexes must be insisted upon. If laymen serve as lectors and acolytes, if they preach and distribute Holy Communion, then women should do the same. Moreover, it is evident, if one faces the problem with consistency, courage and sincerity, that the process of eradicating discrimination must not stop here. The question of women clergy must be faced.[9]

Daly notes that as the functional roles of the priesthood are changing to embrace a broader definition, moving from a "cultic notion . . . to a ministerial one," the specific experiences of women cannot be discounted or ignored.[10] Certainly, as long-established church structure and practice evolve to new forms, women will be heard. Already, women are organizing through the traditional women's groups in many faiths, to focus on new feminist objectives. Within the Catholic Church the Joint Committee of Organizations Concerned about the Status of Women in the Church is currently working to set up an Office of Women's Affairs with the United States Catholic Conference. The usually conservative National Council of Catholic Women has protested to the Bishops' Council that women are "third-class Christians" in the Church. St. Joan's International Alliance, founded in Great Britain early in the 1920s, has since 1965 formed groups in this country to further the equality of women both inside and outside the Catholic Church. And in 1969, the National Coalition of American Nuns was formed to address feminist concerns of social justice and to protest the male priestly domination of the Church.[11]

Many Protestant denominations have formed women's groups, the most militant of which is probably the Unitarian Universalist Women's Federation. Other organizations, such as the venerable Church Women United, the United Methodist Women, the United Presbyterian Church Task Force on Women in Church and Society, now count themselves as part of the new activism. The American Jewish Congress National Women's Division is also involved in advocacy for women. All these organizations are concerned about sex discrimination and all-male leadership; many work on broad-based programs through local branches and chapters. These old-line organizations enjoy a distinct advantage in building a solid base for concerted action. They are in most cases considered eminently respectable to a large segment of the community. Few, however, have addressed themselves specifically to the issues which single women face in their daily lives, and many are strongly biased against divorced women.

An exception to this bias is found among the Unitarian Universalist congregations that have provided serious forums for the discussion of crucial changes in modern family life. One example of this concern is an innovative program deserving special attention. The Unitarian Society of Wellesley Hills, Massachusetts, under the direction of the Reverend Polly Laughland, herself a divorced woman, sponsored a two-week summer program for single people, designed as a residential retreat at a summer beach area available to local churches.[12] Over sixty persons attended, the majority of them divorced women, although there were a few men and two or three widows. They came from all over the East and as far away as Michigan, Florida, and Canada.

The two-week experience included small-group learning sessions focusing on personal issues of goal-setting and value clarification, in which participants could share their feelings about the past and their objectives for the future. Frank discussions on such subjects as human sexuality, intimacy, loneliness, and love were encouraged and were balanced with recreational periods and creative crafts workshops. A children's program was included for the families of single people. The Reverend Laughland publicized the event under the appealing title, "Affirming Singleness," in itself a notable acceptance of changing lifestyles.

The Reverend Laughland feels that her own life experience as a single person has enhanced her professional capability to serve both families and single people. While clergy who are divorced remain part of a tiny minority, the phenomenon is increasing as married ministers and rabbis respond to the same pressures and changing social mores as their congregations. While the Catholic Church maintains that their celibate clergy retain an essential impartiality simply *because* they are not married, among those religious groups whose clergy do marry, the distance between minister and parishioner tends to decrease as clergy increasingly realize that life is an imperfect struggle, one in which they themselves are intimately involved. The efforts to open up churchly dialogue to the issues of everyday living at least had the advantage of recognizing that marriages *do* fail, that bereavement is a complex process, and that family life indeed has taken on new shapes and structures which can and do work regardless of religious positions.

DIVORCED CATHOLICS: A CASE IN POINT

One out of every four Americans is a Catholic in both culture and tradition. In many of the Northern states, Catholics approach half the population and have had an enormous impact on the developing urban cultures of the Northeast. The current Catholic divorce rate is now estimated to be approaching that of other segments of the society, in spite of strenuous efforts of the hierarchy to stem the tide. One out of every three Catholic marriages now ends in separation or divorce. Approximately six million Catholics are now divorced; of these three million have remarried. Most of these second marriages have not received the blessing of the Church, which forbids remarriage except in the following situations: termination of the marriage by the death of the spouse; annulment of the first marriage; special papal dispensation. [13]

There is currently a strong movement within the Church to gain recognition of second marriages of divorced Catholics. Both the National Federation of Priests Council and the Canon Law Society have asked the American bishops to grant official reconciliation for those whose marriage is "dead" and who have demonstrated "proven sincerity" in their desire to live fully Catholic lives. The influential Jesuit publication *America* has endorsed this proposal as have many individual parish priests across the country. [14]

While changing the status of the divorced Catholic in remarriage has been a major objective of many activists, the movement encompasses far more and extends support and charity to all those who are separated or divorced. There are now over one hundred Divorced Catholics groups in the United States and Canada, the majority of which have been started by laypersons with the support of a few priests and nuns. The movement started over twenty-five years ago, largely through the efforts of the Sisters of the Cenacle, who offered spiritual support to divorced women who were alienated and rejected within their parish communities. The obvious poverty of many women alone, and the often large numbers of children in their families, made a claim to the charitable mission of the Church which could not be ignored. Since the 1960s, however, new groups of Divorced Catholics have become much more change-oriented and are characterized by lay leadership and advocacy while other groups within the Church, including Catholic Charities, Family Life Centers, and even diocesan matrimonial tribunals, have become involved in divorce ministries. [15]

The largest, most influential center for divorced Catholics is under the exceptional leadership of Father James Young at the Paulist Center in Boston. Since 1972, the Paulist Center Community has run educational and support programs, acted as a network coordinator and clearinghouse for other groups of divorced Catholics, and has published a widely circulated newsletter. The center not only runs local programming, but has sponsored four national conferences on a broad range of concerns for separated and divorced persons. The most recent conference, in November, 1975, attracted 500 persons from all over the country and introduced the theme of personal and spiritual growth through life transition and urged the laity to activism and reform. An earlier public statement by Father Young summed up the thrust of the movement: "Divorce is an experience that tells you a lot about yourself. What the Church should ask is, 'Is this person growing through this?' The Church should be calling people to health and life and growth."[16]

Other efforts have been sponsored by the networks of Christian Life Centers. In New Hampshire, for example, the Christian Life Centers have set up seven Divorced Catholic groups, spaced geographically around the state, staffed by priest-and-nun teams. And in the St. Paul–Minneapolis Archdiocese, a citywide task force has been working to develop parish-based groups, although some divorced Catholics prefer to meet away from their home parishes—and pastors.[17]

The real strength and cutting edge of the movement has been in the small groups. It is within the small "rap groups" that the distinctly secular flavor of reform is most evident. In addition, the intimate and supportive nature of small-group learning is compatible with the present attitudes of many Catholic women, who are for the most part unused to activism and to the experience of mutual self-help. They have somehow been left out of the mainstream of feminist consciousness-raising. As Catholic women, they have felt themselves to be the principal guardians of the home and family. Often they have never worked outside the home and have few career aspirations. As a result, these women have suffered not only from isolation and poverty, but from pervasive feelings of self-blame, guilt, and personal fault.

We were invited to observe a typical small group of Catholic divorced women who had formed under the inspiration of the Paulist Center and a local priest. (One member tells her story at the end of this chapter.) The group followed guidelines suggested by the Paulist Center; two members had trained through the Center's workshops for group leaders, although the groups are deliberately leaderless and nonstructured. The meetings include sharing experiences and support, and newly separated women are helped by those with more distance from their own crisis.

Outings with the children are planned to help the families to feel less strange in the parish community. Single-parenting and financial management resources are shared over refreshments. The group meets once monthly and tries to attend the larger events at the center as well.

Several striking themes emerged from the group. First, the women had not divorced lightly. For many, there had been prolonged marital strife, physical abuse, histories of alcoholism, and counseling both within and outside the Church had been sought, most often by the wives. Second, it was clear that the women intended to remain in the Church as they built new lives for themselves and their children. And last, there was a real reluctance to challenge the authority of the Church and priesthood. Ingrained habits persist beyond the desire for change, as we observed when the group's chaplain visited for an hour. A sympathetic, even learned, man, he nonetheless spoke formally to the women and conducted a question-and-answer period which was far from satisfactory. It was clear that he took his ministry seriously, but it seemed equally apparent that he was uncomfortable with the new activism of Catholic women, tentative though it was. Dialogue between peers was not yet a reality in this setting, but new and profound learning was taking place and new directions were being explored, both by the priests and the women.

As Father Young said, in a keynote speech in a 1974 conference of divorced Catholics:

I do not think the Roman Catholic Church is going to decide what marriage will be like in American society or even have a major say in what marriage will be like. Marriage in any age, in any culture is an institution shaped by complex social, economic, religious, and cultural forces. There is a new kind of marriage emerging in American culture. As Christian believers committed to an ideal of permanent, faithful, loving marriage, I think we must realistically assess what is happening to marriage in our times, and look upon the result with eyes of hope.[18]

V O I C E S

"I did just about everything this priest told me to do."

The speaker is a thirty-seven-year-old Catholic mother of three children, who is a full-time student in teacher training at a public college, now practice-teaching.

She was divorced three years ago after several separations and some years of family counseling. Her income consists of some child support, food stamps, Medicaid, and a rent subsidy. She is also actively engaged in starting a divorced Catholics' group in her city, the first ever with parish sponsorship and an official spiritual advisor from the rectory.

Things are working out quite well for me because I have parents, especially my father, who was totally for my going to college. He gives me not only moral support but, at times, financial support. However, the first year I was going to college I was going evenings. The WIN program supported me by giving me thirty dollars a month and paid for college tuition and books. I found a young cousin to come in and help and I did the rest myself. It was only when I switched to days that my mother started coming quite often, once a week on some of my worst days, so that the children always had someone to look after them. The littlest one was almost four years old at the time I entered college as a day student—I missed her terribly. Sometimes when the parochial school had vacations and I didn't, I took them all to school with me—lots and lots of times they came to school with me. I mean, it's amazing what you can do if you have to get to class. At the beginning I didn't think how I was going to do it, but this is quite common with so many women, I think, when they have to make a decision. The pieces somehow fit and if you want it enough, it will work. And a little faith, too —I believe in that.

Of course, there was the guilt. It took a whole semester to get over that. I would be in school and feeling so terrible about it—that I was away from the house. The guilt feelings were really bad. But, I also had guilt feelings about being divorced, too. So I had a dual situation. It was terrible. But then I met some of the teachers and professors, other married women and other divorced women in school—because more and more colleges are accepting them, the older women—and we got strength from each other.

At the beginning I thought it was going to be difficult because you have to remember that parochial schoolchildren have double the homework that the public schoolchildren have and they often needed help with their schoolwork. My boy is very much into sports and I thought this would be just another added burden to me because of the time it took driving him back and forth to each game. However, it's worked out fine. . . . People are out there who really want to help, if you can just get yourself to be honest about your situation and to ask them to help you: "Can you drive my son? I'm in a situation where it's very difficult, I'm trying to go to school, I'm trying to get a degree. Can you help me?" And I've found no one has ever refused.

Summertime I used to find most difficult, because of lack of funds, and you can't get away. This can be very difficult. However—I say it again!—there are places you can go for camp, camperships, tuition help. Take advantage of them, that's what they're there for and you usually have to start in April or May. And it's a wonderful opportunity for them to go to two weeks of camp. Like I say, I do have family, lots of family and they're wonderful people and they have taken the children on occasion for weekends. I'm very fortunate that way. I have a sister who has a cottage on the Cape—she's invited them and I've gone myself. I'm lucky. I'm really lucky. As hard as it is, and doing it alone without much money, I still feel very lucky. I think you have to count your blessings.

As far as school goes, I've been fortunate there, too. I have a National Student Loan, and because it's a state college, the tuition is very inexpensive in comparison to an Ivy League college. At this school I attend, if you borrow two hundred and fifty dollars, they will match that with another two hundred and fifty which you do not have to pay back. After payment of tuition, books, and supplies, there is always a little extra for car expenses, clothes, and everyday items.

It's amazing how you can stretch that extra money. I do have a car—it's seven years old, but it's in good condition. And if I have any problems, my father knows a mechanic who usually fixes it for very little. But, here we go again—taking advantage of people and letting them know your situation. I found that most people treat you pretty fair when they know you're raising up a family alone and are on a limited income. You can always reciprocate by a gift at Christmastime.

Some teachers have said to me, they've never seen anyone enjoy school like I do. And my grades are great! It's frustrating, though. I've wanted to throw in the towel many times. But you just have to push forward. I should have been graduating this June, but I did have an operation and I lost a semester. So, hopefully, December's graduation, after five years. And remember, I just had a high school degree. I was thirty-one when I took my SAT'S and achievement tests. It was, for me, the beginning of a new life.

I never used to have any social life and I think that was wrong. I could have tried a little harder, but I was really frightened of the outside world. A single woman alone out there can be very scary—it really was for me. I had to get over a very bad marriage. I had a lot of hangups.

I did have a lot of offers to go out, but I just couldn't. What happened was the reverse. I became very close to the children and included them in everything I did. There's something that's very important about a divorce that I don't think a lot of people understand. It's a death, the death of a marriage, and there's a mourning period, and no matter how many people want to take you out that first year or so, you're not really yourself for quite a while—at least it was like that for me. You can either go one way or the other. You can hang around at a singles' bar every weekend or you can stay in the house till this gets out of your system. And you have to find it out for yourself.

I came out here [to the suburbs] on the suggestion of our priest. We were separated at the time and going to him for counseling—I did just about everything this priest told me to do. I knew down deep the marriage was a disaster from the very beginning, from the time I was on my honeymoon, yet I kept giving it a try and my ex-husband kept promising he'd change, but it just didn't work. The house I live in is owned by this very same priest who gave counseling all my married life—at times it seemed I was out of a marriage more than in it. He suggested making a change in different surroundings—meeting new people, making new friends, and getting away from in-laws. I remember feeling ill because it seemed he was giving another order. It was about this time when I felt tired of listening to him, when I wanted to tell him, "I don't want counseling anymore. I'm old enough to make up my own mind. I'm a human being. This marriage is not going to work." But I said nothing. I even went to a psychologist, and both my ex-husband and I took turns. Finally, even [the psychologist] suggested giving it another try. He, too, was a priest.

Three years ago when I started the divorce proceedings, of course I went through the Church and I signed the papers. You don't have to, a lot of Catholics I know don't. But at this time I was seeing another priest, my parish priest, and he helped me throughout the divorce. It was the first time in eleven years a priest had respected a decision I had made. Shortly after my Church separation, I asked him to come to dinner some night because I thought it would be so nice for the children having a man even if it was a priest. He refused. You have to understand their position, too—usually their pastor is from the old school and priests just do not talk to divorced women, because "What will the people say?" However, they don't all feel that way today. We are living in such a revolution—I really feel bad for those older women alone.

When I first came here, I thought it was terrible. Most people stayed in their houses and they didn't recognize you on the street. Now I love that privacy and I enjoy it. That's something you wouldn't get with relatives back in the city. You have to be accountable and you feel you owe them an accounting—something I just didn't want to go through. I'm glad that I did come out to the suburbs, as hesitant as I was on the decision.

It also gave me the opportunity to grow away from my mother. I love her dearly—she's a precious lady—but, I had to be me, too. My husband was strangling me. She was in her own way too, strangling me, but let me explain why. I was brought up in an Italian, Catholic family, my father and brothers looking after me at all times, my mother running the house. She wanted me to marry and when the marriage failed, she didn't want me to get a divorce. She was ashamed of what "the people might say." It wasn't her fault. It was a time when Catholics who got a divorce were unmentionables. When I look back to the fifties, I can see, for me, there was nowhere to go but to get married. I wanted to go to college then, but there was no money and no scholarships available. I even wanted to be an airline hostess, but my father would never let me go. When I visit my parents and brother, the kids can see both sides but sometimes they can't wait to get home here, so they have both.

Well, a woman here in town approached Father C. one day and said, "We need something here for divorced people. Other churches are doing it and the people here in our parish who are divorced need something." When she called me, she told me Father suggested calling me to see if I would like to put this thing together. I said, "Great!"—here I was convalescing from an operation and out of school and my brother had just died, too. I was very down and feeling very depressed. But you see how God works. It was the right time at the right place. This is why I say faith is so important. All the pieces will fit.

So, we had a very quiet meeting in my living room. They asked me and another divorced Catholic woman if we could go down to the Paulist Center and set up some kind of program. We took a four-week training seminar. Well, people found out about us because on Palm Sunday in the church bulletin it read, "First Meeting Divorced Catholic Group." The repercussions were felt from here to the other end of town. And you have to understand that even though it was a divorced Catholic group for this section of the city, I get phone calls throughout the state from people who know relatives in this town or that town or God knows where else, who would like our help because there is nobody who can help them with their problems. So, the need is great. I have had women who are so-called happily married come to me for help concerning their marriages. This has been kind of a shock. We didn't expect this. I've become a listener and I've become a supporter for these people who are going through so-called happy marriages.

We meet once a month. We got six the first night, which is about par for the course. It's a rap group and we're not psychologists, but we listen and if we can be of any help, give any moral support, we try. We meet in living rooms and there's no president, no vice-president, it's not worked like that. We're trying to become a strong body to help one another. We hope eventually we will grow and be able to help all divorced people in all the parishes in our city. Also, to help all Christians with the same problems because there's nothing for divorced Catholics in our city. When you're going to school, divorced, have a growing family to raise, there isn't much time for anything else. But this divorced Catholic group means more to me. If I can just help someone during that lonely time of divorce proceedings or at any time, then my time was well spent. My neighbors—if I can do anything for them, I will, but the need is not with the neighborhood right now, the need is that of divorced people.

I used to think way ahead a lot and I found that what I want doesn't always happen. I've learned to take one day at a time. I want to graduate, but I found, like last year when I became ill, I became angry. Oh dear, this was the worst thing that could happen to me. But I realized that during that period of illness, I had time to stop and think and contemplate, not in your time but in God's time. And, it's coming. All the pieces are beginning to fit. I really try not to look too far ahead. I really don't because so many things can come into your life. But, in the back of my mind, way down deep, I do want to be married again. I really do. So, I'm just starting to invite people into my home—male people. I have a lot of platonic relationships with teachers who are single, but we just have dinner because we are good friends. I want that, but, on the other hand, I would like to go out once in a while. Someday I would like to get married again.

I was brought up in the fifties. Marriage was the important thing and having children. I still feel that the family is one of the most important and beautiful ways to go through life, the most healthy way to go through life. Maybe I'm terribly wrong, maybe being a bachelor or a single woman can be much more fulfilling, too. I don't think so, I really don't. I feel that the joys of being a mother, a wife, and having a good husband really *are* the most beautiful things of all. So, my first wish is that my children take their time when planning to make a commitment concerning marriage and that I won't encourage them in any way to make *their* decision. But I still have a very deep Italian background that comes out, which is great, right? So I hope they do marry someday and have a family of their own. My second wish is for all women who are bringing up a family alone. To those people, I hope that what I have said will brighten their day just a little because you're not alone with this great responsibility and your children will grow up and be on their own, all too soon. And my third wish? I really hope to be a good teacher: to teach them to look at what they see and appreciate it, to experience all kinds of art, to be sensitive to life, which includes our whole environment because I think too many kids are not taught this from early childhood.

Chapter 11

THE LAW OF MAN

"A married woman making the transition to single personhood often needs much more than simply legal assistance, especially if she is poor and/or has children."—Isabella Jancourtz, attorney

$\mathcal{M}$OST SINGLE women will need legal services at some time in their lives, yet no institution in our society remains less accessible to women than the law. There is almost a consensus among single women that the law is obscure, costly, out of reach—an institution dominated by men, riddled with bias and discrimination, and very nearly incomprehensible. All single women, whether widowed, divorced, or never married, need credit. All single women need housing. Widows need help with inheritance taxes and survivor benefits. Women facing separation and divorce need advocates willing to explain the available alternatives and able to represent their interests. Yet when single women seek solutions to their legal problems, they are confronted by a number of barriers, both personal and institutional. Women are usually woefully ignorant of legal matters. Isolated from the legal profession and the legislative corridors where laws are formulated, bound by stereotypes which contend that the law is a man's world, most women simply do not know their legal rights.

In addition, legal services can be, and usually are, costly, and since most single women are economically disadvantaged, they hesitate to seek the legal services they need. And to compound the problem, the majority of lawyers, judges, politicians, lawmakers, and government officials are men, very often white, well educated, and older, men whose lives are far removed from the lifestyles of single women. Finally, the law itself is permeated with anachronistic, discriminatory, sexist assumptions that make justice for women an illusory goal. Small wonder that when it comes to the law, women feel powerless and alienated.

THE LEGAL PROFESSION: THE MEN'S BAR

Thus whenever we as women come into court for any reason—as accused, as accusor, to settle a claim or as a witness—we face a powerful, male-dominated structure within which judges are pre-eminent. Their personal belief systems cannot help but influence their judgments. If sexism is among a judge's prejudices—and in this society it is highly likely that it would be—a woman appearing before him must expect to have this prejudice affect the entire court process as well as his ultimate ruling, even when the judge may be trying hard to be fair and impartial.[1]

These words, quoted from an exhaustive study of Massachusetts government and courts by the Women's Research Center, point to another target of feminist change. Women, encouraged by the women's movement, have been building their political strengths through the formation of alternative community-based voluntary associations; they have brought continually increasing pressure to bear on public policy through special-interest groups such as child care coalitions and welfare rights organizations. NOW, following the example of the black civil rights activists in NAACP, has set up a legal defense and education fund to finance court suits filed by women victims of discrimination. In short, women have been developing more effective interfaces with the law and lawgivers and have learned to communicate more directly with them, but as yet there are only a few token women in the structure of government and the judiciary.

The statistics are startling. In a 1969 study by the National Conference of Bar Presidents, there were estimated to be not more than 8,000 female lawyers in the United States, 8 percent of all lawyers. Out of almost 10,000 judges, fewer than 200 were women, the majority serving in lower courts. Although there are more women than blacks in the legal profession, and more women have been at it longer, there are now more black men than women in the judiciary, including one black man on the Supreme Court. Only a few token women have been appointed to the federal circuit courts; for forty years, Florence Allen was the sole woman appointed to a federal judgeship.[2]

At the state level, the same dismal picture prevails. When the New York legislature created 125 new judicial vacancies in 1968, *two* women and 123 men were ultimately appointed. In Massachusetts, a state with a high proportion of women college graduates and women holding professional degrees, fewer than 10 percent of all lawyers are women. Only eight women hold judgeships, two are part-time, and only one serves above the district court level. Nor is the prospect for change bright; judges are appointed for life in that state and the turnover is low since there is no mandatory retirement age. And court clerks, registrars of deeds, and other key court personnel are all over 90 percent male.[3]

The discrimination extends to juries as well. Although the majority of cases heard, both civil and criminal, do not have jury trials, juries have until very recently been predominantly male. Women do not appear on jury rolls as frequently as do men; prior to 1949, women in Massachusetts were not permitted to serve on juries at all. Up until 1969, when the law was changed due to persistent pressure by feminists, women could be exempted solely on the basis of being a woman, and present laws usually exempt mothers of children under sixteen, women having the care of such children, and women in religious life. In addition, judges have often excused women from serving on juries which would hear distasteful crimes such as rape or violent assault.[4]

For those women who have chosen the law as their profession, further obstacles have lain ahead. Law schools have refused women admissions outright, or established arbitrary quotas. Law firms discriminate blatantly in their hiring practices, or else place a few token women in research and other less prestigious positions where advancement is limited.[5] One woman lawyer who passed the regional bar examinations among the top ten finalists has had such difficulty in interviewing for positions that the bar examiners have given her special permission to use her ranking in her resume.

Since 1970, however, the women's movement has been responding in force to discriminatory practices in the legal profession. There are now, for example, more women law students than there are woman lawyers. Particularly in the large cities feminist law firms have formed, some of them receiving foundation grants to subsidize civil rights court cases. In 1971, the Professional Women's Caucus filed charges against most of the law schools in the country, charging them with discriminatory practices in hiring, student admissions, and financial aid. A real turning point in many women's consciousness came during the first Nixon term when President Nixon, having four opportunities to appoint a woman to the Supreme Court, failed to come up with a single female nominee although both he and Mrs. Nixon were flooded with applications by feminists. When the American Bar Association in 1972 adopted a resolution calling for affirmative action by both law schools and law firms, the Association of American Law Schools went even further, threatening to remove accreditation from member law schools discriminating against women in recruitment policy and practice.[6]

What is the status of the woman lawyer today? First, she is in that uneasy period of transition where she is no longer a token, yet still is an anomaly. She still earns less than her male colleagues, seldom becomes a full partner in prestigious law firms, and if she is a judge, she usually sits in family courts. She is often besieged by feminist groups to be a speaker on panels, to represent suits for which there is small chance to earn a fee, or to be spokesperson in legislative forums. Many women lawyers feel trapped in conflicts between feminist expectations and the pressure to conform to the ethos of their male colleagues. But the extraordinary expansion of women's organizations has created new working coalitions between those women who are on the inside of institutions and the feminists and women's groups who are supporting them. When the new law students begin to emerge in numbers in local bar associations and in feminist law firms, at least some of these conflicts will begin to be resolved.

And what do these data mean to the lives of single women? Basically, that every time a single woman needs legal services, she must still depend on an institution predominantly male and undoubtedly sexist. It is often at this juncture that single women step into the real world for the first time, a disheartening experience of the way society and its institutions view adult women who are alone without husbands or fathers. The woman who is separating from her husband has urgent problems which demand immediate professional attention, yet the separated and divorced women we spoke with had had, almost without exception, negative experiences with either the legal process or lawyers—usually with both. The following quotations are typical:

• The legal hassle that you have to go through in this state to become separated or divorced is so extensive that if you're a human being, you're going to ask yourself, "Is it worth it?" And I think for me, in the end, I think to myself that if I didn't have the children, I might have given up on the idea. But when I think of the children, I cannot stay with this man. I can't do it to my children. I may do it to myself, but I'm not sure I could ever do it to them.

• My lawyer once said to me, "I'm sure a woman like you, and I don't say this to all my clients, I'm sure you're going to get married again." And my response is: I would never get married again. And I'm pretty firm about it. I mean, if I found another man that I would fall in love with, I might live with him but, unless they change the divorce laws in this state, there is no way I would ever get married again. I just would not go through this again.

Several women muddled along with lawyers who were essentially no help at all because they had no clear-cut understanding of what lawyers can and cannot do. In fact, the situation is much like that encountered by single women and the clergy; the expectations of both sides are unrealistic and neither side fully comprehends the situation. Paul Bohannan comments that the expertise demanded of lawyers in divorce cases "has made lawyers into experts in several aspects of divorce; there are no recognized experts in other aspects of divorce. Therefore, lawyers are called upon to assume responsibility for more and more aspects of the institution—in many, they have no training; in others, there is no possible legal base from which they can operate."[7]

Furthermore, many lawyers (and judges) are extremely biased against divorce and assume conciliatory roles which can be both destructive and costly. As Gettleman and Markowitz point out, "neither lawyers nor judges are warranted (nor should they be permitted) to stop divorce. They are not personally accountable for the high divorce rate; they are 'enablers' in a process they do not initiate."[8]

Another woman in our interview group said she and her husband had been proceeding with a restrained and civilized separation "until the lawyers stepped in." Now they are divorced, but still in litigation over both child support and custody arrangements. A woman whose husband moved to a neighboring state has spent more money trying to collect legal maintenance than she will ever realize in a settlement. Irrationality and unscrupulous behavior on the part of both the client and the lawyer are not uncommon in divorce cases.

Unfortunately divorce proceedings are also costly and it is hardly surprising that many low-income families simply dissolve without legal process. The Women in Transition handbook estimates that an uncontested divorce costs at least $750; a "no-fault" or nonadversary divorce is at least $300 to $400; and a separation can be arranged for around $350. Contested divorces, which can be complex matters, involving several court appearances and custody hearings, can run into the thousands of dollars. The charge for a support hearing alone is about $250 for the plaintiff and $150 for the defendant.[9] While it is obviously to a woman's advantage to pay a flat fee for legal services, most lawyers prefer to charge by the hour with hourly rates that start at $25 and can go much higher.

Thus, it is not surprising that many lawyers are tempted by the financial rewards of divorce litigation and object to knowledgeable clients doing some of the work themselves. Furthermore, despite the financial benefits, divorce lawyers usually make less money than their colleagues in insurance or corporation law and share with the criminal lawyers a low status in the legal profession, dealing as they do with human passions and emotions, a situation that increases the likelihood of having inadequate legal counsel.[10]

Widows, too, face the complexities of the law at a time when their emotions are unstable. Many older widows were taught that it was feminine to be ignorant of their husband's legal and financial status, and in their confusion and bereavement, they are extremely vulnerable—prime targets for bad advice from relatives and the services of unscrupulous lawyers, the latter a problem that the Women's Bureau has long been concerned with. A further difficulty for many widows is the complexity of Social Security benefits legislation, and Lopata urges widow-advocate services be established in all local Social Security offices to help new and confused widows with the bureaucratic red tape of federal programs.[11]

Establishing credit as a single woman can be an unpleasant learning experience. While divorced women are the principal victims of credit discrimination, widows have had problems, too. At the widows' conference that we discussed in Chapter Three, uncertain credit status was one of the participants' main concerns. And a never-married professional woman with whom we talked had to pay $400 in additional legal fees in order to obtain a mortgage on a house as sole owner. Another could not get her credit cards renewed when she changed jobs and moved. And landlords are reluctant to rent to single women, particularly if they are young and attractive or old and liable to ill health.

CLIENTS AS CONSUMERS

One attempt at breaking down barriers between women and the law has been to develop consumer education programs. Women's groups, adult education programs, women lawyers, and politicians have combined forces in informal coalitions to help women grasp some of the complexities of the law. Many women's centers now sponsor workshops and seminars on women and the law, which deal with such typical concerns as how to find a good lawyer, property rights, wills and trusts, credit legislation, and employment. Other groups, specializing in divorce law, sponsor support groups and training programs for women going through separation and divorce. Workbooks and training manuals especially directed to the legal concerns of women have been developed by many feminist organizations. The comprehensive manual of the Women in Transition project helps women to know what questions to ask, and where to go for competent, inexpensive legal services and includes the results of a survey of feminist support groups across the nation that identifies most of those dealing directly with women in the process of divorce. The manual's authors are not lawyers; they are simply women who have demonstrated most effectively that the law can be accessible and understandable to laypersons.[12]

Another useful tool has been the divorce handbook addressed specifically to the law in a particular state. Since separation and divorce law is still far from uniform in the United States, these state-law instructional manuals have been very useful. In Massachusetts, Isabella Jancourtz, a woman lawyer who is divorced, has written *The Massachusetts Woman's Divorce Handbook*, covering the subject from temporary restraining orders to tax consequences and enforcement.[13] These low-cost and explicit legal handbooks have reached large numbers of women through feminist bookstores, women's center libraries, and publicity in the media. All these programs and publications serve to close the information gap that characterizes women's legal problems, and to thereby clarify the legal process.

Other feminists urge a sort of preventative approach whereby women learn about the law before an emergency situation occurs. Lawyer Aileen Belford has urged all adult women to have a regular "legal checkup," in much the same way people have medical examinations. She feels strongly that women should have their own lawyers, and a separate credit rating, whether or not they are married, and stresses the point that women should inform themselves of their rights in four major areas: real estate and credit, estate planning, domestic relations, and consumer rights.

Lynn Caine's experience of widowhood has led her to much the same message for widows. She suggests that married couples set aside a special day each year to review together their tangible assets such as property, investments, and insurance and their outstanding debts. An annual review of this kind would undoubtedly ameliorate the terrible confusions and burdens which many widows face when their husbands die; at the very least, they would have identified their resources and gained some insights into the strengths and gaps of the family assets before they face the crisis of becoming a widow. Lynn Caine's husband, an expert at insurance law, was himself inadequately covered at the time of his death; she feels that her own lack of knowledge and her ensuing money problems exacerbated her grief and forced her into foolhardy decisions. [14]

The emphasis in these suggestions and plans is strictly on the acquisition of knowledge—few of these individuals or groups are suggesting any course of action other than *knowing one's rights* under the law. Increased information to a disadvantaged group certainly is a form of advocacy, but many activists are looking for more positive change.

PUBLIC POLICY: THE INFLUENCE
OF WOMEN IN GROUPS

As Jo Freeman has pointed out in her study of the impact of the women's movement on public policy formation, the critical time period of women's activism has been from 1966 to 1972. Prior to that time, there *was* no policy on women's status and civil rights before the law. As she says, "What is striking about this new national women's policy is not simply that there is still a long way to go, but that the notoriously cumbersome governmental apparatus has done so much so quickly." [15] By 1972, several crucial laws had been enacted in Congress, and many state legislatures had acted to eliminate sex discrimination from state codes. Powerful new feminist lobbies and networks had sprung into being; older, more established women's national organizations had received new life and a sense of advocacy from feminist support. What the women's movement is now attempting is not only personal change, but also structural changes in the institutions of society that perpetuate sex discrimination. To do that, women must enter the realm of practical politics. They must directly address the laws, and the lawmakers, in order to translate feminist objectives into public policy.

The political realm, like law as an institution, has not been hospitable to women. Women have had little access to party machinery and decision-makers, or to the "old boy" system which maintains the power structure. The Women's Research Center study of Massachusetts state government found between 90 and 95 percent of all administrators, legislators, department heads, and major elective officeholders were men. Other states and the national government follow the same segregated pattern. Legislatures, both state and national, are almost exclusively male clubs. In Congress, there are, as of this writing, eighteen women in the House of Representatives and none in the Senate. In the fifty state legislatures, there are around 300 women. Representation varies widely from state to state; in Massachusetts, where state representatives are well paid, there are fourteen women while in neighboring New Hampshire, where legislative salaries are token, there are more than three times that many women in the legislature.[16]

At the administrative level, there is one woman governor in the fifty states, plus a handful of token women in cabinet positions. At the federal level there were no female appointments to the Cabinet during the Nixon administration. And even Republican congresswomen were insulted when Nixon suggested that, since he had been unable to find any qualified women for the Cabinet, Cabinet wives might enjoy attending an occasional meeting.[17]   When the White House Task Force on Women's Rights and Responsibilities submitted its report, urging a national commitment to bring women into key government positions, those recommendations were largely ignored also. The Ford administration has improved the track record somewhat, and Mrs. Ford has proved to be a real advocate at the White House.

Feminists in the Woodwork

Within the federal government itself, however, there are some reservoirs of feminist strength which have proved surprisingly effective when combined with the mounting pressure of "outside" women's groups. The Citizens' Advisory Council on the Status of Women, which we have cited often in this book, is a permanent standing committee of influential women which replaced the ad hoc President's Commission established in the Kennedy administration. The council issues a yearly report on issues and objectives of concern to women, focusing on such diverse issues as employment, voting patterns, women in the military, credit, homemakers, and the Equal Rights Amendment. They have provided the format and mandate for the establishment of similar commissions in the separate states, now federated under the Interstate Association of Commissions on the Status of Women. Independent of any federal agency, the council's role is to "arouse public awareness and understanding, and to stimulate action with private and public institutions, organizations and individuals working for the improvement of conditions of special concern to women."[18]

The other key government agency, also regularly mentioned in this book, has been the Women's Bureau of the Department of Labor. Started after World War I to "promote the welfare of wage-earning women," the Women's Bureau is a major repository of research and statistics defining the participation of women in the labor force.[19] In addition, it is an advocacy force, promoting protective legislation for working women through publications and public forums and supporting the unionization of women workers. The Women's Bureau has also supported the expansion of publicly funded day care for the children of women workers, continuing-education programs for adult women, and flexible working hours for working homemakers.

A third force, aptly described by Jo Freeman as the "woodwork feminists," has emerged in the federal government to support feminist objectives in legislation and reform.[20] These are the women who for years have been working in government agencies and commissions and on legislative staffs. Usually solo or pioneer women in otherwise all-male offices, they had been largely isolated from one another, but one result of the growing women's lobbies and pressure groups has been the emergence of these women as feminist supporters and their group identification with the common cause of equal rights. This new coalition has been especially effective in the drive for the Equal Rights Amendment and for the education reforms aimed at eliminating sex bias from educational institutions and practices.

National Women's Organizations

None of the feminist forces within the government could have accomplished much without the support of the national feminist organizations. Many of them have been mentioned elsewhere in this book, in connection with specific concerns of single women. These nationwide superorganizations, representing thousands of local chapters, are the channels through which the special-interest groups can bring their own subgoals into the mainstream of the women's movement. Only large-scale, well-staffed, nationally based lobbies have been able to forge the links with key government personnel to bring about legislative change. Together with the women and agencies within the federal structure, they have created an identifiable women's "policy system" for the establishment of women's rights.[21]

The National Organization for Women is the largest and certainly the most visible of all the new women's associations. Founded in 1966 by feminist activists in New York City, the organization has grown to some 600 local chapters that are in every state in the country and, as of 1974, had over 40,000 members. Local chapters vary widely both in composition and focus but NOW leadership has been largely upper-middle-class professional women, many with legal or legislative backgrounds. Its particular strengths have been in the political sophistication of its national leaders and its capability for mobilizing its membership into action; NOW has been responsible for most of the major litigation in equal opportunity court cases, supplying both lawyers and funds through its Legal Defense and Education Fund. At the local level, the most important function of the chapters is coordinative; NOW is a good first place to go for information about other women's groups, programs, and activities. Although NOW probably has the largest budget—in 1974 almost a half million dollars—and most secure funding base of all women's pressure groups, it is nonetheless chronically short of funds; the enormous effort which has gone into the ratification of the Equal Rights Amendment and the support of abortion reform is a continual drain on the treasury. NOW members, unlike its leaders, have been heavily drawn from the ranks of working women; and the recent split in the national leadership stems from NOW's acknowledged difficulties in responding to the problems of the housewives, the single mothers, and those in the lower strata of the workforce.

The Women's Equity Action League (WEAL) split off from NOW over the abortion issue in 1968 to form a "conservative" organization. It has devoted its considerable research and legislative capability to support equal employment rights and opportunities for academic women in colleges and universities.

Federally Employed Women, founded in 1968 to help alleviate the isolation of women managers in government service, has chapters in fifty-six cities. Its concerns have been focused on reform in the Civil Service Commission and the promotion of child care centers for government employees.

The National Women's Political Caucus was started in 1971 at a Washington meeting of prominent feminist leaders to help more women enter public office. Almost every state and major city has a local caucus. The membership is made up in large part of women already active in NOW or WEAL or other politically active feminist groups.[22]

The organizations described above share in many cases an overlapping membership of young, politically adroit, well-trained, middle-class white women. There are conspicuously fewer national groups which represent poor, nonwhite, and working-class women. And there is as yet no nationally powerful group which truly represents housewives, nonworking women, and unaligned women as such. The National Congress of Neighborhood Women is the only nationally based group organized to address the concerns of blue-collar and ethnic women living in working-class communities. The National Black Feminist Organization, founded in New York City in 1973, has 2,000 members in some ten cities, and includes a wide range of minority women from many walks of life. Traditional women's organizations, like the Business and Professional Women's Association, the YWCA, and the League of Women Voters, which have large memberships and a broad base of local chapters, have until very recently stayed clear of controversial feminist politics, but they represent an enormous potential for concerted action on women's issues, particularly since they have a heterogeneous constituency. It is to these organizations that many of the small special-interest groups look for housing, program coordination, and funding support.

How to organize these disparate groups into something that has political clout has been the concern of many feminist leaders. In Rhode Island, the women's groups have joined forces to form a Women's Coalition as a mechanism to establish regular communications on matters of political action.[23] The Rhode Island Coalition has established a legislative clearinghouse in order to mobilize action quickly on key bills and crucial public hearings. The organizational structure is simple, with no officers or bylaws, and the group borrows space from participating groups. The coalition is a useful model for other states considering collective political action. The state commissions on the status of women also suggest themselves as a neutral base for effective coalition since they already function as clearinghouses for information on women's activities.

LAWS WHICH AFFECT SINGLE WOMEN

What does this new political activism mean for the lives and concerns of single women? What benefits, if any, will they enjoy from the new and pending legislation to which the feminists are so committed? Laws alone cannot restructure social attitudes nor can they change deeply entrenched assumptions, particularly when they concern such areas as patterns of family life and the sexual roles of men and women. And as we have noted many times in this study, single women are at the intersection of a number of powerful social trends, characterized by multiple choices and conflicting pressures for social change. Definitive solutions to the many problems of single women will not come about solely as the result of legislative reform or of changes in the legal profession itself, though the presence of more women in that field is almost certain to open the way for more change.

There are, however, some direct benefits for single women in the increased political activity of the women's movement. One is that of public education. The public debate over feminist issues that is taking place in the media, the legislatures, and the courts is at last translating the vital needs and goals of women to the country at large. The issues have been irrevocably transformed from the private domestic area to the public domain of national policy. Secondly, the experience of activism, long barred to most women, is now involving more and more individuals; women are thronging the law schools, running for public office in unprecedented numbers, learning new skills, proving their competence to themselves and to others.

And finally, there are some specific concrete benefits to single women within the new laws. If laws cannot change attitudes, they can at least alter the environments in which certain attitudes flourish. The following review touches on a few major areas of legislation which will have some direct effects on single women.

The Equal Rights Amendment

1. Equality of rights under the law shall not be denied or abridged by the United States or by any State on account of sex.
2. The Congress shall have the power to enforce, by appropriate legislation, the provisions of this article.
3. This amendment shall take effect two years after the date of ratification.
—Article the Twenty-Seventh, U.S. Constitution: proposed by Congress March 22, 1972, ratified by thirty-four states. [24]

The Equal Rights Amendment is not a new issue. First proposed by the National Women's Party in 1923, it has been introduced in one form or another in every subsequent Congress. The main objection to passage in the earlier period was from organized labor and working-class women, who felt that it jeopardized the state protective laws which working women and their unions supported. But since 1971, when equal employment opportunity legislation superseded most states' laws protecting the hours and working conditions of women workers, this opposition has been largely stilled. The AFL-CIO now endorses the ERA, as does a broad spectrum of women's organizations, including most religious associations, the Business and Professional Women, the American Association of University Women, NOW, the League of Women Voters, and the National Women's Political Caucus; over fifty national associations and networks now endorse the ERA.

The opposition is made up largely of some conservative groups; the Daughters of the American Revolution, the John Birch Society, the National Council of Catholic Women, all oppose the ERA, and many groups have been set up solely to defeat the amendment. By far the most active is Stop ERA, headed by Phillis Schlafly, a conservative Republican leader, writer, and law student. Stop ERA opposes the ERA on the grounds that it "will destroy the institution of marriage and family life," and a recent Roper poll shows that 14 percent of adult Americans agree.[25] It's important to note that Mrs. Schlafly, the opposition spokesperson, represents a way of life quite foreign to most single women: she is married, affluent, white, and middle-class; has household help, a successful husband, and an independent income. The institutions she purports to defend have been more hospitable to her than to single women.

The Roper poll found that 61 percent favored the passage of the ERA, including most of the men interviewed. What will be the impact of a constitutional amendment which makes explicit the rights of women? First, it will supersede all states' laws making distinctions between men and women. It will provide a new set of sex-neutral guidelines for almost every area of public life: education, domestic relations, property ownership and management, crime and jury duty, employment, military service, housing, and all public accommodations. In some specific examples, the ERA will influence custody awards to allow fathers to be considered equally with mothers in divorce actions; credit will be awarded on the basis of a universal yardstick; existing laws on equal employment will be reinforced.

The rights of women to be supported by husbands is rapidly becoming a specious issue, since fewer than half the states now require this support. And, as we have seen, maintenance cases have been difficult to enforce in any state. As for the argument of "being treated like a woman" which Stop ERA employs to some effect, one feminist said, "Sure, I'd like to have the car door opened and my cigarette lit for me, but not if it costs me three thousand dollars in salary." Most of all, then, the passage of ERA will provide a new climate for women, in which women will have a better chance for self-sufficiency in a changing society.

The Equal Credit Opportunity Act

Now, when I read those figures about the economy, how much credit there is around, it worries me. I once had a real problem with retail credit. My first job I stayed at for a long time because it was so exciting, but it paid badly. Finally, I decided I had to do something about money so I changed jobs, bought a car, and applied for a gas credit card. They turned me down. And I was very upset. So I called them up and asked why did they turn me down? What they said was that they had found that people who worked for a long time in one job and then changed jobs tended to start a pattern of instability! Well, anyway, I didn't let them get away with it, and I got a charge card.

Now, I'm aggressive, and I have a strong sense of justice. I deserved that credit card and I was about to get it. Once I've made up my mind to go after something, I can always think of some strategy for going after it. My observation is that a lot of women don't act that way, and it also seems to be true of some of my young male colleagues.
—Never-married woman

The Equal Credit Opportunity Act, passed in 1974 by Congress, prohibits credit discrimination on the basis of sex, marital status, race, religion, national origin, or age. Creditors are broadly defined to include all retail stores, banks, credit unions, and credit-card issuers. Specific regulations were to be formulated by the Federal Reserve Board in early Fall of 1975. When the board's first set of regulations was issued for public comment, feminist organizations reacted en masse, accusing the board of a "sell-out to the banking hierarchy," [26] because the provisions covering women's part-time earnings did not allow them to be a factor in assessing an applicant's credit-worthiness, and the provisions banning requests for information on childbearing intentions and requirements for a spouse's signature for business loans were not sufficiently explicit, particularly since credit applicants could not demand a written explanation for refusal. The provision which allows both husband and wife to open joint accounts in both names if they wish, however, has been approved by the board, a critical matter for women since a wife frequently has no previous credit history enabling her to get credit if she becomes widowed or divorced.

Without the rigorous, informed critique of the national women's networks, the whole issue of credit reform would probably have remained in limbo, phrased in ambiguous terms that carried no real force. Now single women can purchase a house or a car on credit or establish charge accounts on the basis of alimony and child support. Many of the states have since passed equal credit laws that go beyond the scope of the federal legislation.

Equal Employment Opportunity Laws

Given the importance of work in the lives of single women, the recent legislation concerning employment of women has an overriding importance.[27] Most of the landmark bills have been passed in one decade, as a result of unremitting pressure by feminists both in and out of government. The Equal Pay Act, passed in 1964 as an amendment to the Fair Labor Standards Act, requires the same pay for men and women in jobs that are "substantially equal" and permits wage differentials only if there is a bona fide seniority or merit system, or a system based on factors other than sex alone. It specifically prohibits discharging or discriminating against persons who file a complaint. The act covers almost the entire workforce with the exception of employees in small retail or service establishments where, unfortunately, many women are employed.

Even more pivotal has been Title VII of the Civil Rights Act of 1964, which prohibits workplace discrimination on the basis of sex. In revised guidelines published in 1972, hiring in most jobs is prohibited if it is based on stereotyped characterizations of the sexes. The last crucial addition to equal opportunity law was the so-called Executive Order 11246 which extended coverage to almost every work situation including the federal government and all federal contractors. Together this body of law constitutes a rampart against unfair practices in hiring, recruitment, in employment agencies and labor unions, and in promotion and career development practices. Federal contractors must show compliance with these laws by developing "affirmative action" plans which spell out specific remedies to existing discriminatory practices. In addition, almost all states have enacted their own legislation, some of which goes even further than the federal law.

In spite of the many safeguards built into the law to encourage individuals to take action, few women have found it feasible to initiate cases. For most women, the costs, emotional strain, and even harassment that are the inevitable accompaniments of discrimination suits are too high a price. In addition, most state enforcement agencies are two to three years behind in their caseloads, of which over a third are estimated to be sex discrimination suits. The "class action" suits, usually initiated by feminist organizations, which seek to address institutional sexist practices, have been far more satisfactory. The American Telephone and Telegraph case in 1973, awarding women employees some $15 million in a one-time back-pay settlement, was perhaps the most stunning victory in a series of class action suits. In this agreement Ma Bell made with the federal enforcement agencies, around 1 percent of the entire nation's workforce was brought under affirmative action. In another landmark settlement Delta Airlines agreed to change employment policies and practices that were found to discriminate against both women and minorities. These cases have set a precedent for a new strategy for approaches to equal employment opportunity, reducing the necessity for case-by-case reform and increasing the chances of success and leading enforcement officials to seek to establish institutional patterns of discrimination in whole industries or an entire labor union structure.[28]

The track record of enforcement has been spotty, in spite of both state and federal legislation. Women's interests are still secondary to those of minorities in the minds of many agencies and individuals charged with compliance, even though women constitute the largest minority in the workforce. According to a report of the General Accounting Office on enforcement of antidiscrimination rules in the federal government, the compliance agencies have been so deficient that it is not even possible to assess what progress has been made and the Joint Economic Committee of the Congress, to whom the report was submitted, stated that "In a program that is ten years old, the deficiencies uncovered by the G.A.O. boggle the mind."[29] For most single women, the problems are multiple; few are in a position to jeopardize existing jobs or have the time, energy, and funds to initiate action against employers. Young unmarried, well-educated career women have been in the vanguard of those filing suits, but many feel it was hardly worth it in terms of the real costs and depletion of emotional energy. As we have seen in the analysis of the present workforce in Chapter Seven, equal employment is on the books, but is not yet a reality in the lives of most women.

Divorce Law Reform

The laws above demonstrably provide real-world economic benefits for single women and have been supported not only by feminists but by a broad stratum of American life, including many men. In the area of divorce law, however, support has been fragmentary, and the women's movement itself is bitterly divided. The movement has been unable to arrive at a consensus in its position on matters pertaining to family life, structure, and roles, and in child care, abortion, and divorce reform; and this conflict has been largely responsible for the steady proliferation of the small special interest groups formed around the pro's and con's of these particular questions. *Women have not yet found a common ground in determining a feminist policy on the family.*

These conflicts are reflected in the whole matter of divorce law reform. Divorce law, traditionally a morass of conflicting state regulations, capricious settlements, and bitter custody battles, has two especially difficult areas—alimony and the question of custody. But the first attempts at divorce law reform did not originate with the women's movement; indeed, that is hardly to be expected, given the male-dominated structure of both the legislatures and the legal profession. The National Conference of Commissioners on Uniform State Laws has written a model bill called the Uniform Marriage and Divorce Act. While the model bill has no official standing, it represents a wide body of respected legal opinion attempting to reconcile the glaring differences in the many state laws, but the American Bar Association has refused to endorse the bill, largely due to its stand on no-fault divorce, one of the centers of the debate on reform.[30]

No-fault divorce essentially means that either partner to a marriage may get a divorce without grounds, merely declaring that the marriage has suffered "irretrievable breakdown." Since 1970, when California adopted the first "no-fault" statute, forty-five states have passed some version. The difficulty comes in the vagueness of most such legislation. Little or no provision has been made which ties in "irretrievable breakdown" to the economic realities of the wife-homemaker and the support of minor children. NOW, once in the forefront of divorce reform, has now refused to take a stand on no-fault laws until economic safeguards for women and children are spelled out.[31] It is ironic that the benign intent of much divorce law reform legislation merely preserves the old inequities in a different form; single women, who might have had some leverage under adversary divorce laws, find they can be cut adrift without guarantees of funds or child support.

Some feminist groups and some women lawyers see a real need for transitional guidelines to be built into divorce law reform. Short-term awards to allow a woman to establish herself in a new life or an allowance for further education or retraining, have been suggested. A thorough overhaul of child support practices and some allowance made for the unpaid contributions of the mother and homemaker are both needed. It is foolhardy to assume that since the goal of feminism is women's economic self-sufficiency, that goal is instantly attainable. It is not, given the segregation and discrimination of the workplace and the lack of work experience and skills of many women who had prepared solely for family life.

Another area of divorce reform that arouses concern is the concept of mandatory counseling for couples contemplating divorce. Those who favor conciliatory efforts maintain that it gives the couple time to cool off and to review the differences dispassionately and to many judges, the idea of conciliation counseling is enormously appealing since it represents an attempt to "save the home." Gettleman and Markowitz feel such sympathy is misplaced and that any official intervention in the process comes too late to be of any real use. They feel it is an invasion of both privacy and free will—that couples should have the right to make divorce decisions in private without the intervention of the state.[32] Most feminists feel that the quality of conciliation procedures is at fault and that male conciliators, particularly if they are lawyers, are biased against women. Practically speaking, in states like New York, which require some kind of predivorce counseling, most people simply do not see the counselors. The size of the potential caseload and the costs of doing a thorough job simply preclude the development of effective programs, although there is nothing inherently wrong in the concept of a divorce forum. Divorce law reform presents a mirror image of the way in which society currently views divorce. During this period of social transition, single women are once again caught in conflicting currents of change.

Other laws and pending legislation are beginning to affect single women's lives particularly in areas of health services reform and the provision of adequate housing for low-income families. Social Security changes are being pushed by older citizens and their advocates. Consumer protection laws and equal educational opportunities have already started to impact on the quality of women's lives.[33] But until women see themselves in some positions of power and authority, they will still be very much on the outside of the law trying to push inside to full participation.

V O I C E S

"We have managed as a completely female family—and managed well."

The speaker is a forty-seven-year-old mother of three teenage girls. She has been divorced for eleven years and works as a middle-level manager in business, supporting herself and her children from her earnings. She has received intermittent amounts of child support through the years, but remains the prime earner and sole custodial parent.

When I first left my husband, it was such an unthinkable thing for me that my marriage would break up. It was such a horrible experience and the circumstances at the time seemed so awful to me that every time I thought about the future, all I could see was a black curtain. And if anyone had told me then that eleven years later I'd be living as I am now, not married and working full time, I really couldn't have imagined it.

Sometimes I come home at the end of the day with a good deal of built-up tensions . . . sometimes I feel very glad and very grateful and very on top of the world. I'm thankful I can make my own decisions, and my children are definitely better off in a stable environment with somebody who loves them and who can give them at least the basics.

I wasn't married until I was twenty-eight. I had a long experience of being single. Oh, I was all set to be the most perfect little wife you ever saw. I feel sorry for my husband in retrospect because I was so determined to be perfect I pretty much neglected his emotional needs. I was going to sit back and be supported and any income I got was just found money. I didn't have to work for money. I kept my hand in because I wanted to—it was necessary to me and it was just sheer luck that I was in a kind of work that could be done part time at home. It was luck, not planning. I was married for seven years. I was part of a couple— even though my marriage wasn't happy, I had a status that made me acceptable wherever we happened to live.

I still suffer from this feeling that I don't fit in anywhere. There isn't any niche for me. The attitude I've met with right along since I've been divorced and alone with the children has been one of extreme caution, if not suspicion. People's first honest innate reaction, not to us personally but to the circumstances, is to draw away. They're afraid we will be a burden, in one way or another—we might make unreasonable demands. I've felt that many couples have sort of regarded me as a possible threat because I didn't have an overt sex partner, somebody they knew was there. They weren't quite sure what I was doing. That made them a little leery or, unfortunately, made for the kind of experimentation where the husbands of close friends drop in to see how I am and to see what they can get away with. So you slap them down kindly, sweetly, firmly, and keep on going. It used to upset me. It doesn't seem so serious anymore, but it does seem to me that the whole situation prevents you . . . there are barriers you have to break down before people can get to know you as a person. They're suspicious, they're cautious, or they're curious. They want to see if you're available for a little fun, and you have to break down all these walls before you can ever get to know people as people.

And the lifestyle I'm leading now drains me. What I do when I come home is too similar to what I do at work. I'm managing—I'm setting up situations in which other people can function. I'm arranging for the girls to go to college or to take skating lessons or to go to music and dancing lessons. They're all talented and their activities are important. It's also important to me that if they have the talent and they are self-disciplined and they want to give the time, the least I can do is provide the set-up, but it's been at the expense of my own interests. I made the deliberate choice and maybe it's masochistic—I don't know—but it seemed to me it would only be for a few years.

On the weekends, we do housework. If I've had a good week and my energy level is high, I whip through it Friday night and Saturday and then I have at least Saturday night and Sunday to feel frisky. If it's a bad week and my energy level is low, it takes me the whole damn weekend to just get through the essentials. This in spite of the fact that the kids do a lot. We've had a pretty rigid division of labor ever since I went to work full time. They all have posted lists of chores, and menus are posted two weeks ahead of time. Every other weekend we try to do a little yardwork, and I enjoy that. It's a big yard with a lot of lawn-mowing and leaf-raking and a garden which we share with other tenants. I take every chance I can get to get out—riding my bike, walking. Actually, one of the problems in my life is that I've always loved to be alone, and I'm better off emotionally if I *can* be alone, but nowadays without enough time and the way things are set up, I practically never am.

Does it come through as drab and grim? There are times when I feel really glad we live this way, considering the alternatives—remarriage to people I knew would not have worked out. And I certainly couldn't have stayed married. I don't *feel* grim, and I don't feel very resentful, but I'm perfectly aware that I'm suppressing a lot of myself. Things are changing already, because the children get older all the time, and the older they get, the freer I get. I think the biggest worry has been that I didn't want them to grow up feeling guilt ridden because mother had been such a martyr.

When they were tiny, I would sometimes long for them to grow up so I could feel irresponsible. And then I have to laugh, because when the oldest one left for college three weeks ago, I missed her so much I nearly went out of my mind—I went moping around the house for a couple of days. We all missed her terribly. Her baby sister went and got the great big high school graduation picture and she was going to tape it to the dining room chair. That was too much. I realized then that I was going to have more ambivalent feelings than I was prepared for, when they are all grown up.

But I'm just thrilled that she has this opportunity. Three years ago—no money—and I didn't even see that the kids would get to college. I really didn't think they would. I went through a year or two not sure that I wasn't going to be on welfare, from day to day. For many years I had shared a home with my sister who was also divorced, and we shared all the expenses, which was a big financial help. And I was then getting child support money from my ex-husband and earning a tiny sum at home. And then she left to remarry, which was just great. At about the same time my ex-husband lost his job, and was never ever able to find another one. I just lost my child support like that . . . I didn't have anything. And I just leaped into the first job I could find, which paid very little, but it did have medical insurance, that kind of thing. Then I gradually worked into something better and then something better. All that time I didn't know what I was doing, I really didn't. I just kept pretending I understood things, and found out how to do things, and kept on doing them. I was terrified, as I told the kids. But, it worked out.

I guess I just came on the single-parent scene earlier than most people. There I was with my little kids, two under the age of three years, and there wasn't a day care center within twenty miles. And I sort of feel that's been the story right along. I have gotten there ahead of the wave of need, and had to do things on my own. I can tell you exactly what will happen in the next five years in the women's movement, because it will be what I need right now that isn't there—and that is some kind of counseling for women already in business—with role models provided.

There's lots of talk now about entry-level positions, but if you're in management, as I am, you have different questions. And women don't yet know the answers. I have been in many situations where I didn't know what to do next, flying absolutely blind. I wish there were some experienced women who might have told me what to do next or what to expect. Right now, for instance, I'm stuck with this strictly executive job at quite a good salary for a woman, but with a very low-level job title. It's terribly unfair. What techniques do we use to improve such a situation? I have from time to time tried to reach out to groups that are now helping women and found that they are dealing with problems I had had to work out by myself years ago.

I like the people I work with very much. Many of them are very congenial. But out of the group of about twenty people I work with, there are only two of us who have children living at home. Most of the people are single, or young couples without families, so my life is very different from theirs. I have some married friends I'm very close to and see quite a bit of, and a couple of single women that I pal around with on weekends, and an occasional date. On the whole, I'd say the friendships I've made on my own have been the most supportive.

I sure don't feel I've met any support from any institution in society. During my married years and at the time I was divorced, I was very religious. It didn't take me long to discover how the Episcopal Church felt about divorced women. I think I hung on for two or three years and then I just couldn't stand it. And then I tried a few standard organizations like Parents Without Partners, and they just didn't fill the bill. It seemed silly to me, a bunch of people in their thirties and forties going to mixers and dances—like being a freshman in high school again. They didn't fill my needs, and I went ahead on my own. I was lucky I had work I could do, and found a few really sweet kindred souls, women and men. . . . Maybe it's different now for younger women, but I felt just absolutely isolated.

My kids have liked it out here. It's prettier and more pleasant than our last home and the schoolwork is a lot more interesting. The youngest one still misses the old community where she had more friends. They've all found it rather hard to make friends here, partly because I think we're quite unsophisticated really. We've never had any money to speak of—quite a low income—we've really been bootstrapping it for years. We didn't have any resources except what I could earn. I don't think the kids miss their father much, but they have from time to time suffered just from the general status. They have felt, as kids will, left out of it—if it was Daddy's night at the Girl Scouts, things like that. Which can be tough.

One reason we moved here was that we had lived in a strongly Catholic community and there weren't many other children of divorced families. I could see that my girls were growing up with the attitude that our family was very unusual and, somehow, they were beginning to pity themselves. The other kids thought our living arrangements were a little bit strange. This wasn't true of people who really got to know us.

But, the children have always felt self-conscious in a new community, and we have moved oftener than many families do. Quite frankly, thinking back over the five apartments we've lived in since I was divorced—a lot of the moving was due to this quest for a quiet neighborhood because we never could pay very much in rent—it was economic. But I don't think that the children have any more than the normal problems, and in some ways fewer: it's too soon to be self-congratulatory about this, and as far as I'm concerned, this is one end product that you never see.

It's a lifetime project, and you don't look for returns. I would love, though, to talk to other women about this business of having teenage girls who are starting to menstruate just about the time when I myself am going into menopause—it's a kind of fraught emotional environment! The only thing I've known how to do is try and be very honest about feelings in the family. Let's put it this way. I don't encourage uncontrolled display of feelings, crying sessions, tantrums, that whole bit. When people step out of line, we all sort of push each other back again. I do want us to be open and speak up. I don't encourage fighting or saying things to hurt people's feelings, but if we don't level with each other, we're not going to find that support outside.

For many years, I wanted to get married again. I'm *not* sorry I'm divorced. But it's very sexually frustrating if you have normal urges. It's hard because, if you're going to have an affair, you either have to be very furtive about it or you risk embarrassing your children. The most serious affair I had, the man used to come to the house. With all the talk about liberation, well, the girls accepted it. They liked the man, they were glad I was happy, but they didn't want their friends to find out about this. Anyway, that's one reason I did want to remarry—I couldn't see any sort of satisfactory sex life outside. But I'll tell you, I would never marry again under the kind of terms of my first marriage, which just embodied the worst of conventional marriage. I'd go way out, if I were to marry now, with things like a five-year renewable contract with divisions of labor spelled out quite specifically. And more than that. I have no reason to marry except for joy. It would have to be strictly for emotional satisfaction—deep joy and companionship and love. It would have to enhance what I already have. My consciousness has risen so gradually over the years. I've never been part of the movement in any organized way, but I think I'm one hundred percent with it right now. It seeped in somehow. I used to be so embarrassed because we were an all-woman family. I used to think we were deprived—I was sorry for myself because I never had a son and my husband didn't love me, and all that. And I used to feel sorry for the girls too. But, you know, my attitude has totally changed and so has theirs, and now I'm really proud that we have managed as a completely female family—and managed well. We have no debts. We have no major problems. I have a daughter going to college. I didn't think any of them would make it. So, I'm thrilled. I'm proud. I guess that's really true.

Chapter 12

STRUGGLES OF THE PAST, WORK OF
THE PRESENT, WISHES FOR THE FUTURE

"In the first decade of the movement, from 1965 to 1975,
women learned they had the power to change their lives. And
in the next decade, we will see women working to change the
institutions in which they work."—Florence Howe

*J*N THE last half of the nineteenth century, groups
of women began to come together in formal associations for a common
purpose. Many factors were at work behind this drive, but nothing gave
it more impetus than the twin issues of Civil War and slavery. Women's
protest has always been peculiarly linked to black civil rights; in 1860
Elizabeth Cady Stanton noted, "The prejudice against color, of which
we hear so much, is no stronger than that against sex. It was produced
by the same cause, and manifested very much in the same way. . . . The
few social privileges which the man gives to the woman, he makes up to
the Negro in civil rights."[1] The nineteenth-century feminists were repeatedly urged to put the suffrage of black men before the rights of
women, both black and white, and out of a naïve sense of philanthropy
the majority did just that. After the Civil War hostilities had simmered
down, white feminists continued to support a number of causes that
came under the heading of "social reform" rather than focusing on the
basic issues of women's rights, their role in marriage and the family,
their status in the larger society. "Volunteer organizations run by and
for women," another writer said, "can be faulted for serving everyone
but themselves in the past."[2]

Some characteristics of the earlier women's groups are strikingly
relevant to the present wave of collective action by women. Formal histories are scarce, but the archives of the major surviving federations and

networks contain some documentation that occasionally reaches a wider public in promotional brochures celebrating an important milestone of a particular group. The YWCA, for example, published a modest volume in 1970 entitled *One Hundred Years of a Great Idea*, which covered the history of the Y and contained some biographies of prominent leaders of that organization; and there are many other such small in-house literary efforts which have had a limited circulation, confined largely to the organization's membership. One or two historians have recorded the events in which the early women's groups played so prominent a role, notably Eleanor Flexner in *A Century of Struggle* and William O'Neill in *Everyone Was Brave*. There are also some important collections of materials: the Schlesinger Library at Radcliffe and the Sophia Smith collection at Smith house a number of valuable if obscure items pertaining to these early examples of women's activism, and the Women's History Research Library in Berkeley has collected many of the raw materials of feminist history, both past and recent, in comprehensive files for scholarly perusal.[3]

THE FIRST WAVE OF FEMINISM

The most thoroughgoing analysis of the nineteenth-century feminist activism can be found in O'Neill's *Everyone Was Brave*. This history of the first wave of feminism in America examines women's organized groups in the nineteenth and early twentieth centuries, analyzing the way in which actions related to the goals of the movement—viewing the strategies in light of the objectives and examining those objectives critically.[4] O'Neill chose five large nationally based feminist groups which represent the range of women's interests and the direction of the feminist thrust. The General Federation of Women's Clubs claimed some 150,000 members by 1900, and by 1920 could truthfully say that over a million women were involved in the club movement. The Association of Collegiate Alumnae, later the American Association of University Women, smaller because it restricted membership not only to the small number of women who were college graduates but solely to those from certain selected institutions, had at the time of the First World War around 6,000 members, over half of whom had never married. The National Federation of Settlements involved thousands of young women over the period between 1890 and 1920 who came and went in the growing numbers of settlement houses, usually until marriage changed their work plans. The National Consumers League, founded by a small cadre of elite, well-educated women, had by the early 1900s ninety local leagues in various cities, twenty state leagues, thirty-five auxiliary leagues, and many branches on college campuses. The National Women's Trade Union League, founded somewhat later, worked directly with the existing unions to help organize the then five million women in the workforce.[5]

In addition, there were powerful groups of women within such disparate organizations as the Young Women's Christian Association, the Women's Christian Temperance Union; the Women's Party, the National American Woman Suffrage Association, which later became the League of Women Voters, the National Council of Women, and . . . the National Association of Women Opposed to Woman Suffrage.

While such enterprises provided educated women with opportunities for "fellowship and constructive enterprise," in O'Neill's phrase, the majority of women in these groups were deflected from the substantive reform of women's status and rights which had been the goal of the earlier feminists. Middle-class women, unlike the few radical feminists who were seeking a "fundamental evaluation of women's roles in American life," seemed to be seeking some justification for their investment in higher education, and were tempted to remain legitimate through some moral notion of social reform, which O'Neill calls "social feminism."[6] Such altruism proved to be extremely difficult to translate into public policy. Nevertheless, the women involved in the clubs and federations were also learning valuable new skills: public speaking, organization and management, some understanding of the ways in which legislation and public policy change were effected.

The movement also brought together for the first time sizeable numbers of educated upper-class women and women from the working classes, although it was the former who had the leisure to do the enormous tasks of organizing. The National Federation of Settlements brought college-educated women into close contact with poor, slum-dwelling women and their families. The National Women's Trade Union League and the Consumers League worked directly with the five million or more employed women for protective legislation and the unionization of women workers. All these organizations together formed a formidable base from which the feminists could launch a national campaign for equal rights.

That they failed to do so is due to a number of reasons. First, their goals were diffuse and hard to reconcile and furthermore ignored the basic feminist imperative to examine marital and parental roles of women critically. Their own altruism and genuine moral concern also proved to be their undoing. As O'Neill remarks, "The striking thing about organized women was the degree to which they upheld the traditional womanly concern for altruism and benevolence, to the point where almost everything they did was justified in these terms. . . . Society discouraged them pursuing their own advantage, and few of them wished to, in any case."[7]

Another commentator on women's organizational activism, Jo Freeman, says that in limiting their goals to the symbolic vote, women lacked imagination. The suffragettes ultimately dismantled the first women's movement by their assertion that "political equality could only help women better perform their domestic functions."[8] They never seriously questioned their own role in that domestic setting; the few radicals who did were driven underground or denounced as eccentric old maids, since so many were single women, (Casting aspersions on the femininity of strong feminist leaders has a long history and exists still today, as can be seen clearly in modern women's groups.)

What does the first wave of feminist activism tell us about the chances for success of later women's organizations? O'Neill says that what history really tells us is that women cannot gain equality regardless of what strategies they devise and what organizations they construct.[9] Given the present structure of society, with its economic and emotional investment in traditional forms of marriage and parenting, he believes the best tactic for women would be to ally themselves with some political ideology such as socialism with overt goals of restructuring basic societal institutions. Since most women do not want to revolutionize domestic life nor do they feel it necessary, and in any case they will not commit themselves to radical action, this lesson of history leaves women at an impasse.

It is important to note that most of the early feminists, like women today, were not radicals. In fact, the reverse was true with the majority of groups described above. Nor did all women's organizations intend to be political, although the very fact of women working collectively carried a political implication. Many women were against universal suffrage, the symbolic goal of the feminists, and organized primarily to prevent the achievement of that goal. The movement was never homogeneous and it *was* frequently fragmented and easily diverted. Its importance, however, lay in the sense that women were slowly beginning to have, largely by reason of their improved education, that they were part of a broader society with concerns that reached beyond the hearth and cradle. Industrial development, the rise of urban centers, and vast new groups of immigrants from other cultures were even then changing the old rules and stable traditions; and the early feminist stirrings were a response to these changes.

There was, however, some real value in the personal achievements of early feminists in their collective action outside the home. Certainly the practical skills and techniques of advocacy represented a real breakthrough in traditional assumptions about women. And although it may have been strategically unwise to have been identified with broad issues of moral and social reform, it was not a total liability. If an influential number of persons in a society come out for an ideology based on humanistic goals and the achievement of personal freedom, the society must somehow be affected. Finally, while one cannot measure the effect on society of changed individual attitudes, there is no doubt such personal changes remain just below the surface, fermenting and transforming, until a later opportunity for realization presents itself.

BREAD AND BUTTER FEMINISM

In the past decade just such an opportunity seems once again to have surfaced. Not since the nineteenth century has this country seen such a burgeoning of voluntary organizations among such vastly different segments of the population. This new "social initiative," in Robert Nisbet's apt phrase, has come from youth and age alike, from all levels of social and economic class and the complete spectrum of political thinking. Forming cooperative self-help groups is not exclusively the style of the new feminism. There are youthful communes developing new models for cooperative shelters, technologically displaced engineers designing programs for mid-life career change, elderly businessmen extending their work lives and usefulness to the community; and all have some characteristics in common with both the problems and objectives that the mutual-aid groups for single women have developed.[10]

The most important factor in the drive of single women toward activism has been its urgency. The single women in this book have turned to collective action, not from ideological conviction or rhetoric, but because suddenly they found there are so many of them with pressing economic, legal, social, and emotional needs which society has been entirely unprepared to meet. In one decade there are suddenly large numbers of young women in the most marriageable ages choosing to "go it alone," at least through their twenties. And the women in the oldest age group, who now outnumber men three to one, have health, housing, and income problems demanding immediate solutions. The rising divorce rate continually enlarges the ranks of the single with large numbers of adult women, women suddenly heads of households, often with young children, needing jobs, child care, low-cost health care, decent housing, legal and financial expertise, home-management skills. In addition to these basic survival issues, all single women, those of all ages and those who have never married, need support, social life, protection from bias and even harassment. Most importantly, single women are seeking some framework in which to validate, legitimize, and comprehend the singleness of their lives—as a social status, as a family style, as a life plan.

Single women are looking for institutional change *at the same time* that they are painfully acquiring a new sense of self, a new identity as an adult. Perhaps one process tends to have a synergistic effect on the other, in a way not experienced by women in more traditional roles. Single women, far more than the ideological feminists, have shown us where women really are in our society.

Not all the women in this book, however, considered themselves feminists, in spite of the pervasive and energizing force of the women's movement which they all recognized. At the risk of oversimplification, one could say that the never-married women were "natural feminists" insofar as they had planned their lives without tying those plans to marriage and personal relationships, while the separated and divorced women seemed to be "instant feminists," suddenly recognizing and accepting their single status—a point that may come when buying a car, moving to a new apartment, confronting the welfare office. The widows seemed the most reluctant to be labeled as supporters of "women's lib," as they called it, particularly the elderly women, although one sixty-seven-year-old woman reported gleefully that she was now a "libber" since she had just passed her driver's test and was licensed to drive for the first time in her life. And another widow, twenty years younger, reported that she would not marry again under the terms that characterized her first marriage although it had been a satisfying one. Widowhood had made her value her independence; she felt it would be foolish to surrender it.

Yet single women are turning to collective action to meet their needs for many of the same reasons that more self-conscious, more political feminists have organized. The once sharp divergence between housewives and most young militants simply no longer exists in many communities. The current debate in NOW illustrates the change. A group of former and present leaders of the organization, including Betty Friedan, have broken off from the elected leadership in order to broaden the priorities of the movement's largest, most comprehensive association. While nominally still part of NOW, the new network calls itself Womensurge, and rejects the revolutionary agenda of the new NOW leadership. One Womensurge member said:

> If you polled the 60,000 members of NOW, you'd find by an overwhelming majority that the priorities are E.R.A. ratification, enforcement of equal rights, and non-sexist education. Marriage and divorce, older women, homemakers are increasingly priorities in many chapters. These are the kinds of things that are grassroots interest, and are being ignored because they are not radical chic. They are hard-core guts issues and don't lend themselves to what has become fashionable.[11]

These bread-and-butter issues were not early priorities of the new feminism. They have been thrust forward in large measure by the gathering numbers and growing political force of single women. Jo Freeman, who has studied women's groups extensively, calls the proliferation of new women's organizations "the primary means by which feminism enters new segments of the population." The "mushroom effect," as many have called it, is the result of the way various groups of women deal with the implications of feminism for their own life situations, and Freeman feels that the constant formation and dissolution of small special-interest groups within the movement have been both its strength and its weakness. [12]

When Every Woman's Equal

Many women we spoke with have been sacrificing scarce resources of time and energy in collective efforts they believe will bring about both personal and institutional change. Such self-sacrifice has been a continuing problem: how much time can a single working mother donate to garnering votes for public day care? How much energy does an elderly woman have to devote to legislative monitoring? Our tentative answer: quite a lot more than we would have predicted. In contrast to the early feminists of both eras who were either affluent and leisured or young and unattached, these activists are frequently neither, yet they have so fixed their priorities that somehow, despite the time-consuming nature of the work, they make the efforts.

One reason the work takes so much time is found in the structure of most women's groups we observed; in a wide variety of organizations, from widows' support programs to feminist credit unions, there is a determination to shun bureaucratic hierarchal processes in favor of participatory democracy, where all participants would share equally in the decisions and the routine support work. This horizontal organization, while not unique to the women's movement, has been a hallmark of women's voluntary associations, and it has been enormously effective in achieving individual change, the task of "consciousness raising," which was a first objective of many groups. Such change takes place over time, and requires a considerable emotional investment, but specific tasks and long-term external goals are harder to develop under diffuse leadership, since so much effort goes into the maintenance of group learning and solidarity. Nonetheless it may be worth the work; if a group has a single specific task which in itself defines the structure, such as a publication, or the delivery of a service, successful operation is more certain. [13] In addition, many of the larger groups and networks leave themselves extremely vulnerable to takeover by radical, disciplined political groups whose goals are objectionable to the original membership[14] while the fear of such takeovers can create distrust and a kind of group paranoia, especially where gay women are involved, as the experiences of NOW have demonstrated repeatedly.

Many feminist organizers and group members have been uneasy about the implications of group governance. Florence Howe and her colleagues are especially concerned with the problems of leadership and power within women's activism. [15] Many women seem to fear power—the assertiveness it requires, the compromise and sacrifice it entails, the abandonment of cherished ideals of humanism and trust. Even more do they sense a threat to their self-concept of feminine values. A sincere dedication to sisterhood often conflicts with practical business decisions, as we saw in the credit unions, who loan more money for car purchases than for abortions.

The leadership problem is compounded by the issue of pay—pay for services, pay for wages. Frequently the larger groups such as multiservice cooperatives, women's centers, or health projects will have a few paid staff workers and a large number of volunteers serving as both workers and advisors. A complex management mix requires a new set of guidelines in order to function but it can be feasible. It involves a number of interrelated processes, as the paid director of a successful service pointed out:

There again, it depends to some extent on how much you trust the other people, and the integrity of the other people involved. There are a lot of decisions which out of necessity I make after consulting one or two others who spend a lot of time here and who know the day-to-day operation, which is meaningless to the board. There are some people on the board who say, "We want to know about every decision," and I say, "It doesn't mean anything to you." And to what extent some of them may feel threatened, I really don't know. I'm as conscientious as I feel I can be about informing them. The thing about trust works both ways. First of all, that they're trusting certain people to make certain kinds of decisions, but in terms of my relinquishing what is essentially my power, it's very difficult for someone who considers herself competent to consider someone else as competent. It's also difficult to fire someone who's not paid, you know.

We have discussed elsewhere the related problems of fees, which many of the service groups are now facing. With support or planning groups, all participants are voluntary members, perhaps paying token dues. But many groups such as the women's counseling services, the health centers, the law collectives, have clients, inevitably other women, who need and receive concrete services for which they would have to pay in other settings. Though these groups see themselves as alternatives to traditional institutions, in actuality such groups may be open to being manipulated by the system into delivering services which are needed but unfunded. In a sense these services are offering gratis what society should be obligated to provide. Certainly, the referrals from welfare departments to credit unions, educational counseling programs, and free health services can create burdens that an underfunded women's group can ill afford to bear. The ultimate result often is that the original change-oriented objectives of the group are submerged in a volunteer-for-service pattern, or in all too many cases the group may disappear entirely.

Many of the women's groups interviewed for this study are now facing crucial financial decisions which are embedded in the premises of feminism. For example, the health collectives have for the most part adamantly refused to charge for health services which they believe should be provided solely on the basis of need and they consequently receive referrals of indigent clients from both public and private agencies. In effect, they are acting as an unfunded arm of the welfare service within a health services system that is essentially based on free enterprise. Some are reluctantly beginning to establish sliding fee schedules, others are cautiously forming liaisons with local governments in order to distribute costs and thereby surrendering some of their autonomy.

Long-term goals inevitably become deflected under the pressures of immediate service needs. To compound the problem, financial support from the private sector, such as businesses or foundations, has never been either reliable or sufficient for most women's groups. It is estimated that no more than 4 percent of private foundation monies went to women's organizations and programs prior to the 1974–1975 recession years, and most of these dollars went to established programs such as the Girl Scouts and the YWCA.[16]

As a result, the service-oriented women's groups have performed more effectively as innovative models and pacesetters than they have as long-term alternative agencies. Perhaps this is the chief function of such groups, and it is an important one. Providing society with a critical view while presenting feasible alternatives is a valuable contribution, both for women needing the service and for those who want to see the system change. The movement has been a mediator in the diffusion of new ideas, raising the community's consciousness to women's social situations.

The diffusion of new ideas has been implemented by the seemingly endless capacity of the women's movement to build networks and extend communications. The *New Women's Survival Catalog* lists 163 feminist publications in its pages, ranging from magazines for single mothers to radical newsletters for the elderly. Together these publications form a unique feminist media, far more than the commercially successful *Ms.* magazine. Comprehensive training and resource manuals such as the *Women in Transition* handbook and *Our Bodies, Ourselves*, a women's self-help health manual, have grown from underground paperbacks to establishment best sellers and the popular press, never insensitive to success, has itself become part of the new network, following the powerful cutting edge of the underground publications. Although some observers, like Jo Freeman, feel that the "endless fission" of the women's movement signifies that it is expanding, not building, more and more women are being reached and encouraged to participate in some kind of mutual self-help group or program. Thus, private disputes and interests become translated into public debate; the subgoals of small groups are clarified and become integrated into the more general goals of society. It is on this process that the critical mass of single women is now making a substantial impact.[17]

Volunteerism or Voluntarism

Is the current activism of women simply a new version of the venerable institution of volunteerism, refurbished with a fashionable rhetoric? Are women being asked once again to extend their motherhood to the community in order that vitally needed human services can be provided through unpaid volunteer labor? Are the voluntary associations of the women's movement merely a thinly disguised manipulation of the male-dominated society intended to keep women distracted and contained while the real business of the country goes on? Such questions are particularly crucial to the self-help efforts of single women, who are both the clients and the caregivers in many new organizations and services.

Traditional service-oriented volunteerism has been seen as detrimental to women's quest for equal rights, a "hybrid of work and role-playing" that reflects many women's profound ambivalence toward their place in the labor market. Doris Gold, the eastern coordinator of the NOW Task Force on Volunteerism, estimates that there are at least 13 million volunteers in America, nine out of ten of them women. The monetary worth of volunteer labor has been estimated at some $14.2 billions of dollars—more than sufficient reason for volunteerism to have been an action priority of the Nixon administration, which with a $7 million media campaign established the National Center for Voluntary Action, giving volunteering an attractive new package. The majority of volunteers serve in social welfare agencies and institutions; it is no accident that most of these serve clienteles of women, children, the elderly, whose needs are persistently given low priority in government budgets.[18]

While the stereotype of the volunteer is the over-forty "empty-nest" housewife with time on her hands, a 1970 survey of volunteers in New York City indicated that in that city this concept is no longer accurate; although 77 percent of the volunteers were women, only 22 percent were married women and 55 percent were single women, a genuine indicator of the trends noted in this study, at least for large, urbanized areas.[19]

No group has been more critical of women and volunteerism than NOW. Through its Task Force on Volunteerism, NOW spokespersons have issued a position paper which declares that volunteerism is incongruent with feminist objectives. First, the "volunteer mystique" serves to reinforce the second-class status of the woman by exploiting her labor in the nonworkforce. NOW further feels that most volunteer jobs are jobs removed from the labor market, jobs which could be filled by poor women who need them. They argue that such nonpaid work depresses the entire level of women's salaries, already unreasonably low. Volunteers are thus both resented and feared by paid staff, who see their own responsibilities delegated to middle-class service workers without credentials or other background. That the majority of volunteer jobs fall into the areas where government has been negligent serves to strengthen the feminist argument.

The NOW position paper makes the crucial distinction between *service-oriented* volunteering and *change-directed* voluntarism. Their statement defines the difference:

We wish to make a rough dichotomy between two kinds of volunteerism, which are separate and distinct. One is *change-directed*. We have no quarrel with this kind of self-expression, which is the cornerstone of a democratic society. Without such volunteer effort, women could not liberate themselves. The other kind is *service-oriented* volunteerism. This seeks to complement insufficiently funded social services with non-paid labor in order to alleviate social ills. In addition it blunts the pressure for a more equal distribution of the nation's wealth, by muting the unrest which threatens the economic privileges and power of the well-to-do.[20]

Consequently, NOW opposes legislation which would support service volunteers, including such proposals as reimbursements for travel and child care, tax relief for volunteers in social service, and other token subsidies. Instead, they seek better real funding in the entire sector of human services, which would strengthen both the job market for women and the need for client support.

Another woman, a volunteer we talked with, had this to say:

What is the sacrifice? We decided it was important to pay at least one person, because, after all, the amount of work that women have done throughout history for no pay is phenomenal. On the other hand, there is a lot of shitwork that has to be done around here. There are a million envelopes and forms that have to be stamped. Someone's argument is, well, shitwork has been done by women all these years. But the fact remains that we're women and what does it mean if the work is "meaningless"? It's meaningless if you're doing it for someone else, but maybe it's not so meaningless if you're doing it for a cause.

Gold and her colleagues look ahead to the new kinds of change-oriented collective actions which have been described in this book. Other, less militant commentators on the volunteer problem are coming to agree with this position. In a new book, *Women, Work, and Vol-*

unteering, Herta Loeser, a coordinator of volunteer services, warns that the feminists may be throwing out the baby with the bathwater since volunteer work can and does contribute to women's personal growth by providing opportunities for the acquisition of new skills and pathways into the paid labor market. Loeser is particularly concerned about the older women, often alone, who have never adopted feminist objectives, yet want and need to be engaged in useful, socially valid activities; for such women volunteer placement is a setting conducive to new learning which the women's movement has been unable to offer. As Loeser says, "Feminist women can use the volunteer structure for their own ends, experimenting with its training and mind-expanding opportunities to nourish a more conscious identity." [21]

Inevitably, it is harder to document and measure the kinds of personal change which have been experienced by single women who are working for collective solutions to their common concerns. Their voluntary associations have been both a forum for the debates and an instrument for social change. The extent to which their action influences public policy can be measured by legislation passed or failed, but personal attitudes are elusive—we have only some sense of a society in transition, some sense of where women alone are located within that continuum of change.

THREE WISHES FOR THE FUTURE

Because more and more women in every age group and social situation will be experiencing longer periods of singleness in their adult lives, whether by choice or by chance, all women must begin to prepare for responsible, autonomous adulthood early in their lives, finding opportunities to weigh the advantages of singleness rather than experiencing it as a disaster. As women explore lifestyles that are no longer solely linked to marital decisions, what they are learning is being transmitted to society, for more women are finding, in the face of severe economic constraints, conflicting and punitive laws, and the lack of clear behavioral guidelines, that singleness has its own rewards. As women seek actively for new, alternative resources to gratify their needs, resources once found only in marriage, they are designing new models for social service and for change, which will in turn influence the larger society.

The responses of the larger society to date have been minimal and lag far behind the urgent need for change. Certainly the early educational experiences of women must soon begin to match the realities of family life in the last quarter of the century. Career and vocational training and guidance for women and the expansion of nontraditional work opportunities, allowing women full adult participation in the work life of the nation, are essential. Adequate, publicly funded, community-controlled child care must support the choice of mothers to be self-sufficient, but it is equally important that we compensate those mothers and homemakers whose unpaid work maintains the working family members and cares for the family's children. The bias of the government for the traditional family must give way to new alternatives and new sanctions for women, children, the elderly, and families.

We have seen how single women are trying to change personal attitudes toward women's status in the society as well as the formal institutions which perpetuate that status. Through the collective action of growing numbers of voluntary associations, single women are in the forefront of those who seek such change. Through their own efforts, single women are raising the consciousness of their communities to new possibilities for living satisfying lives, and to the fragility of traditional marriage.

One question remains. What do single women want for themselves in a time of rapid social transitions and expanding options? When a single woman sees a number of possibilities, which one does she choose? When we asked each woman about the three wishes she'd choose to be granted, a striking number of these diverse individuals wanted those two things which Freud said were essential to a good life: love and satisfying work. Almost half wanted rewarding work to do or to have a good, close relationships with a man, and many wanted both. But only two women, both of them Catholics, wanted to get married or remarried. To see one's children happy, to find personal contentment, and to grow as a person came next. In spite of the precarious nature of many women's finances, only four wanted economic security, and all four were over forty-five.

These responses are not conclusions to the complex concerns which have been explored in this book. But they do give some sense of where single women might be going. We have written about single women because their lives and experiences present certain vital questions for our society most clearly, highlighting the impact of changing social mores and traditions in a way that other women's lives cannot. But the knowledge we have now does not answer all these questions. We do not know, for example, if our present workforce can absorb ever-increasing num-

"If You Had Three Wishes—"

Wish	Number*	Percentage
Find a good man	10	45
Satisfying work/career	10	45
Children happy	5	23
Personal growth	5	23
Find contentment	5	23
Economic security	4	18
Altruistic .	3	13
Wish for autonomy	3	13
Travel	2	9
Own one's home	2	9
Others:		
Better health	1	
Survival	1	
Turn the clock back	1	
Cabin in the mountains	1	

*Of the twenty-seven women interviewed, not all made all three wishes. The elderly widow was not asked this question, one or two others refused to answer, and several more had two wishes only.

bers of women, at least at their present level of skills. We do not know if the nation can afford quality child care for all the children who need it, or whether we should pay women to stay home. And although it has been clearly established that women need better training and more educational opportunities early in life, we do not know how fast educational institutions can respond and move toward career development for women. Or: what kinds of housing and communities must be built in the future to accommodate varied family structures and a multigenerational population?

At the beginning of this book, we spoke of our hope that a study that highlights the present social situation of single women would have an "advocacy effect" of its own, an effect we hope will not only stimulate single women themselves to become more autonomous, to become their own advocates, but will also encourage both the public and the private sectors to build new approaches that will meet single women's needs. Our wish is that women who have been largely isolated from the concerns and problems of other women will begin to develop a sense of bonding. One of the tasks of this study was to identify the common interests and concerns within the divers ranks of single women and those shared needs were indeed present—the economic instability of single women's lives; the sense of social stigma and discrimination; and for many, the problems of single parenting.

But it was important to learn how single women themselves perceived their life experience, and in this area many differences appeared. Elderly widows simply felt differently about themselves than did young divorcees; parents' problems are different from those of nonparents. Yet the work of single women's voluntary associations clearly demonstrates the theme we have repeatedly emphasized: single women can accomplish major changes by perceiving common causes and then acting on those perceptions to establish their own priorities, services, and advocacy. When women divide against each other because of prejudice and misplaced pride, no one's cause will prosper.

But it remains true that many single women have not seen that they can alter their social situation through their own efforts; they choose instead to endure life rather than engage it. In other words, the common issues in single women's lives that we have found are more or less imperfectly perceived by single women themselves. This, however, is not necessarily a disappointing outcome. The future for women must accommodate the pluralism of our society, the life stages that all adults go through, and must be flexible enough to offer survival and a decent life to women of all ages and persuasions.

RESOURCES

NOTES

INTRODUCTION

1. Such a woman, the sole wage earner and decision-maker of the family with a legal husband present, is *not* the head of household in the United States Census Bureau. There is also a further distinction between female heads of households and female heads of families. For example, a widow living alone, or with a sister or other adult, may be a head of household, but if she has children under eighteen, she is also a head of family. Conversely, a divorced woman with children who lives with her parents is neither, for her father is head of both the family and the household. Women's Bureau, U.S. Department of Labor, "Facts About Women Heads of Households and Heads of Families" (Washington, D.C.: Government Printing Office, April 1973).

2. Abbott L. Ferriss, *Indicators of Trends in the Status of American Women* (New York: Russell Sage Foundation, 1971); for a discussion of unreported desertion *see* Leslie A. Westoff, "Two-Time Winners," *New York Times Magazine*, August 10, 1975, pp. 10ff; for a general discussion of incomplete divorce statistics *see* Joseph Epstein, *Divorced in America: Marriage in an Age of Possibility* (New York: Dutton, 1974); for a complete analysis of the 1970 Census figures on marriage and divorce *see* Hugh Carter and Paul C. Glick, *Marriage and Divorce: A Social and Economic Study* (Cambridge: Harvard University Press, 1973).

3. Isabel Sawhill, "Discrimination and Poverty Among Women Who Head Families," paper presented at Conference on Occupational Segregation, Wellesley College, May 1975; figures comparing female-headed families by race and with two-parent families come from U.S. Department of Labor, Women's Bureau, "Facts About Women"; the Census Bureau statistic on decreasing size of families was announced in *New York Times*, July 13, 1975.

4. Ruth A. Brandwein, "The One-Parent Family as a Viable Life Style," paper presented at the conference of The National Council of Family Relations, American Academy of Marriage Counselors, October 1974.

5. Brandwein, "The Single-Parent Family: Linking Research to Action," working paper, Women's Research Center of Boston, 1974.

6. Eli Ginzberg, *Educated American Women: Self-Portraits* (New York: Columbia University Press, 1966).

CHAPTER 1

1. Ellen Goodman, "The 'Single' Newly Defined," *Boston Globe*, August 22, 1975.

2. Ferriss, *Indicators of Trends*; Women's Bureau, "Facts About Women." Ferriss notes inaccurate reporting and decreased marital decisions among young women.

3. Jessie Bernard, "The Paradox of the Happy Marriage," *Woman in Sexist Society*, ed. Vivian Gornick and Barbara K. Moran (New York: Basic Books, 1971); references to studies cited are found on pp. 85-98.

4. Douglas T. Hall, "A Model of Coping with Role Conflict: The Role Behaviour of College-Educated Women," Yale University, Department of Administrative Sciences, Report No. 35 (undated).

5. Ruth Chaskell, "Changing Patterns of Services for Unmarried Parents," *Social Casework*, 49, *1* (1974), pp. 3-10.

6. Mignon Sauber and Janice Pareth, "Unwed Mothers Who Keep Their Children," *Social Work Practice*, selected papers of National Conference on Social Welfare (1965), pp. 94-106.

7. Birgitta Linner, *Sex and Society in Sweden* (New York: Random House, 1967).

8. Chaskell, "Changing Patterns."

9. Lanie Jones, "New Pride in Being a Single Mother," *Los Angeles Times*, March 23, 1972.

10. *SPACE, Newsletter for Single Adoptive Parents*, 1, *1* (July 1975), lists self-help organizations; estimated number of single adoptive parents is found in an undated news release of the Child Welfare League of America.

11. Undated brochure of the National Council for the Single Woman and Her Dependents.

12. Margaret Adams, *Single Blessedness: Observations on the Single Status in Married Society* (New York: Basic Books, 1976); Mirra Komarovsky, *Blue Collar Marriage* (New York: Vintage Books, 1967).

CHAPTER 2

1. Westoff, "Two-Time Winners," provides the estimate of the percentage who remarry and divorce; information about those who don't remarry is in Ruth A. Brandwein with Carol A. Brown and Elizabeth M. Fox, "Women and Children Last: The Social Situation of Divorced Mothers and Their Families," *Journal of Marriage and the Family*, 36 (August 3, 1974), pp. 498-514.

2. Jessie Bernard, "No News but New Ideas," *Divorce and After*, ed. Paul Bohannan (Garden City: Anchor Books, 1971), pp. 3-29.

3. Ibid., pp. 26-7.

4. William O'Neill, *Divorce in the Progressive Era* (New Haven: Yale University Press, 1967), in the preface.

5. Margaret Mead, "Anomalies in American Post-Divorce Relationships," *Divorce and After*, Bohannan, pp. 123-4.

6. Michael Wheeler, *No-Fault Divorce* (Boston: Beacon Press, 1974), pp. 172-3.

7. William Goode, *Women in Divorce*, 2nd ed. (New York: Free Press, Macmillan, 1969).

8. Anne C. Schwartz, "Reflections on Divorce and Remarriage," *Social Casework*, 49, 4(1968), p. 213.

9. Brandwein, "The Single-Parent Family: Linking Research."

10. Susan Gettleman and Janet Markowitz, *The Courage to Divorce* (New York: Simon & Schuster, 1974).

11. Sonya Rudikoff, "Marriage and Household," *Commentary*, 55 (June 1973), pp. 56-64.

12. Gettleman and Markowitz, *Courage to Divorce*, p. 57.

13. For a comprehensive survey of research in this area, see Elizabeth Herzog and Cecelia Sudia, "Fatherless Homes: A Review of Research," *Children*, 15 (September-October 1968), pp. 177-82.

14. Private communication from Dorothy Burlage of the Laboratory of Community Psychiatry, Harvard Medical School, June 4, 1975.

15. E. E. LeMasters, *Blue Collar Aristocrats* (Madison: University of Wisconsin Press, 1975).

16. Carol A. Brown, Women's Research Center of Boston, "The Effects of Resources on Lifestyles: Case Histories"; Gettleman and Markowitz, *Courage to Divorce*, pp. 56-7, cite instances when children are told the ex-spouse is dead.

17. This material comes from a proposal to private foundations drawn up by Justice for Divorced Mothers, Inc., Boston/Cambridge, 1971.

18. This material comes from public releases and private correspondence with the Women in Transition project and an interview with staff members; see also *Women in Transition: A Feminist Handbook on Separation and Divorce* (New York: Scribner's, 1975).

CHAPTER 3

1. U.S. Department of Commerce, Bureau of the Census, *Preliminary Figures, United States Census, 1970* is the source of the comparison with divorced persons; Helena Lopata, *Widowhood in an America City* (Cambridge: Schenkman Publishing, 1973), pp. 17 and 21, provides the figures for the average age and life expectancy of widows; Phyllis Silverman, "The Widow's View of Her Dependent Children," paper presented at the Symposium on Dying and Bereavement, Berkeley, California, March 1973, provides the estimate of the number of children under sixteen whose parents die.

2. Conference for the Widowed, sponsored by the Massachusetts Psychological Center and the Massachusetts Funeral Directors Association at Simmons College, Boston, April-May 1975.

3. Lynn Caine, *Widow* (New York: Morrow, 1974).

4. Silverman, "Widowhood and Preventive Intervention," *The Family Coordinator*, January 1972, pp. 97-8.

5. Lopata, "Keynote Speech, Conference on Older Women Alone," sponsored by the Institute for the Study of Women in Transition, Bretton Woods, New Hampshire, September 1975.

6. Silverman, "Mutual Help and the Elderly Widow," paper presented at the Boston Society for Gerontological Psychiatry, May 1974.

7. Lopata, *Widowhood*, p. 263.

8. Ibid., p. 90.

9. Lopata, "Speech, Older Women Alone Conference."

10. Ibid.; Silverman, "Services for the Widowed During the Period of Bereavement," working paper.

11. Silverman, "Widowhood and Preventive Intervention," pp. 97-8.

12. This material comes from published and unpublished papers of Dr. Phyllis Silverman and interviews with her and participation in a five-week program on widowhood that she coordinated; her comments on the professionals who do not help are found in "Forum: Mental Health," *Boston Sunday Globe*, September 28, 1975; the best resource on mutual self-help groups for the widowed is Silverman, *Helping Each Other in Widowhood* (New York: Health Sciences Publishing Corp., 1974).

13. Silverman, ed., *Helping Each Other*, p. 84.

14. Roberta Kevelson, *Annual Reports: The Women's Center* (Fall River, Massachusetts: Bristol Community College, July 1975).

15. Lopata, *Widowhood*, in "Conclusions."

CHAPTER 4

1. U.S. Department of Labor, Women's Bureau, "Fact Sheets," using "Census of the Population, 1970: General Social and Economic Characteristics" of the Bureau of the Census and "Women Workers in Regional Areas and in Large States and Metropolitan Areas, 1971"; Lopata, *Widowhood*, pp. 24-5, 28-9.

2. Alfred C. Kinsey and Wardell B. Pomeroy, Clyde Martin, and Paul Gebhard, *Sexual Behavior in the Human Female* (Philadelphia: W.B. Saunders Co., 1953); Sidney Abbott and Barbara Love, "Is Women's Lib a Lesbian Plot?" in *Sexist Society*, Gornick and Moran, p. 438.

3. Abbott and Love, ibid., 446-7.

4. American Psychiatric Association, "Resolutions on Homosexuality," December 15, 1973; Task Force on Gay Liberation, "SRRT/ALA," Philadelphia, n.d.

5. *Time*, September 8, 1975, pp. 32-43.

6. Ibid.

7. Unitarian-Universalist Association, Department of Education and Social Concern; *Time*, September 8, 1975, pp. 32-43.

8. Homophile Community Health Service, "Statement of Purpose," Boston, n.d.

9. Excerpted from *Off Our Backs*, March 1975.

10. Jill Johnston, *Lesbian Nation: The Feminist Solution* (New York: Simon & Schuster, 1973); "Report of the Woman Alone Conference," in Kevelson, *Annual Reports: Women's Center.*

11. Robert Fulton says the widowed are the fastest-growing segment of the population in Silverman, *Helping Each Other*, pp. 147-57; for organizing among the elderly, *see* "The Organized Elderly," *New York Times*, June 22, 1975, p. 1.

12. Lopata, *Widowhood*, pp. 262-3.

13. U.S. Department of Health, Education, and Welfare, Office of Human Development, Administration on Aging, "Older Americans Are a National Resource," March 1974.

14. "Organized Elderly," *New York Times.*

15. Conference on Women in the Suburbs, workshop on "The Elderly Suburbanite," Wellesley College, May 31, 1975.

16. This material comes from publications of and commentary by the Gray Panthers.

17. The Task Force on Older Women, National Organization of Women, Tish Sommers, coordinator.

18. Jewish Vocational Service/Jewish Occupational Council, "The Older Worker," 1974.

19. Personal interview, Project Retain, Brookline, Massachusetts, June 6, 1975.

20. ELDERHOSTEL, University of New Hampshire.

21. Rosie's Place is in Boston. See "Useful Addresses."

22. Lopata, *Widowhood*, p. 263.

23. Shirley Hill Witt, "Native Women Today: Sexism and the Indian Woman," *Civil Rights Digest, A Quarterly of the U.S. Commission on Civil Rights*, Spring 1974, p. 35.

24. *New York Times*, June 29, 1975, editorial page.

25. Lourdes Miranda King, "Puertorriqueñas in the United States," *Civil Rights Digest*, Spring 1974, p. 27.

26. Roper Organization, Inc., "The Virginia Slims American Women's Opinion Poll," vol. III, 1974.

27. *Civil Rights Digest*, Spring 1974.

28. Carol B. Stack, *All Our Kin: Survival Strategies in a Black Community* (New York: Harper and Row, 1974).

29. Consuelo Nieto, "Chicanas and the Women's Rights Movement," *Civil Rights Digest*, Spring 1974, p. 38.

30. Suzanne Lipsky et al., *Pre-Conference Report on Higher Education for Urban Women* (Boston Study Group on Continuing Education for Urban Women and John Hay Whitney Foundation, February 1973), p. 15.

31. King, "Puertorriqueñas, p. 27.

32. Catherine Stimpson, "Thy Neighbor's Wife, Thy Neighbor's Servants: Women's Liberation and Black Civil Rights," *Sexist Society*, Gornick and Moran, pp. 452 ff.

33. Geraldine Rickman, "A Natural Alliance: The New Role for Black Women," *Civil Rights Digest*, Spring 1974, pp. 57 ff.

34. Lucy Komisar, "Where Feminism Will Lead," *Civil Rights Digest*, Spring 1974, p. 9.

CHAPTER 5

1. Gettleman and Markowitz, *Courage to Divorce,* chapter 1, deal with the "relentless pressure" for marriage and the nuclear family, surveying the media, the churches, family life, professionals, and consumer patterns in America; Chaskell, "Changing Patterns," details the situation of unwed mothers; Carol A. Brown, "The Effects of Resources on Life Styles: Case Histories, A Working Paper" (Cambridge: Women's Research Center of Boston, 1974), details bias against divorced women.

2. Silverman, "The Role of Mutual Help Groups in the Prevention of Emotional Difficulties" (Leonia, New Jersey: Behavioral Science Tape Library: Sigma Information, Inc., 1974), discusses lower status; Caine, *Widow*, p. 90, recounts being set aside because others feared her grief.

3. Adams, "The Single Woman in Today's Society: A Reappraisal," *American Journal of Orthopsychiatry*, 4, 5 (1971), p. 482.

4. Herzog and Sudia, "Fatherless Homes," *Children*, discuss bias of researchers; Andrew Billingsley, *Black Families in White America* (Englewood Cliffs, New Jersey: Prentice-Hall, 1968); Brandwein et al., "Women and Children Last," pp. 498-514; Brandwein, "The One-Parent Family."

5. Goode, *Women in Divorce*, pp. 243 ff.

6. Arthur Miller, "Reaction of Friends to Divorce," *Divorce and After*, Bohannan, pp. 63-86.

7. Caine, *Widow*, p. 90.

8. Lopata, *Widowhood*, pp. 176 ff.

9. This material is based on interviews with leaders and members of the organization and a site visit to its Newton (Massachusetts) office.

10. Massachusetts Department of Commerce and Development, "City and Town Monograph for the City of Newton," rev. in 1973.

11. Dorothy Uhlig, "Together and Alone in Suburbia," unpublished paper, Harvard Divinity School, 1972.

12. This material is based on interviews with participants and site visits to the Project and its Single Mothers Group, in Somerville, Massachusetts.

13. Massachusetts Department of Commerce and Development, "City and Town Monograph for the City of Somerville," rev. in 1973.

CHAPTER 6

1. Brandwein, "The One-Parent Family," p. 13.

2. Carol Jenks, "Guidelines for Self-Help Groups," (Boston: Paulist Center DCG Program, n.d.).

3. Irving R. Stuart and Lawrence E. Apt, *Children of Separation and Divorce* (New York: Grossman, 1972).

4. Gettleman and Markowitz, *Courage to Divorce*, pp. 127 ff., discuss expectations for remarriage; Brown, "Effects of Resources," discusses the negative images; Goode, *Women in Divorce*, chapters 17-18.

5. Lopata, *Widowhood*, pp. 177 ff.

6. The Bibliography lists "survival manuals" that seem less offensive, patronizing, and opportunistic than most; some are useful in certain self-help areas.

7. *SAGE Guide: A Bimonthly Guide for the Unattached. See* Useful Addresses.

8. Parents Without Partners, Boston Chapter No. 3, *Newsletter*, May 1975; *The Single Parent: Journal of Parents Without Partners*, 18, 5 (June 1975).

9. Kinsey, *Sexual Behavior in the Human Female*; Paul Gebhard, "Post-Marital Coitus Among Widows and Divorcees," *Divorce and After*, Bohannan, pp. 89-106.

10. Kinsey quoted in LeMasters, *Blue Collar Aristocrats*, in Introduction; Lopata, *Widowhood*, pp. 60-61.

CHAPTER 7

1. Ferriss, *Indicators*.

2. Ibid.

3. Jo Freeman, *The Politics of Women's Liberation* (New York: McKay, 1975), pp. 29, 33-4.

4. Interview, Project Retain, June 6, 1975; Milwaukee County Welfare Rights Organization, *Welfare Mothers Speak Out: We Ain't Gonna Shuffle Anymore* (New York: Norton, 1972), p. 22.

5. Marian P. Winston and Trude Forsher, "Non-Support of Legitimate Children by Affluent Fathers" (Los Angeles: Rand Corporation, 1971), p. 5.

6. Louis Kriesberg, *Mothers in Poverty: A Study of Fatherless Families* (Chicago: Aldine Publishing Co., 1970).

7. Winston and Forsher, "Non-Support," p. 83; Milwaukee County WRO, *Welfare Mothers*, p. 83.

8. Milwaukee County WRO, *Welfare Mothers*, p. 81.

9. Ibid., pp. 73-6; studies of cost evaluation are found in U.S. Department of Labor, Manpower Administration, *Manpower Research and Development Projects*, 1973 ed.

10. Blanche Bernstein with William Meezan, *The Impact of Welfare on Social Stability* (New York: New School for Social Research, Center for New York City Affairs, June 1975), p. 100.

11. Ibid., p. 2.

12. *New York Times*, June 15, 1975.

13. David Kevin, "Group Counseling of Mothers in an AFDC Program," *Children*, 14 (March-April 1967), pp. 69-74.

14. University of Southern California, Regional Research Institute, undated poll; "Resources Issue," *MOMMA* magazine, 1974, p. 48.

15. Gettleman and Markowitz, *Courage to Divorce*, p. 223.

16. Wheeler, *No-Fault Divorce*, p. 54.

17. Gettleman and Markowitz, *Courage to Divorce*, pp. 224-5.

18. Wheeler, *No-Fault Divorce*, p. 66.

19. Bohannan, *Divorce and After*, pp. 48-52.

20. Brandwein, "Women and Children Last: The Social Situation of Divorced Mothers and Their Families," *Journal of Marriage and the Family*, 36, *3*, p. 501.

21. U.S. Citizens' Advisory Council on the Status of Women, *Women in 1973: Report to the President*, May 1974, pp. 66-77.

22. Roslyn Feldberg and Janet Kohen, "Divorce: Is It Inevitable?," unpublished paper of the Women's Research Center of Boston, 1974.

23. Winston and Forsher, "Non-Support," p. 3.

24. *New York Times*, March 21, 1975, and August 9, 1975.

25. Wheeler, *No-Fault Divorce*, p. 67; *see* this book and Gettleman and Markowitz, *Courage to Divorce*, for a fuller analysis of the DuBroff proposal.

26. Wheeler, *No-Fault Divorce*, p. 53.

27. Council on the Status of Women, *Women in 1973*.

28. *New York Times*, April 19, 1975.

29. Ralph Nader and Kate Blackwell, *You and Your Pension* (New York: Grossman, 1973).

30. *New York Times*, October 24, 1975.

31. Bernard, *The Future of Motherhood* (New York: Dial Press, 1974), p. 280.

32. U.S. Department of Labor, Women's Bureau, "Highlights of Women's Employment and Education," May 1975.

33. Ibid.

34. Roslyn Willett, "Working in a Man's World," *Sexist Society*, Gornick and Moran, p. 369.

35. U.S. Department of Labor, Women's Bureau, "Steps to Opening the Skilled Trades to Women," June 1974.

36. Ibid., pp. 6-7.

37. Willett, "Working in a Man's World," p. 369, and Adams, "The Compassion Trap," both in *Sexist Society*, Gornick and Moran.

38. Vicki Breitbart, *The Day Care Book: The Why, What, and How of Community Day Care* (New York: Alfred A. Knopf, 1974), chapter 3; U.S. Department of Labor, Women's Bureau, "Day Care Facts," pamphlet 16, rev. 1973.

39. Ibid.; Bernard, *Future of Motherhood*.

40. The Massachusetts Early Education Project, "The Costs of Day Care: Money and Other Resources" (Washington, D.C.: Day Care and Child Development Council of America, 1972), p. 42

41. Ibid., pp. 2-3.

42. Bank Street College of Education, Network Coordinator, Child Care Resource Center and the Day Care Consultation Service, "Child Care Support Network: A Proposal," n.d.

43. *New York Times*, September 19, 1975.

44. This material comes from an interview and site visit to the Massachusetts Feminist Credit Union.

CHAPTER 8

1. The above discussion has been deeply influenced by the writing and teaching of Ira Goldenberg, president of Franconia College; for a statement of his thinking about the relation between social change and social service institutions *see* his *Build Me a Mountain* (Cambridge: M.I.T. Press, 1971), especially chapters 3 and 11; Ginzberg, *Educated American Women*, discusses the cost of social change in his conclusions; for a discussion of overworked caseworkers *see* Adams, "Compassion Trap," *Sexist Society*, ed. Gornick and Moran.

2. Goldenberg, *Build Me a Mountain*, pp. 472-84.

3. The significance of the medical model is discussed in Erving Goffman, "The Moral Career of a Mental Patient," *Asylums* (New York: Doubleday, 1961), and in Thomas T. Szasz, *The Myth of Mental Illness* (New York: Harper and Row, 1961); discussions of the political investment of the helping professions are found in R. D. Laing, *The Politics of the Family and Other Essays* (New York: Vintage, 1969), and Seymour Halleck, *The Politics of Therapy* (New York: Harper and Row, 1971). Studies showing mental health seen as an adjustment to existing community norms are reviewed in Gettleman and Markowitz, *Courage to Divorce*, chapter 4 (the bias for "normal family patterns" is noted on p. 70); Kenneth Keniston is quoted from a guest editorial in *Woman's Day*, August 1975.

4. Women's Research Center of Boston, "Who Rules Massachusetts Women?" (Cambridge, August 1972).

5. Phyllis Chesler, "Patient and Patriarch," *Sexist Society*, ed. Gornick and Moran, discusses bias in therapeutic services; Nancy Schlossberg and John J. Pietrofesa, "Perspectives on Counseling Bias," *Counseling Psychologist*, 4, *1*, pp. 44 ff., discuss bias in vocational and educational guidance.

6. Szasz, *The Community Mental Health Movement: The Modern Inquisition* (New York: Harper and Row, 1967), discusses the medical model in community mental health agencies; Adams, "Compassion Trap," *Sexist Society*, ed. Gornick and Moran, discusses the sex and class of its professionals.

7. Phyllis Silverman and Hope G. Murrow, "The Care-Giver During Critical Role Transition in the Normal Life Cycle," paper presented at National Institute of Mental Health Continuing Education Seminar on Emergency Mental Health Services, June 1973.

8. This material comes from a site visit to the Elizabeth Stone House in Jamaica Plain, Massachusetts, an interview with its coordinator, Mary Raffini, and several published papers of the program.

9. Karen Lindsay, "Creating a Communal and Feminist Therapy," *Boston Phoenix*, March 4, 1975.

10. Suzanne Lipsky with Lucia Bequaert, Rosamund Rosenmeier, and the Boston Study Group on Continuing Education for Women, *Pre-Conference Report: On Higher Education for Urban Women* (John Hay Whitney Foundation, February 1973); Alice Chrichlow and Alice Evans, "Counseling and Other Supportive Services for the Urban Woman," the *Pre-Conference Report: On Higher Education for Urban Women*.

11. The following material is based on the author's work as a board member of the Women's Inner-City Educational Resource Service in Roxbury, Massachusetts, and on its annual reports to the Fund for the Improvement of Post-Secondary Education, Department of Health, Education, and Welfare (1973-1975), and on a taped group interview with the counseling staff, May 1975.

12. O'Neill, *Divorce in Progressive Era*, Preface.

13. Rita Whiteley, "Women in Groups," *Counseling Psychologist*, 4, *1*, p. 27.

CHAPTER 9

1. Quoted in the *Newsletter* of the Association of Feminist Consultants, September 1975, p. 2.

2. U.S. Department of Labor, Women's Bureau, "Women Workers Today," rev. 1974.

3. Bernard, *Future of Motherhood*, pp. 253 ff.

4. "News of the Week in Review," *New York Times*, August 23, 1975.

5. Women's Bureau, "Women Workers Today."

6. Esther Matthews, ed., *Counseling Girls and Women Over the Life Span* (Washington, D.C.: National Vocational Guidance Association, APGA, 1972), p. 10.

7. Esther Westervelt, "A Tide in the Affairs of Women," *Counseling Psychologist*, 4, *1*, p. 3.

8. Erik Erikson, *Childhood and Society*, rev. 2nd ed. (New York: Norton, 1963).

9. Gail Sheehy, "Catch-30 and Other Predictable Crises of Growing Up Adult," *New York Magazine*, February 18, 1974.

10. Roger Gould, "The Phases of Adult Life: A Study in Developmental Psychology," *American Journal of Psychiatry*, 129, *5* (November 1972); Daniel J. Levinson et al., "The Psychological Development of Men in Early Adulthood and the Mid-Life Transition," paper to appear in *Life History Research in Psychopathology*, vol. 3, ed. D. F. Ricks, A. Thomas, and M. Roff (Minneapolis: University of Minnesota Press, 1974-).

11. Matthews, *Counseling Over Life Span*, p. 28.

12. Levinson, "Psychological Development of Men," p. 19.

13. The following material comes from the author's experience as a career counselor with New Environments for Women, Associates, in Arlington, Massachusetts; the records from which the data are compiled have been changed slightly to preserve anonymity in research use.

14. Matthews, *Counseling Over Life Span*, p. 23.

15. See "Less Time, More Options," *The Carnegie Commission on Higher Education Report* (New York: McGraw-Hill, 1971); Elizabeth Koontz, "Counseling Women for Responsibilities," *Journal of the National Association of Women Deans and Counselors*, 34 (1970), p. 13.

16. The most comprehensive program has been sponsored by the Department of Labor and the State of Wisconsin through the University of Wisconsin.

17. Westervelt, ed., *Releasing Women's Potential: The Two-Year College as a Catalyst* (Albany: State University of New York, 1969).

18. Ibid.

19. The author is an advisor to the Women's Opportunity Research Center, Middlesex Community College, Bedford, Massachusetts.

20. Kevelson, *Annual Reports: Women's Center*.

21. Sara Davidson, "The Myth of Happily Ever After," *Woman's Day*, May 1974, p. 28.

CHAPTER 10

1. O'Neill, *Divorce in Progressive Era*, pp. 35-8.
2. Gettleman and Markowitz, *Courage to Divorce*, p. 67.
3. O'Neill, *Divorce in Progressive Era*, pp. 35-8.
4. Lopata, *Widowhood*, p. 250.
5. Gettleman and Markowitz, *Courage to Divorce*, p. 72, point out the description of divorce as an affliction; Lopata, "Speech, Older Women Alone Conference," and Silverman, *Helping Each Other in Widowhood*, p. 5, note that Jewish widows felt their clergy inadequate.
6. Silverman, "Role of Mutual Help Groups."
7. Georgia Dullea, "Married Couples Take a New Look at Life Together," *New York Times*, June 24, 1975.
8. Mary Lou Thompson, ed., *Voices of the New Feminism* (Boston: Beacon Press, 1970), pp. 136-7.
9. Mary Daly, "Toward Partnership in the Church," *Voices of the New Feminism*, Thompson, ed., p. 140.
10. Ibid., p. 150.
11. Ibid., p. 147; Freeman, *Politics*, p. 163.
12. Interview with the Rev. Polly Laughland, June 1975.
13. Michael Novak, "Black and White in Catholic Eyes," *New York Times Magazine*, November 16, 1975, p. 33, discusses the impact of Catholics on the Northeast; Father James Young, quoted in *New York Times*, November 18, 1975, estimated the divorce rate; Charles M. Whelan, S.J., "Divorced Catholics: A Proposal," *America*, December 7, 1974, p. 363, discusses remarriage.
14. *New York Times*, March 13, 1975, reports the movement for reconciliation; editorial, *America*, December 7, 1974, p. 362.
15. *Divorce: A Publication of the Divorced Catholics Group, The Paulist Center Community, Boston*, 2, *1*, pp. 1-2, is the source of current information about the groups; James J. Rue and Louise Shanahan, *The Divorced Catholic* (Paramus, New Jersey: Paulist-Newman Press, 1972), discuss the historical background.
16. *New York Times*, November 18, 1975; Father Young is quoted in Michael Ryan, "Uncoupling Catholics," *Boston Magazine*, April 1975, p. 49.
17. *Divorce: Publication of Divorced Catholics*.
18. Address at the Third Annual Divorced Catholics National Conference, October 26, 1974.

CHAPTER 11

1. Women's Research Center of Boston, "Who Rules Massachusetts Women?," p. 29.
2. Doris L. Sassower, "The Chief Justice Wore a Red Dress," *Woman in the Year 2000*, ed. Maggie Tripp (New York: Arbor House, 1974), pp. 147, 149.
3. Ibid., p. 148; Women's Research Center, "Who Rules," p. 29.
4. Women's Research Center, "Who Rules," p. 33.
5. Sassower, "Chief Justice," *Woman in 2000*, ed. Tripp, p. 149.
6. Sassower, "Chief Justice," *Woman in 2000*, ed. Tripp, pp. 149-50; Dr. Pauli Murray, a black woman professor of constitutional law at Brandeis University, told a graduate student audience at the Harvard Graduate School of Education in November 1971 that she had submitted her *vitae* to Mrs. Nixon and had received a form acknowledgment.
7. Bohannan, *Divorce and After*, p. 44.
8. Gettleman and Markowitz, *Courage to Divorce*, pp. 200-1.

9. *Women in Transition* handbook, p. 137.

10. Bohannan, *Divorce and After*, p. 47.

11. Interview with Vivian Buckles, director, Women's Bureau, Region I office, April 22, 1975; Lopata, *Widowhood*, p. 276.

12. *Women in Transition* handbook; Roberta Greene, "Till Divorce Do Us Part" (Pittsburgh: KNOW, n.d.); Barbara B. Hirsch, *Divorce: What a Woman Needs to Know* (Chicago: Regnery, 1973); *Women's Yellow Pages*, editions in New York City and Boston.

13. Isabella Jancourtz, *The Massachusetts Woman's Divorce Handbook* (Boston: New England Free Press, 1974).

14. Aileen Belford, "Address," to the Woman Alone Conference, Easton, Massachusetts, February 1975; Caine, *Widow*, p. 163.

15. Freeman, *Politics*, p. 171.

16. Personal communication from VIP (Voter's Information Program), League of Women Voters of Massachusetts, December 1975.

17. Freeman, *Politics*, p. 206.

18. Interstate Association of Commissions on the Status of Women, "Statement of Purpose," Washington, D.C.

19. Marcia Hovey, "A Doughty Lady Turns 50," *Manpower*: official publication of the Manpower Administration, U.S. Department of Labor, March 1970.

20. Freeman, *Politics*, pp. 228 ff.

21. Ibid., p. 226.

22. Ibid., pp. 159-62.

23. Personal communication from Miriam Kapsinow, State Coordinator, NOW, Rhode Island, February 1975.

24. *The National Voter: The Official Publication of the League of Women Voters of the United States*, 25, *3* (Fall 1975), pp. 6-8.

25. *New York Times*, December 15, 1975, p. 44; *see also* Council on the Status of Women, *Women in 1973*, for a list of all those groups that endorse or oppose ERA.

26. Karen deCrow, NOW president, quoted in *Women Today*, 5, *19* (September 1975), p. 111.

27. U.S. Department of Labor, Women's Bureau, "Laws on Sex Discrimination in Employment," rev. May 1973.

28. Council on the Status of Women, *Women in 1973*; Harvey Shapiro, "Women on the Line, Men at the Switchboard: Equal Opportunity Comes to the Bell System," *New York Times Magazine*, May 20, 1973.

29. *New York Times*, May 5, 1975, reports on the response to the G.A.O. report; Freeman, *Politics*, p. 186, points out women are the largest minority in the workforce.

30. Wheeler, *No-Fault Divorce*, pp. 125-6; Wheeler's book is the most complete reference on the subject.

31. Steve MacDonald, "The Alimony Blues," *New York Times Magazine*, March 16, 1975, p. 40.

32. Gettleman and Markowitz, *Courage to Divorce*, pp. 194 ff.

33. U.S. Congress, House of Representatives, *Legislation Affecting Women Enacted or Pending*, 93rd Cong., 1974-1975 (available through your congressman).

CHAPTER 12

1. Stimpson, "Thy Neighbor's Wife," *Sexist Society*, ed. Gornick and Moran (originally in Susan B. Anthony, *The History of Women's Suffrage*), pp. 456-7.

2. Doris Gold, "Women and Voluntarism," *Sexist Society*, ed. Gornick and Moran, p. 396.

3. "One Hundred Years of a Great Idea" (New York: Young Women's Christian Association, 1970); Eleanor Flexner, *The Century of Struggle: The Women's Rights Movement in the United States* (Cambridge: Harvard, Belknap Press, 1959); many women's organizations, such as the American Association of University Women, The General Federation of Women's Clubs, and The YWCA, maintain archives at their national headquarters.

4. O'Neill, *Everyone Was Brave: The Rise and Fall of Feminism in America* (Chicago: Quadrangle Books, 1969).

5. Ibid., pp. 82-4, 90-4, 96-100.

6. Ibid., pp. 102, 355, and chapter 3.

7. Ibid., p. 351.

8. Freeman, *Politics*, p. 19.

9. O'Neill, *Everyone Was Brave*, p. 358.

10. Robert Nisbet, from his book *Twilight of Authority*, excerpted in *New York Times,* September 23, 1975, op-ed page; Rosabeth M. Kantor, "Getting It All Together: Communes Past, Present, and Future," *The Future of the Family*, ed. Louise Kapp Howe (New York: Simon & Schuster, 1972), pp. 311 ff., discusses communes; John C. Crystal and Richard N. Bolles, *Where Do I Go From Here with My Life* (New York: Seabury, 1974), discuss mid-life change; and SCORE: Service Corps of Retired Executives is an ACTION program of the Department of Health, Education, and Welfare.

11. Enid Nemy, "13 NOW Leaders Form a Dissident Network," *New York Times*, November 15, 1975.

12. Freeman, *Politics*, p. 151 and chapter 7; Sheehy, "Divorced Mothers as a Potential Force," *Future of the Family*, ed. Howe, pp. 55 ff.

13. Freeman, *Politics*, pp. 150-1, 123-4.

14. Ibid., pp. 129 ff.

15. Sheehy, "Divorced Mothers," *Future of the Family*, ed. Howe.

16. *Women's Studies Newsletter*, November 1974.

17. Freeman, *Politics*, p. 143; *The New Woman's Survival Catalog* (New York: Coward, McCann and Geohegan, 1973); Boston Women's Health Collective, *Our Bodies, Ourselves* (New York: Simon & Schuster, 1971).

18. Gold, "Voluntarism," *Sexist Society*, ed. Gornick and Moran, pp. 393, 385.

19. Ibid., p. 398.

20. Kerstin Joslyn and Tish Sommers, "Volunteerism and the Status of Women: A Position Paper" (NOW Task Force on Volunteerism, n.d.).

21. Herta Loeser, *Women, Work, and Volunteering* (Boston: Beacon Press, 1974).

SELECTED BIBLIOGRAPHY

A partial list of useful references for and about single women. For a more complete list, see the notes for each chapter.

WOMEN ALONE

Adams, Margaret, "The Single Woman in Today's Society: A Reappraisal," *American Journal of Orthopsychiatry*, 4, *5* (October 1971).
——, *Single Blessedness: Observations on the Single Status in Married Society* (New York: Basic Books, 1976).
Brandwein, Ruth A., with Carol A. Brown and Elizabeth Maury Fox, "Women and Children Last: The Social Situation of Divorced Mothers and Their Families," *Journal of Marriage and the Family*, 36, *3* (1974), pp. 498-514.
Butler, Robert N., *Why Survive? Being Old in America* (New York: Harper and Row, 1975).
Caine, Lynn, *Widow* (New York: Morrow, 1974).
Forman, Lynn, *Getting It Together—The Divorced Mother's Guide* (New York: Berkeley Publishing, 1974), paperback.
Goode, William J., *Women in Divorce*, originally published as *After Divorce* (New York: Macmillan, Free Press, 1956).
Johnston, Jill, *Lesbian Nation: The Feminist Solution* (New York: Simon & Schuster, 1973).
Lopata, Helena Z., *Widowhood in an American City* (Cambridge: Schenkman Publishing Co., 1973).
Martin, Del, and Phyllis Lyon, *Lesbian Woman* (San Francisco: Glide Publications, 1972).
Sauber, Mignon, and Janice Paneth, "Unwed Mothers Who Keep Their Children: Research and Implications," *Social Work Practice*, National Conference on Social Welfare, selected papers (1965), pp. 94-106.

Silverman, Phyllis, ed., with Dorothy MacKenzie, Mary Pettipas, and Elizabeth Wilson, *Helping Each Other in Widowhood* (New York: Health Sciences Publications Corp., 1975).

————— , "The Role of Mutual Help Groups in the Prevention of Emotional Difficulties" (Leonia, New Jersey: Behavioral Science Tape Library/Sigma Information, 1974).

Strugnell, Cecile, *Adjustment to Widowhood and Some Related Problems*, foreword by Phyllis Silverman, a selected and annotated bibliography (New York: Health Sciences Publishing Corp., 1974).

Taves, Isabella, *Women Alone* (New York: Funk and Wagnalls, 1968).

Tunstall, Jeremy, *Old and Alone* (London: Routledge, Kegan, Paul, 1966).

Wakin, Edward, *Living as a Widow* (Chicago: Claretian Publications, Jubilee Paperback, n.d.).

Women in Transition, Inc., *Women in Transition: A Feminist Handbook on Separation and Divorce* (New York: Scribner's, 1975).

THIRD WORLD WOMEN

Billingsley, Andrew, *Children of the Storm: Black Children and American Child Welfare* (New York: Harcourt, Brace, Jovanovich, 1972).

Cade, Toni, ed., *The Black Woman: An Anthology* (New York: New American Library, Signet Books, 1970).

Civil Rights Digest: Special Issue on Sexism and Racism, Quarterly of the U.S. Commission on Civil Rights (Spring 1974).

Comer, James P., and Alvin F. Poussaint, *Black Child Care: How to Bring Up a Healthy Black Child in America* (New York: Simon & Schuster, 1975).

Lerner, Gerda, *Black Women in White America* (New York: Vintage Books, 1973).

Lewis, Oscar, *La Vida* (New York: Random House, 1965).

Lipsky, Suzanne, Lucia Bequaert, Rosamund Rosenmeir, et al., *Pre-Conference Report: On Higher Education for Urban Women* (Boston Study Group on Continuing Education for Urban Women and John Hay Whitney Foundation, February 1973).

Reid, Inez Smith, *Together: Black Women* (New York: Emerson Hall Publishers, 1972).

Stack, Carol B., *All Our Kin: Survival Strategies in a Black Community* (New York: Harper and Row, 1974).

FAMILIES IN TRANSITION

Bernstein, Blanche, and William Meezan, *The Impact of Welfare on Family Stability* (New York: New School for Social Research, Center for New York City Affairs, June 1975).

Bohannan, Paul, ed., *Divorce and After: An Analysis of the Emotional and Social Problems of Divorce*, with Bernard, Burch, Cohen, Gebhard, Kay, Mead, Miller, and Rheinstein (New York: Doubleday, Anchor Book, 1970).

Carter, Hugh, and Paul C. Glick, *Marriage and Divorce: A Social and Economic Study* (Cambridge: Harvard University Press, 1970).

Epstein, Joseph, *Divorced in America: Marriage in an Age of Possibility* (New York: Dutton and Company, 1974).

Feldberg, Roslyn, and Janet Kohen, "Divorce: Is It Inevitable?," unpublished paper of the Women's Research Center of Boston (1974).

Gettleman, Susan, and Janet Markowitz, *The Courage to Divorce* (New York: Simon & Schuster, 1974).

Glick, Paul C., and Arthur J. Norton, "Perspectives on the Recent Upturn in Divorce and Remarriage," *Demography*, 10, *3* (August 1973), pp. 301-14.

Herzog, Elizabeth, and Cecelia Sudia, "Fatherless Homes: A Review of Research," *Children*, 15 (September/October 1968), pp. 177-82.

Howe, Louise Kapp, ed., *The Future of the Family* (New York: Simon & Schuster, 1972).

Hunt, Morton M., *The World of the Formerly Married* (New York: McGraw-Hill, 1966).

Klein, Carole, *The Single Parent Experience* (New York: Avon, 1973), paperback.

Kohen, Janet, "Meeting Emotional Needs in the Family: Pressures to Divorce," working paper (Cambridge: The Women's Research Center of Boston, 1974).

Kriesberg, Louis, *Mothers in Poverty: A Study of Fatherless Families* (Chicago: Aldine Publishing Co., 1970).

Milwaukee County Welfare Rights Organization, *Welfare Mothers Speak Out: We Ain't Gonna Shuffle Anymore* (New York: Norton, 1972).

O'Neill, William, *Divorce in the Progressive Era* (New Haven: Yale University Press, 1967).

Ross, Heather L., and Isabel V. Sawhill, *Time of Transition: The Growth of Families Headed by Women* (Washington, D.C.: Urban Institute, 1975).

Rue, James J., and Louise Shanahan, *The Divorced Catholic* (Paramus, New Jersey: Paulist-Newman Press, 1972).

Simon, Anne W., *Stepchild in the Family: A View of Children in Remarriage* (New York: Odyssey Press, 1964).

Skolnick, Arlene, and Jerome Skolnick, *Intimacy, Family, and Society* (Boston: Little, Brown, 1974).

Stuart, Irving R., and Lawrence E. Abt, eds., *Children of Separation and Divorce* (New York: Grossman Publishers, 1972).

U.S. Commission on Civil Rights, *Women and Poverty*, staff report (Washington, D.C., June 1974).

U.S. Department of Labor, Women's Bureau, "Facts About Women Heads of Household and Heads of Families" (Washington, D.C., April 1973).

Wilkerson, Albert E., *The Rights of Children: Emergent Concepts in Law and Society* (Philadelphia: Temple University Press, 1973).

Winston, Marian P., and Trude Forsher, "Non-Support of Legitimate Children by Affluent Fathers as a Cause of Poverty and Welfare Dependence" (Los Angeles: Rand Corporation publication, December 1971), p. 4665.

THE FEMINIST EXPERIENCE

Bardwick, Judith, et al., *Feminine Personality and Conflict* (Belmont, California: University of Michigan, Brooks/Cole Publishing Co., 1970).

Bem, Sandra L., and Daryl J. Bem, "Case Study of a Non-Conscious Ideology: Training the Woman to Know Her Place," in D. J. Bem, *Beliefs, Attitudes, and Human Affairs* (Belmont, California: Brooks/Cole Publishing Co., 1970).

Bernard, Jessie, *The Future of Motherhood* (New York: Dial Press, 1974).

Boston Women's Health Collective, *Our Bodies, Ourselves* (New York: Simon & Schuster, 1973).

Chesler, Phyllis, *Women and Madness* (New York: Doubleday, 1973).

Citizens' Advisory Council on the Status of Women, *Women in 1972: Report to the President* (Washington, D.C.: Government Printing Office, April 1973).

Citizens' Advisory Council on the Status of Women, *Women in 1973: Report to the President* (Washington, D.C.: Government Printing Office, May 1974).

Ferriss, Abbott L., *Indicators of Trends in the Status of American Women* (New York: Russell Sage Foundation, 1971).

Freeman, Jo, *The Politics of Women's Liberation* (New York: McKay, 1975).

Gornick, Vivian, and Barbara K. Moran, eds., *Woman in Sexist Society* (New York: Basic Books, 1971).

Graham, Ellen, ed., *What Do Women Really Want? Articles from* The Wall Street Journal (Chicopee, Massachusetts: Dow Jones Books, 1974).

Howe, Florence, with Adrienne Rich, Arlie Hochschild, and Aleta Wallach, *Women and The Power to Change* (New York: McGraw-Hill, 1975).

Janeway, Elizabeth, *Man's World, Woman's Place: A Study in Social Mythology* (New York: Morrow, 1971).

Morgan, Robin, *Sisterhood is Powerful* (New York: Random House, 1970).

O'Neill, William, *Everyone Was Brave* (Chicago: Quadrangle Books, 1969).

Rennie, Susan, and Kirsten Grimstad, *The New Women's Survival Catalog* (New York: Berkeley Publishing Co., 1973).

Thompson, Mary Lou, ed., *Voices of the New Feminism* (Boston: Beacon Press, 1970).

CAREER AND LIFE PLANNING FOR WOMEN

Bird, Caroline, *Born Female: The High Cost of Keeping Women Down* (New York: McKay, 1969).

———, *What a Woman Needs to Know to Get What She's Worth* (New York: McKay, 1973).

Cotton, Dorothy Whyte, *The Case for the Working Mother* (New York: Tower Publications, 1970); written by the editor-in-chief of *Parents' Magazine*.

The Counseling Psychologist, special issue: "Counseling Women," 4, *1* (April 1974).

Davidson, Sara, "The Myth of Happily Ever After," *Woman's Day* (May 1974).

Eyde, Lorraine D., "Met and Unmet Needs of Women: Implications for Continuing Education for Women," paper presented at the National University Extension Association (Columbia, South Carolina, April 1972).

Hedges, Janice Neipert, "Women at Work: Women Workers and Manpower Demands in the 1970s," *Monthly Labor Review* (June 1970).

Loeser, Herta, *Women, Work, and Volunteering* (Boston: Beacon Press, 1974).

Matthews, Esther E., et al., *Counseling Girls and Women Over the Life Span* (Washington, D.C.: Vocational Guidance Association, 1972).

Pogrebin, Lettie Cottin, *Getting Yours: How to Make the System Work for the Working Woman* (New York: McKay, 1975).

U.S. Department of Labor, Women's Bureau, *Careers for Women in the 70s* (Washington, D.C.: Government Printing Office, 1973).

Wells, Jean A., *Continuing Education for Women: Current Developments* (Washington, D.C.: U.S. Department of Labor, Women's Bureau, 1974), 17 pages.

CHILD CARE

Breitbart, Vicki, *The Day Care Book: The Why, What, and How of Community Day Care* (New York: Knopf, 1974).

Care and Child Development Council of America, *Costs of Child Care: Money Resources and Alternative Funding* (Washington, D.C., 1972).

"Child Care Support Networks: A Proposal," Day Care Consultation Service, Bank Street College of Education, Acting Network Coordinator, New York.

Nye, Ivan, and Lois Hoffman, *The Employed Mother in America* (Chicago: Rand McNally, 1963).

Ruderman, Florence, *Child Care and Working Mothers* (New York: Child Welfare League of America, 1968).

U.S. Department of Labor, Women's Bureau, *Children on Campus: A Survey of Pre-Kindergarten Programs at Institutions of Higher Education in the United States* (1973).

——— , *Day Care Facts*, pamphlet 16, rev. (Washington, D.C.: Government Printing Office, 1973).

——— , *Day Care Services: Industry's Involvement*, bulletin no. 296 (Washington, D.C.: Government Printing Office, 1971).

Women's Research Action Project, *Corporations and Child Care* (Cambridge, Massachusetts).

SINGLE WOMEN AND THE LAW

DeCrow, Karen, *Sexist Justice: How Legal Sexism Affects You* (New York: Random House, 1974).

Goldstein, Joseph, with Anna Freud and Albert J. Solnit, *Beyond the Best Interests of the Child* (New York: Macmillan, Free Press, 1973).

Greene, Roberta, "Til Divorce Do Us Part" (Pittsburgh: KNOW, Inc., n.d.).

Hirsch, Barbara B., *Divorce: What a Woman Needs to Know* (Chicago: Regnery, 1973).

Jancourtz, Isabella, *The Massachusetts Woman's Divorce Handbook* (Boston: New England Free Press, 1974).

Kanowitz, Leo, *Women and the Law: The Unfinished Revolution* (Albuquerque: University of New Mexico Press, 1969).

U.S. Department of Labor, Citizens' Advisory Council on the Status of Women, *The Equal Rights Amendment and Alimony and Child Support Laws* (Washington, D.C., January 1972).

U.S. Department of Labor, Women's Bureau, *Laws on Sex Discrimination in Employment* (Washington, D.C.: Government Printing Office, 1973).

Wheeler, Michael, *No-Fault Divorce* (Boston: Beacon Press, 1974).

USEFUL ADDRESSES

* indicates publisher of a periodical

Alliance for Displaced Homemakers
4223 Telegraph Avenue
Oakland, California 94609

Amazon Quarterly
554 Valle Vista
Oakland, California 94610

American Psychiatric Association
Division of Public Affairs
1700 18th Street N.W.
Washington, D.C. 20009

Child Care Support Network
Bank Street College of Education,
    Acting Coordinator
610 West 112th Street
New York, New York 10025

Child Care Switchboard and Single
    Parent Resource Center
3896 24th Street
San Francisco, California 94114

Child Care Task Force
1400 East 53rd Street
Chicago, Illinois 60615

Child Welfare League of America
67 Irving Place
New York, New York 10003

Consortium on Early Childbearing and
    Child Rearing
Suite 618
1145 19th Street N.W.
Washington, D.C. 20036

*Day Care and Child Development
    Council of America
1012 14th Street N.W.
Washington, D.C. 20005

Divorce
Paulist Center Community
Boston, Massachusetts 02108

ELDERHOSTEL
Office of Residential Life
7 Stoke Hall
University of New Hampshire
Durham, New Hampshire 03824

*Gray Panthers
3700 Chestnut Street
Philadelphia, Pennsylvania 19104

Interstate Association of Commissions
on the Status of Women
District Building
Room 201
14th and East Streets N.W.
Washington, D.C. 20004

Joint Committee of Organizations
Concerned about the Status of
Women in the Church
1600 Sunset Street
Apartment 115
Waukegan, Illinois 60085

*KNOW News
KNOW, Inc.
P.O. Box 86031
Pittsburgh, Pennsylvania 15221

*Labor Pains Newsletter
P.O. Box 72
Cambridge, Massachusetts 02138

*The Lesbian Tide
373 N. Western Avenue
Room 206
Los Angeles, California 90004

Massachusetts Feminist Credit Union
186½ Hampshire Street
Cambridge, Massachusetts 02139

*Massachusetts Woman's Divorce
Handbook*
27 Warren Avenue
Weston, Massachusetts 02193

*MOMMA
P.O. Box 567
Venice, California 90291

National Association of Banking
Women
111 Wacker Drive
Chicago, Illinois 60601

National Black Feminist Organization
370 Lexington Avenue
Room 601
New York, New York 10017

National Congress of Neighborhood
Women
National Center for Urban Ethnic
Affairs
4408 8th Street N.E.
Washington, D.C. 20017

National Organization for Women
1957 East 73rd Street
Chicago, Illinois 60649

National Welfare Rights Organization
1424 16th Street N.W.
Washington, D.C. 20036

*Off Our Backs
1346 Connecticut Avenue
Room 1013
Washington, D.C. 20036

*PRIME TIME
168 West 86th Street
New York, New York 10024

Project Retain
83 Centre Street
Brookline, Massachusetts 02146

Rosie's Place
357 Columbus Avenue
Boston, Massachusetts 02116
  or
c/o Warwick House
St. Philip's Parish
1 Warwick Street
Roxbury, Massachusetts 02120

*SAGE Guide
P.O. Box 39
Belmont, Massachusetts 02178

St. Joan's International Alliance
435 West 119th Street
New York, New York 10027

*Senior Citizens News
National Council of Senior Citizens
1511 K Street N.W.
Washington, D.C. 20005

*The Single Parent
Parents Without Partners, Inc.
7910 Woodmont Avenue
Washington, D.C. 20014

*Single Parents for Adoption of
Children Everywhere
Box 742
Pinewood Drive
Webster, Massachusetts 01570

*Sisterhood of Black Single Mothers
P.O. Box 155
Brooklyn, New York 11203

Task Force on Gay Liberation
Box 2383
Philadelphia, Pennsylvania 19103

Task Force on Older Women
Tish Sommers, Coordinator
434 66th Street
Oakland, California 94609

Unitarian Universalist Association
Department of Ministerial and
    Congregational Services
25 Beacon Street
Boston, Massachusetts 02108

Unitarian Universalist Women's
    Federation
25 Beacon Street
Boston, Massachusetts 02108

Womanpower
Betsy Hogan Associates
222 Rawson Road
Brookline, Massachusetts 02146

The Women's Center
Bristol Community College
Fall River, Massachusetts 02722

Women's Equity Action League
National Press Building
Room 538
Washington, D.C. 20004

Women's Opportunity Research Center
Middlesex Community College
Springs Road
Bedford, Massachusetts 01730

Women's Research Center of Boston
123 Mount Auburn Street
Cambridge, Massachusetts 02139

Women's Studies Newsletter
The Feminist Press
Box 334
Old Westbury, New York 11568

Women Today
Today Publications News Service
National Press Building
Washington, D.C. 20045

CHART I

Fully Employed Women Continue to Earn Less Than
Fully Employed Men of Either White or Minority* Races

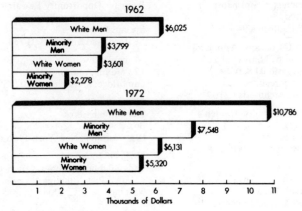

1962

White Men	$6,025
Minority Men	$3,799
White Women	$3,601
Minority Women	$2,278

1972

White Men	$10,786
Minority Men	$7,548
White Women	$6,131
Minority Women	$5,320

1 2 3 4 5 6 7 8 9 10 11
Thousands of Dollars

*Includes all races other than white.

Source: Prepared by the Women's Bureau, Employment
Standards Administration, U.S. Department of Labor, from
data published by the Bureau of the Census, U.S. Department
of Commerce.

CHART II

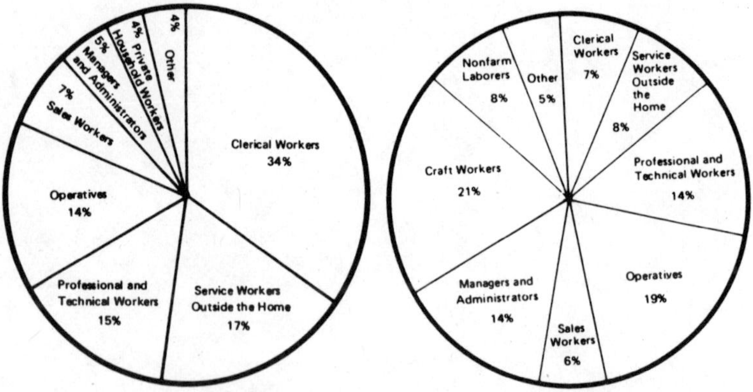

WOMEN

- Clerical Workers 34%
- Service Workers Outside the Home 17%
- Professional and Technical Workers 15%
- Operatives 14%
- Sales Workers 7%
- 5% Managers and Administration
- 4% Private Household Workers
- 4% Other

MEN

- Craft Workers 21%
- Operatives 19%
- Professional and Technical Workers 14%
- Managers and Administrators 14%
- Nonfarm Laborers 8%
- Service Workers Outside the Home 8%
- Clerical Workers 7%
- Sales Workers 6%
- Other 5%

From "Women Workers Today," Women's Bureau, Employment Standards
Administration, U.S. Department of Labor, 1974, revised.

INDEX

Legal services: cost, 188; and sexism, 191-192
Legislation: affecting single women, 199-206; civil rights, 57, 203, 213; for elderly, 61-62, 64; sex discrimination and, 195, 196-197; supporting service volunteers, 224
Lesbian women: 55-60, 97-98; with children, 58-59
Levinson, Daniel: 156, 157
Life cycle of women: 155-165; adolescence, 159, 164-165; and education, 161-164; and careers, 159-161; search for self, 157-159
Life planning: 155, 165
Loeser, Herta: 225
Loneliness: 14, 44, 45, 76, 82
Lopata, Helena: 42, 47, 48, 53, 66, 84, 85, 102, 156, 174, 193
Lutheran Service Society: 51

Man, eight stages of: 155
Markowitz, Janet: 26, 137, 192, 206
Marriage: counseling viewpoint of, 137-138; divorced women's view of, 100-101, 186; "happy," 26; isolation in, 168; options to, 155; in other cultures, 23; secular concepts of, 173-174; single woman's view, 18, 104-106, 152; society's view, 21, 23, 97, 158
Marriage Encounter Movement: 175-176
Married women: 158, 163
The Massachusetts Woman's Divorce Handbook: 194
Maternal and Infant Care program: 16
Matthew, Esther: 155, 157, 159
Mead, Margaret: 23
Media: 15, 24, 25, 69, 124
Medicare: 61, 62, 125
Men: and feminism, 59; and gay activism, 58; needs, 12-13, 62, 157; singleness in, 96, 157
Mental health field: 58, 137, 140
Mental Patients' Liberation Front: 145
Middle-class communities: 82
Middle-class mothers: 33
Ministry, women in: 176-178
Minority women: adoptive parents, 71-76; ambivalence of, 67, 70-71; blacks, 54, 66, 68-71; Chicanas, 66, 68; elderly, 60-66; in farm life, 55; Native Americans, 66, 68; profile of, 54-55, 66-71; Puerto Ricans,

67-68, 69; status of, 55-56, 58-59, 61, 68; and women's movement, 56-57, 67, 69
MOMMA: 17, 59, 121
Mothers in Poverty: 117

Nader, Ralph: 63, 125
NAIM: 51-52
National Association of Banking Women (NABW): 132-133
National Black Feminist Organization: 71, 199
National Congress of Neighborhood Women: 199
National Council for the Single Woman and her Dependents: 19-20
National Organization to Insure Support Enforcement (NOISE): 123
National Welfare Rights Organization (NWRO): 118, 120
National women's organizations: 197-199
National Women's Political Caucus: 198
Native American women: 66, 68
Never-married women: adoptive mothers, 17-18, 71-76; characteristics of, 11, 20, 98-113; as a choice, 9-10, 18; organizational needs of, 19-20; pension benefits, 125; in religious life, 11-12, 18; sexual needs, 15; social life of, 112-113; society's view, 8, 80-81; statistics, 10; unwed mothers, 10, 15-17, 80; view of marriage, 18, 104-106, 152
New Environments for Women (NEW): 157-159
New morality: 15, 100-102
New Women's Survival Catalog: 222
The New York Times: 66, 119
Nixon, Richard M.: 129, 190, 196
Noble, Elaine: 58
"No-fault" divorce: 122, 205
Nonsupport action: 122, 123
NOW (National Organization for Women): 35, 57, 71, 123, 176, 198, 205, 219; Task Force on Older Women, 64, 126; Task Force on Volunteerism, 223-224
Nuns: 11-12, 14, 170-171

Occupational aspirations: 158, 159
Old Age Assistance: 116, 125
Older Americans Act of 1965: 61
Older Women's League: 123
O'Neill, William: 23, 149, 214-216
Open Marriage: 105

66; group counseling, 148-150; versus professional counseling, 140-141; widows, 47-53
Survivor benefits: 124-126
Sweden: 16
Szasz, Thomas: 137

THEOS: 51
Therapy: 91
Transition: for adoptive mothers, 73; in divorce, 30, 139, 156, 184; group counseling in, 149-150; home to college, 160; for newly separated, 28, 139-140; returning to school, 146; timetable for widows, 41-42, 140

Uniform Marriage/Divorce Act: 205
Unitarian-Universalist Association: 58, 178
United Methodist Church: 58
Unwed mothers: social services for, 16-17; stigma, 10, 15, 80

Vocational counseling: in colleges, 161; new models for, 151
Vocational Readiness Program: 164-165
Voluntary associations: for blacks, 71; for elderly, 62-63; in inner-city, 71; structure of, 219-220; for widows, 47-53
Volunteerism, or voluntarism: 223-225

Welfare: advocacy groups, 120-121; mothers, 33; myths about, 116, 117-118; quality of, 119-120; statistics, 117
Welfare Mothers Speak Out: 120
Westervelt, Esther: 155
"Widowed Service Line": 50
Widows: and the church, 172; counseling, 140; elderly, 44-45, 48, 115-116; financial problems of, 43-45, 48-49, 53, 115-116, 122, 125-126; friendships and, 81, 84; identity, 42, 218; Jewish, 174; the law and, 193, 194; in other cultures, 39; role models for, 39-40, 47; social life of, 43, 95, 97; society's view of, 39, 42, 80; statistics, 40; transition for, 41-42, 140; view of divorcees, 46-47; voluntary

associations for, 47-53; young, 43, 45, 156
Widows' Exchange Project: 53
Widow-to-Widow Project: 49-50
Willett, Roslyn: 129
WINNERS: 146-148, 164
Witt, Shirley Hill: 66
Women in Apprenticeship: 128
Women in Transition (WIT): 37-38, 58, 124, 149, 192; Handbook, 37, 192, 194, 222
Women, Work, and Volunteering: 224-225
Women's Bureau, of Department of Labor: 127-128, 129, 153, 197
Women's Center: 163, 166
Women's Coalition: 199
Women's Cooperative, Inc.: 86-89
Women's Equity Action League: 198
Women's movement: and Catholic women, 180; and child care, 131; early groups in, 214-215; expansion of, 222; in federal government, 196-197; future considerations, 225-228; history of, xii, 213-217; issues in, 217-225; leadership, 219, 220-221; and legal profession, 190, 195; and lesbians, 56-57; media image, 69; and minority women, 67, 69; national organizations, 197-199; and never-married women, 12, 18, 218; opposition to, 31, 67, 69; and sexuality, 15; structure of, 219-220; and volunteerism, 223-225; and work force, 153, 155
Women's Refuge Center: 144-145
Women's Research Center: 26, 83, 123, 137-138, 156, 189, 195-196
Women's Survival Manual: A Feminist Handbook on Separation and Divorce (WIT): 37, 192, 194, 222
Womensurge: 219
WORC (Women's Opportunity Research Center): 162-163
Work: 109-111, 153-154; versus home and marriage, 155, 166; limited options in, 126-129
Work Incentive Program: 118, 182
Working-class communities: 82

Young, Father James: 179-180, 181